AMERICA'S SILVER AGE

Books by
Gerald W. Johnson

•

RANDOLPH OF ROANOKE

A LITTLE NIGHT-MUSIC

AMERICA'S SILVER AGE

•

HENRY CLAY

". . . a statesman who was very sure that he was no god,
and by no means certain that he was right as a man."

Gerald W. Johnson

✰ ✰

AMERICA'S SILVER AGE

The Statecraft of
Clay - Webster - Calhoun

✰ ✰

ILLUSTRATED

Harper & Brothers Publishers

NEW YORK *and* LONDON

1939

CONTENTS

✩

[v]

Contents

Contents

ILLUSTRATIONS

✶

AMERICA'S SILVER AGE

CHAPTER I

ON THE EVIL FAME OF PEACE-LOVING STATESMEN

The singular disrespect accorded Henry Clay as the member of the Triumvirate identified with pacifism

YOUNG Henry Clay, with a commission as United States Senator in his pocket, was approaching Washington when Destiny spoke to him. Mr. Clay paid little heed, for Destiny was disguised as one of his fellow-travelers, a pessimistic and somewhat querulous soul, who discoursed of politics cheerlessly. Things, in the opinion of this traveler, were terrible. The year 1806 was drawing to a close. It was a time of tremendous commercial, and especially of industrial, expansion, but politically a period of stagnation had set in. The driving power that had characterized President Jefferson's first administration was slackening, and affairs were drifting into the hands of those who, while not exactly opposing the Jeffersonian reform program, felt that we had gone too fast and too far, and that the country should have a breathing spell. "Do nothing" was already an attractive idea in Washington, and soon it was to become the order of the day.

About the larger aspects of this situation, Mr. Clay's fellow-traveler apparently was not greatly concerned, but he was much annoyed by certain details. There was, for example, the matter of a bridge across the Potomac at Washington. Everyone understood the need for it, nobody was openly opposing it, and yet the necessary legislation had been hanging fire in Congress for years. Even at this moment the hopes of business men, who ardently desired the bridge, seemed doomed to another defeat; the bill was pending in the Senate, but the do-nothing party characteristically had moved another postponement and, as far as political observers could tell, the votes were evenly divided.

"Everything," said the man gloomily, unconscious that at this moment he had begun to speak with the voice of Destiny, "depends on this new man from Kentucky, this Clay. He can break the deadlock, but nobody knows how he will vote."

Young Mr. Clay heard this with a pleasure that fixed the incident permanently in his mind, for he remembered it and told the story many years later; but even he had no idea how accurately the stranger was predicting the future.[1]

It was not merely the matter of a bridge that depended upon this man Clay. The pessimistic traveler would have been more astonished even than Mr. Clay had he been given a glimpse of the future that would reveal to him how much depended upon the coming to Washington of this long, loose-jointed young Westerner, almost startlingly ugly, with his bulging forehead, long nose and wide mouth, but filled with gay good humor and ready to meet any friendly advance with a flashing smile that transfigured his face and made it, for the moment, almost handsome. Mr. Clay would have admitted readily, on that December day in 1806, that he had not a care in the world. Twenty-nine years old, coming to Washington to fill out the remaining part of the term of a Senator who had resigned and with his pockets full of money received as retainers from clients whose interests he was to represent before the Supreme Court, he approached the national capital jauntily, in the mood described in Kentucky as "ready for a fight or a frolic" nor caring which he found. Even the political record he might make within the next three months troubled him little, for he had no idea of seeking re-election.

Yet before he arrived at the rather dismal little city by the Potomac, he learned from the lips of a talkative stranger, unaware of his identity, that already he was important.

Possibly Mr. Clay would have done better had he fixed his

[1] Incidentally, when he got to Washington, he voted right and the bill authorizing construction of the bridge was passed. It was what was known as "Long Bridge" and stood almost exactly where the modern bridge crosses the river carrying the road to Alexandria.

attention on another factor of the situation—he was regarded as important, yes, but he was also regarded doubtfully. The mouthpiece of Destiny in the traveling coach had hopes of Henry Clay, but felt no assurance that he could be relied on; and in that he was taking the attitude assumed by thousands of men within the next half-century. This is, however, the wisdom of hindsight, which is cheap. Is it fair, or sensible, to expect a man of twenty-nine, successful, self-confident, good-humored, pleased with the world and with himself, to act as Socrates might have acted when he was old and disillusioned? Mr. Clay missed the note of dubiety, exactly as you or I would have missed it, had we been in his place; and he did perceive the evidence of his importance, exactly as you or I would have perceived it. Shall we raise sanctimonious eyebrows and blame the boy, because we know what is coming in the next fifty years, and therefore know that he might have been wiser, while he certainly had no knowledge and probably had no intimation of what lay ahead? But that is not only an ungenerous approach to history, it is one that affords no clue to comprehension of the men who made it. All his life long Mr. Clay might have been wiser; but he wasn't, and that is why we have the story as it is.

Mr. Clay was not even aware, as the coach rolled into Washington that day in 1806, that he was on the threshold of a career different not merely in particulars, but in essence, from any that had been carved by an American. With two others, he was to create a new type in our public life, the national statesman, as opposed to the Virginian, or the New Englander, or the Pennsylvanian, become American only by dint of necessity. Washington, indeed, had been American, made so by war, but his Americanism was frankly a concession to the needs of the times and his retreat to Mount Vernon and Virginia seemed to him a just reward for his patriotic assumption of a difficult and unnatural character. John Adams fled back to Massachusetts as to a haven of refuge, where he might salve the wounds incurred during his period of acting as a national figure. Jefferson, like Franklin, had a cosmopolitan outlook, but he was more the internationalist than the nationalist; and above all, he was the Virginian. All of the earlier statesmen felt more at ease in addressing the people of their native States than in speaking from the national rostrum.

Clay, however, was to represent, not Kentucky, but the West, Calhoun the South, not South Carolina alone, and Webster spoke, not for either New Hampshire or Massachusetts, but for the North. These three were really at home in Washington—as much so as in Frankfort, in Columbia, or in Boston. They were to refashion the republic along lines not dreamed of by its founders. They were to fix the minds of their fellow-citizens in certain moulds that endure to this day and that still shape, in great measure, all our political thinking.

Henry Clay was not merely the first of this group to arrive on the scene, but the first in many other ways. Clio, Muse of history, has never quite made up her mind about him; she seems to share the confusion once expressed by his great colleague, Calhoun, when he said, "He is a bad man, an impostor, a creature of wicked schemes. I won't speak to him, but, by God, I love him!"

Even his most violent opponent, Andrew Jackson, speaking in wrath, paid a curious tribute to Henry Clay. Near the end of his life he declared that twice he had failed the American people —he had neither hanged Calhoun nor shot Clay. General Jackson was always careful to select his punishments in strict accordance with his estimate of the offender's quality. When Senator Lacock irritated him, he threatened to cut off the senatorial ears. Calhoun and Clay he would have executed; but note that to Clay he would have granted a soldier's death, reserving the rope for Calhoun. This concession, from Andrew Jackson, was the equivalent of an outburst of admiration from a less magnificent hater.

With such estimates from his two greatest opponents, it is unnecessary to turn to Clay's friends for evidence of his uncanny personal charm. This evidence is so overwhelming indeed that it swept the ordinarily cool and cautious Rhodes into an extravagant encomium: "Other Americans have been intellectually greater, others have been more painstaking, others still have

[4]

been greater benefactors to their country; yet no man has been loved as the people of the United States loved Henry Clay."[2]

One may cherish some doubts as to whether it was really the people who loved Henry Clay without questioning the obvious fact that he was endowed with an extraordinary personal magnetism that swept men along sometimes counter to the force of their own judgment. The man of the period dearest to the hearts of the masses was Andrew Jackson; but what he was to the plain people, Clay undoubtedly was to the aristocracy.

Yet, now that he has been dead nearly a hundred years, people shake their heads sadly over Henry Clay. "A very strong leader, he was not a safe guide," mourns his chief biographer:[3] while the notoriously educated Henry Adams dismissed him as Southern and therefore not worth serious study.[4] Even Gamaliel Bradford, most benevolent of biographers, prefers to commit himself no further than to describe Clay as "distinctly and warmly human";[5] it is interesting to note that at the end of the same essay he breaks into a panegyric of the next great Westerner, "the child of his own Kentucky, the supreme embodiment of the Western spirit, the savior of the union, Abraham Lincoln." Bradford ignores the probability that Lincoln would have found no union to save had it not been for the bad man, the impostor, the creature of wicked schemes.

In fact, it has occurred to so few people[6] that one is conscious of a certain temerity in advancing the idea. Yet the facts seem to be plain enough. It is no longer disputed that from the beginning of the rise of industrialism, that is to say, roughly, from

---

[2] James Ford Rhodes, *History of the United States from the Compromise of 1850 to the Final Restoration of Home Rule at the South in 1877*, vol. i, p. 120. (Hereafter cited as Rhodes.)

[3] Carl Schurz, *Life of Henry Clay*, vol. ii, p. 409. (Hereafter cited as Schurz.)

[4] "Clay's character belonged to the simple Southern, or Virginia type, somewhat affected, but not rendered more complex, by Western influence—and transparent beyond need of description or criticism." Henry Adams, *History of the United States*, vol. ix, p. 52.

[5] Gamaliel Bradford, *As God Made Them*, p. 45.

[6] Among the exceptions must be noted the latest biographers of Clay, Messrs. Mayo and Van Deusen. See *Henry Clay*, by Bernard Mayo and *The Life of Henry Clay*, by Glyndon G. Van Deusen, both published in 1937.

1830, the economic and military strength of the South steadily dwindled relatively to that of the rest of the country; yet in the sixties the South put up a desperate struggle lasting four years. Half a dozen times the Confederacy came dangerously close to winning, and had the odds been only a little less, it seems highly probable that Lee, instead of Grant, would have dictated the terms of surrender. At any time prior to 1861 the odds would have been appreciably less, hence postponement of the war to that date unquestionably contributed decisively, if indirectly, to the salvation of the union.

But who staved off the war? There are no two opinions as to that. It was the transparent Southerner, the unsafe guide, the man who should have been shot. If no other, then at least Jefferson Davis, President of the Confederate States of America, had cause to agree that Old Hickory failed in a great crisis when he neglected to place Henry Clay in front of a firing squad; for that simple precaution might have assured that the South would fight while it was yet strong enough to win. But Clay lived to contrive the compromise of 1850; and thereafter the South was doomed.

Clay, as Rhodes remarks,[7] is linked with peace; and it seems to be the bitter truth that maintaining the public peace is as thankless a task as a statesman can undertake. However religious history may exalt Jesus, Buddha, Confucius as princes of peace, secular history is enraptured by the killers. The statesman whose greatest triumphs were pacifistic may receive guarded praise, but it is invariably commingled with some measure of contempt; the man of war is forgiven every sort of atrocity in view of the brilliance of his campaigns while the weaknesses and follies of the man of peace are excoriated ruthlessly and frequently celebrated far more widely than his virtues. Talleyrand was no greater rogue than Napoleon; but his glory

[7] Rhodes, vol. vi, p. 35. The reference is to James G. Blaine's observation that Henry Clay, Stephen A. Douglas and Thaddeus Stevens were the three greatest American parliamentary leaders. Rhodes, after quoting it, comments, "There is a distinction which Blaine did not draw between Clay on one side and Douglas and Stevens on the other. Recalling Clay suggests peace, recalling Douglas and Stevens suggests the sword."

was that of a pacifist, hence easily extinguished by his crimes. Washington's foibles were as many and as absurd as Jefferson's, but the glory of his military career makes men think it shameful to consider his defects.

This ineradicable tendency of human nature has been remarked by countless philosophers. Parton, for example, noted that "men of books contemplate with mere wonder the fact, that during a period when Webster, Clay, Calhoun, Wirt and Preston were on the public stage, Andrew Jackson should have been so much the idol of the American people, that all those eminent men united could not prevail against him in a single instance."[8] But what would Parton have made of the fact that it is precisely "men of books" who have united for a century in depreciating the Great Pacificator not in comparison with warriors only, but also in comparison with statesmen whose policy led to war? John C. Calhoun, for example, may be denounced for the policy that led to the Civil War: but even those who regard his career with hatred, usually exhibit great respect for the man. Calhoun, it is true, was austerely virtuous in his private life, while Clay was not. Yet it is not the Kentuckian's fondness for the ladies, wine and the gaming table that the world condemns. In these respects, Daniel Webster is as vulnerable as he; but only once, on March 7, 1850, did Webster make any memorable effort to preserve the peace, while Clay was always at it. His function was to quell fighting which is a great crime in the public estimation for, when all is said and done, humanity loves a fight.

Nine months before his death, in a letter to Daniel Ullman, he cited the fourteen points of his career which he considered worthy to be inscribed on a gold medal friends in New York had struck in his honor:[9] and of the fourteen, seven had to do with the maintenance of peace, in one way or another. To Clay himself this was an honorable record. No doubt he would have been genuinely shocked had anyone suggested to him that in the years to come it might serve to tarnish, rather than brighten his fame. Yet this possibility is far from inconceivable. Less than ten years

[8] James Parton, *Life of Andrew Jackson*, vol. iii, p. 696.
[9] Schurz, vol. ii, p. 407.

after Clay's death the war, which he had been largely instrumental in postponing three times, burst upon the country. It raged for four years with a destructiveness up to that time unparalleled, and it developed emotional fixations which have not even yet been entirely removed. North and South, men devoted themselves to one cause or the other with the utmost intensity of which the human heart is capable. Half a million of them died for these causes; and by the time it was over the country had been, as the psychologists say, "conditioned" to belief in the war not as the natural outcome of political stupidity but as a collision of eternal moral principles, foreordained and inevitable.

Men committed to such a belief are by that very fact rendered incapable of regarding the statecraft of Henry Clay as sound; because if Clay was right, then the men who led the country into the Civil War were wrong. If they were wrong, then on both sides we wasted our blood and treasure, disrupted the government, poisoned the country with hatred for a century and laid a staggering burden of debt on the succeeding generation, all for a program that was idiotic from its inception and therefore necessarily absurd in its execution and disastrous in its results. This, though, we cannot admit without an intolerable psychic upheaval. It is an emotional necessity to this country that Clay should have been wrong; and against an emotional necessity, facts form but a feeble counter-agent.

The case of Calhoun is different. As Southerners, we can maintain that Calhoun was right, and not infrequently we do.[10] As Northerners, we perceive clearly enough that Calhoun was wrong as regards his postulates, but we can admit him to a certain standing as a sort of *advocatus diaboli*, whose attacks were a necessary step in the final establishment of the truth. Whatever else he may have achieved, Calhoun has the historical merit of having done all he could to bring on a terrific fight, and much can be forgiven a politician whose statecraft led to war.

Calhoun merits favorable treatment, also, from the moralistic standpoint. In his language, as his remark about Clay shows, he

[10] See, for example, *The Attack on Leviathan*, by Donald Davidson, and *The Pursuit of Happiness*, by Herbert Agar.

occasionally stepped aside from the path of strict rectitude, but otherwise the most rigid Puritan can find little in his public or private life at which to cavil. Calhoun was a stranger to all the more lurid vices. It is not recorded that the gaming table had any attraction whatever for him. At a period in which heavy drinking was the rule, rather than the exception, among men in public life he was notably abstemious. Not only was he entirely faithful to his wife in the physical sense, but he seems to have been genuinely devoted to her to the end of his days. He is an ideal subject for exordiums and exhortations to the young—the poor boy who rose to eminence through rigid adherence to the maxims inculcated in every properly regulated Sunday school.

It must be admitted that Clay is not by any means so well-adapted to the use of conventional moralists preparing edifying discourses for the young. It is true that his lapses were enormously exaggerated by political opponents in those days when campaign pamphleteers stuck at nothing; but there was unquestionably some fire behind the great smoke. There may be doubt of the truth of the story that he lost $8,000 in one evening at cards, but there is no doubt that he did gamble heavily in his younger days. He was never involved in a notorious scandal, but his relations with several pretty women were unquestionably something more than fraternal; he lived to the age of seventy-five and even then did not die of cirrhosis of the liver, but his attentions to the wine bottle were frequently more ardent than discreet. By no rational interpretation of the record can it be made to appear that Henry Clay was a model of correct living, except as regards finances. On that point, he is definitely clear of suspicion. No one has ever presented any evidence that a single dollar of public money ever stuck to Clay's fingers. He remained a relatively poor man when he was holding positions that might easily have been turned to such account as to bring him a fortune. His enemies, unscrupulous as many were, did not charge him with any sort of financial dishonesty, for they knew such a charge would have been ridiculed.

But he was charged with almost every form of duplicity that did not involve money, and in a formidable array of instances the charge was proved to the hilt. Clay was a politician which means, as Abraham Lincoln has assured us, that he was at least one long step removed from an honest man. Throughout his public service he was the center of a succession of political intrigues. He played the game according to the rules as he found them, and the fact that it was frequently a sordid game did not deter him. He desired the Presidency so avidly that he stooped to some practices worse than doubtful to get it; but he stooped in vain. He believed in compromise and this, although it is frequently presented as proof of his insincerity, was perhaps the most honest thing about him. He really believed in it.

Now this, plainly, is no suitable hero of copybook maxims. It would be silly, as well as useless, to try to argue that Clay has been misjudged by history, and that the sniffish reception given him by writers for nearly a hundred years is based on a total misconception of his character. The last two generations may, indeed, have felt a strong emotional need to cry Clay down in order to justify their fathers who turned their backs upon Clay and toward war; but it does not follow that they were ignorant of what manner of man he was. From the standpoint of the teetotaler, he was bad. From the standpoint of the prude, or of the Victorian moralist, he was bad. From the standpoint of the prudent man who eschews gambling, he was bad. From the standpoint of the candid man, he was bad. From the standpoint of the strictly truthful man, he was bad. From the standpoint of the authoritarian, who thinks every man in public life should have a complete set of principles to which he adheres rigidly, he was almost fabulously bad.

Let us then concede the point. Let us set up as one of the stipulations, to borrow a word from the lawyers, that Henry Clay was a bad man.

At that, we have not done with him. Calhoun, even when he would not speak to him, loved him. Andrew Jackson, who hated him, yet would have granted him a soldier's death. This generation, taught from infancy to deplore him, nevertheless when it thinks of Clay, thinks of peace. Undoubtedly, he was more than merely bad.

On the Evil Fame of Peace-Loving Statesmen

To orderly souls, who like to have their historical characters all neatly labeled and filed under the appropriate index number, Clay is a dreadful annoyance. He doesn't fit into any of the more convenient categories. His career doesn't work out according to the ancient maxims. He was a trifler and an idler; at Ghent, for example, with the fate of nations in his hands, he maddened poor John Quincy Adams with his all-night card parties and other frivolities;[11] yet he evolved a philosophy and a polity which has been adopted by the party in power in this country for the better part of a century. He was called an ignorant man,[12] yet he had a grasp of reality that was not possessed by Calhoun, alumnus of Yale, nor by John Quincy Adams, alumnus of Harvard. He drank, he gambled, he flirted with every pretty woman who came by, he made outrageous jests upon the most awful subjects,[13] yet he prospered, his financial affairs were always in order and conducted with a prudence not excelled by that of John Quincy Adams himself.[14] If we somehow resent Clay, is that not natural? We like to impose a pattern upon history, we like to see things work out logically, we like to see our assumptions justified by the event; and Clay defeats us, remaining the unsolved problem, the equation that conforms to no formulae,

[11] See John Quincy Adams, *Diary* for September 8 and 21, 1814.

[12] "He is, like almost all the eminent men of this country, only half educated." John Quincy Adams, *Diary* for March 9, 1821. "Superficiality remained one of his weak points through life." Schurz, vol. i, p. 11. "He knew men well, but he had no knowledge of books." Rhodes, vol. i, p. 120. "He had the very elementary education of a common school in Virginia of that day, and added little to it later." Gamaliel Bradford, *As God Made Them*, p. 47. And so on, the testimony on this point being practically unanimous; even an uncritical biography plainly intended for use as a campaign document touches the question of Clay's learning coyly: "It is by no means rare that the greatest minds are not those which are most conversant with the trifling details of legal decisions. Genius delights in open space. It is the Eagle, that dashes freely abroad through sun and storm, and not the Canary, that is content to nibble at its narrow cage in the parlor window." George D. Prentice, *Biography of Henry Clay*, p. 12.

[13] Witness his remark when Washington was being rocked to its social foundations by the Peggy Eaton affair: "Age cannot wither, nor can custom stale her infinite virginity."

[14] Except in the matter of indorsing notes for friends and relatives, as will appear later.

remaining as mocking and elusive as life itself. A pestilential fellow!

In politics, above all, he defies the rules and upsets the judgments that we usually assume to be correct. He was an unprincipled man. This is, Heaven knows, nothing unusual in politics; public life is today and has always been full of men whose acts square with no set of principles. What startles and disturbs us in the case of Henry Clay is not that he refused to be guided by principle in act, but repudiated such guidance in speech. At the very climax of his career, after more than fifty stormy years in politics, when he was already in that sunset of life that usually turns men's thoughts to philosophy, he lauded compromise, not rigid adherence to principle. In the great debate leading to the compromise that postponed the war for the last time, he declared, "I go for honorable compromise wherever it can be made. Life itself is but a compromise between death and life, the struggle continuing throughout our whole existence, until the great destroyer finally triumphs. All legislation, all government, all society is founded upon the principle of mutual concession, politeness, comity, courtesy; upon these everything is based. . . . Let him who elevates himself above humanity, above its weaknesses, its infirmities, its wants, its necessities, say, if he pleases, I never will compromise, but let no one who is not above the frailties of our common nature disdain compromise."[15]

This may be common sense, but it is not the conventional attitude for a politician to take. What we expect of a man in public life is public proclamation of his intransigent devotion to principle, whatever may be the tenor of his acts. Fame, they say, is a woman, and some philosopher has observed that women may delight in a man who is moral in word and deed, or in one who is immoral in word and deed, or in one who is moral in word and immoral in deed, but they can in no wise endure one who is immoral in word, but moral in deed. It is possible that Henry Clay may fall under this ban. He proclaimed his repudiation of principle in favor of compromise; but compromise was his principle, and he lived up to it. Thus one may argue that

[15] Speech of April 8, 1850. Henry Clay, *Works*, vol. vi, p. 412.

while he talked like a man devoid of principle, his acts were consistently faithful to the principle of compromise—immoral in word, he was moral in deed.

This would account for his evil fame, but there is really no necessity, at this late day, to account for it, or palliate it, or explain it away. Good, bad, or indifferent—what does it matter now? The man lived, promulgated certain ideas, accomplished certain ends, left certain impressions on the history of the country. He appeared on the national stage at a moment when it was occupied, for the most part, by men who were certain. It was, incidentally, the period of greatest brilliance in the history of American politics. It was Clay's fortune to contend for decades with a succession of extraordinarily powerful men who were beset by few doubts, if any. His greatest opponent, Andrew Jackson, had none at all. Calhoun, next in order of Clay's antagonists, had but few, and Webster, sometimes an ally, occasionally an opponent, had no more than Calhoun. John Quincy Adams, the one political leader whom Clay served faithfully throughout the period of his leadership, was a New England Puritan whose steely rigidity in his adherence to principle rivaled that of Calhoun. In this milieu Clay was the great protagonist of uncertainty—not the uncertainty that is common enough among politicians, the uncertainty of limber souls who cannot make up their minds which way the cat is going to jump, but a vastly deeper and more significant thing, an uncertainty as between right and wrong.

Clay was frequently called arbitrary, opinionated, arrogant; and toward his party associates and followers he did exhibit these qualities; but he escaped the greatest arrogance of all, the arrogance of believing that God had endowed him with a peculiar and infallible capacity to distinguish between good and evil. He was under no necessity of following the course Cromwell recommended to the Scotch Presbyterians—he did not need to pray that it might be revealed to him that it was possible for him to be mistaken. He knew it.

He had his lapses, to be sure, and two of the three great mistakes of his career are attributable to them. When he was very

~~young he~~ played a prominent part in precipitating the War of 1812. Perhaps the catastrophic results of that adventure, under-taken in a moment when he had forgotten his fallibility and knew he was right, did much to fix him in his course thereafter. The other was his defense of the Bank in 1836, when he acted as if he were certain of his own righteousness, although it is prob-able that secretly he cherished many doubts. The defense of the Bank, however, was an essay in personal politics. The object, regardless of Clay's protestations, was as much to embarrass the administration as to protect the country, and whenever he played personal politics Clay got into difficulties. The third great mistake was his weakness in permitting his desire for the Presidency, originally perfectly natural and even praiseworthy, to become so inordinately keen as to make him ridiculous.

This humility of the arrogant man, this openness of mind in an age of certitude is, however, precisely what makes Clay wor-thy of study although he has been in the grave for almost a cen-tury. Most of the controversies in which he engaged have long been settled. Most of the issues on which the country divided then are as dead now as Henry Clay himself. A great deal of that which he proclaimed passionately seems, after so many years, utterly trivial and the sonorous periods with which he wrung tears not only from hard-bitten frontiersmen, not only from hard-boiled politicians, but, as Bradford notes with just amazement,[16] even from newspaper reporters, appear to the modern reader to be "sound and fury signifying nothing."

Clay himself has given biographers a striking outline of what he considered the important achievements in his career. Just be-fore his death some of his friends in New York had a medal struck commemorating his public services and they asked him what to have engraved on the reverse. He sent them this list:

Senate, 1806.
Speaker, 1811.
War of 1812 with Great Britain.
Ghent, 1814.
Spanish America, 1822.

[16] *As God Made Them*, p. 71.

[14]

Missouri Compromise, 1821.
American System, 1824.
Greece, 1824.
Secretary of State, 1825.
Panama Instructions, 1826.
Tariff Compromise, 1833.
Public Domain, 1833–1841.
Peace with France Preserved, 1835.
Compromise, 1850.

In all this there is nothing to agitate the minds of men in 1939 except, perhaps, the vast, vague dream that Clay called the "American System." Men of letters have examined the career of Clay assiduously. There are at least seven important lives[17] and innumerable essays and other short writings. His *Life and Speeches* appeared in two volumes in 1854, his *Correspondence* fills another and his *Works* appear in seven. There is a new light, however, in which it may be worth while once more to look at Henry Clay. This is the light of our own times.

The old issues are dead, but the old spirit is immortal. The twentieth century, no less than the nineteenth, is prolific of statesmen with no doubts, men of principle in whose eyes compromise is loathsome. This is an affliction, not of the United States only, but of the century. Rarely, if ever, before has the world held so many rulers who are not only determined to help God run the universe, but who apparently would display no hesitation in taking over the entire job. Not since the days of the Caesars have we had so many military chieftains who seem to aspire not merely to empery but to deity. Napoleon himself was content to be imperial, but his modern imitators apparently would be divine.

Surely, in a world so solemn, so humorless, so bloody, there may be profit in considering for awhile a statesman who was very sure that he was no god and by no means certain that he was right as a man. "The significance of his large humanity" was what led Bradford to write his essay on Clay nearly ten

---

[17] Those of Colton, Prentice, Rogers, Schurz and Thomas Hart Clay, with the recent ones of Mayo and Van Deusen.

years ago; and that significance has increased, rather than diminished, in the last decade.

Clay was elected Speaker of the House of Representatives in 1811, among other reasons because of the general belief that he was the only man who could curb the terrible John Randolph of Roanoke.[18] In this he was but indifferently successful, although he carried his efforts to the length of putting a bullet through Randolph's coat; but he was eminently successful in arousing the violent animosity of that most violent hater. Yet not even the eccentric Virginian wholly escaped the magic of Clay's personality. In the course of that insane odyssey which he made as he was dying, in 1833, Randolph came to Washington and visited the Senate chamber, where Clay happened to be addressing the chair. "Raise me up," said Randolph to his attendant, "I want to hear that voice again."[19]

Perhaps there is a parable here for a world as sick and crazy as ever John Randolph was. The man who said, "I would rather be right than President," sadly suspecting that he would never be either, is certainly a figure out of a different age from one filled with strident disharmonies of men who know they are right, and whose devotion to principle is proclaimed, not merely by their yells and tub-thumping, but by the rumbling of caissons as the artillery wheels into position, by the droning of bombers, and the tramp of millions of armed men. When we think of Clay, we think of peace; so a fevered and horror-haunted world may well cry out with old John, "I want to hear that voice again!"

[18] George D. Prentice, *Biography of Henry Clay*, p. 62.
[19] William Cabell Bruce, *John Randolph of Roanoke*, vol. ii, p. 36.

CHAPTER II

KENTUCKY INTERLUDE

A short dissertation on the background and early life of Mr. Clay

THE question of the moral character of our hero is not, logically, a matter of prime importance in a study of this kind; yet at least a superficial acquaintance with his background is desirable, if only to avoid needless bewilderment in observing some phases of his career.

The notion that Henry Clay was a proletarian who raised himself to eminence against terrific odds is largely buncombe. The idea was sedulously cultivated during his lifetime, and for an excellent reason—he was opposing a man who *was* a proletarian, in the most literal sense, and it was desirable for political effect to give the impression that Clay had overcome handicaps at least as heavy as those that fate laid upon Andrew Jackson.

But it is not true. He had, for the time and region in which he was born, a relatively good start in life. His childhood was, indeed, far from luxurious, but that was because he had the misfortune to be born in one of the devastated regions during a great war, where life was hard for everyone. He was not dictating his autobiography, but taunting the rich John Randolph, when he declared on the floor of the Senate, "I was born to no proud patrimonial estate. I inherited only infancy, ignorance and indigence"; and the statement is more alliterative than accurate. His father was a Baptist clergyman, and the world does not commonly associate wealth with Baptist clergymen; but this one, while not rich, apparently was a man of some substance, and he married a woman who brought him more. The Rev. John Clay is said to have disposed in his will of some thirty Negro slaves,[1]

[1] Joseph M. Rogers, *The True Henry Clay*, p. 146. (Hereafter cited as Rogers.)

over and above his landed estate; and in Virginia, in 1781, a man who possessed thirty Negroes was a long way indeed from being a pauper.

However, if one bears in mind that "infancy, ignorance and indigence" were words shouted by a Senator in the heat of debate with a particularly exasperating opponent and subtracts from them the discount that the circumstances require, they are not hopelessly far from the truth. The inheritance of every child born in Hanover County, Virginia, in the fateful year 1777, consisted largely of infancy, ignorance and indigence. War was raging, and while Henry was still a toddler it swept into Hanover County. Not once, but repeatedly, the country was harried by the redoubtable Tarleton and his British dragoons. One of his biographers[2] declares that Clay's home was raided on the day in 1781 that his father was buried and that a dragoon contemptuously thrust his saber into the loose soil of the new-made grave. At any rate, it is certain that the tides of war swept back and forth across the country for several years; and it is equally certain that, when such conditions prevailed, property as mobile as slaves had a habit of taking to its heels and vanishing forever. It is, therefore, not difficult to believe that Rogers,[3] declaring that "The widow had considerable difficulty in getting along, in spite of her nominally large estate," put it conservatively. If any doubt remains, it is abolished by the additional fact that she was left with seven children, two of them younger than Henry.

A country boy, born the fifth of seven children in a war-racked region, undoubtedly gained early in life an intimate knowledge of the meaning of hard work. Henry was born April 12, 1777,[4] and the treaty of peace was not signed until 1783,

[2] Rogers. He must have picked up the tale in Kentucky, for neither Prentice, Colton nor Schurz seems to have heard it. Schurz says (vol. ii, p. 3) that "while the body was still in the house" Tarleton left a handful of gold and silver on the table as compensation for some property requisitioned; which the widow indignantly cast into the fire as soon as he was gone.

[3] Rogers, p. 146.

[4] In later years it was vehemently asserted that the date was actually 1775, but as the object was to establish that Henry Clay was then too old to be nominated for President again, the story may be dismissed as one of the daintier products of American political campaigning.

while Hanover County was years longer in recovering from the effects of the war; so indigence and ignorance were the common lot. There is little reason to question the assertion that he followed the plow barefoot; everybody did. Hanover, even in time of peace, is by no means one of the richest counties in Virginia[5] and the section in which Clay was born is not the best of Hanover. It is a level plateau some twenty-five miles northeast of Richmond. There is so little slope to the land that drainage is difficult even today, and at that time after every brisk shower water stood for hours, or perhaps days, in great, shallow lakes wherever there was the slightest depression. These spots, too wet for agricultural land and too dry for true swamps, were known as "slashes" and there were so many of them around Clay's home that the neighborhood was known as "The Slashes."

The corn from a wide area of Hanover County was commonly ground at Daricott's Mill, on the Pamunkey River. The usual method of transport was to fill a sack half-full of shelled corn, tie the mouth tightly, and throw the sack across the back of an animal—a pony, a horse, in later years usually a mule—in such a way that half the loose corn fell on each side, forming a sort of packsaddle. Then one of the farm boys was mounted on top of the whole and with a rope bridle rode sedately off to the mill. Doubtless Henry Clay did this often; every farm boy did; but one is permitted to cherish a doubt that it earned for him then, as one of his biographers says,[6] the nickname of "The Mill-Boy of the Slashes." That sounds much more like something manufactured by a political press-agent in later years.

The incident is emphasized here because it illustrates the great difficulty of getting at reality in the life of Henry Clay. What in modern times is termed "the build-up" is by no means a modern invention. It is certainly as old as election by popular vote, and probably far older. The genealogy that traced Augustus' descent from Aeneas was certainly a build-up; and "when that the poor have cried, Caesar hath wept" is an almost perfect example of what the publicity section of a modern National

[5] For a fine picture of its worst features consult Ellen Glasgow's *Barren Ground*.
[6] Schurz, vol. i, p. 4.

Committee tries to do for the head of the ticket. Here, then, is a man who for nearly fifty years was not merely a partisan, but a party leader; for the better part of five decades the interests of countless men were more or less intimately bound up with the political fortunes of Henry Clay; which is to say, for many years some of the shrewdest political manipulators in America were exhausting their ingenuity in efforts to make the man appear to be whatever they thought would appeal to the largest number of voters. In this they were powerfully and consistently assisted by the man himself, for Clay was a politician and an extremely able one. Is it any wonder, then, that there has been erected around him a scaffolding that makes his true contours and dimensions difficult to determine?

Republicans are inclined to preen themselves on their freedom from the patent frauds that a monarchical system renders inevitable, when a human being is erected into a symbol of the sovereignty of the state. But it is to be doubted that our self-gratulation is as well justified as we think. It may be true that we escape the necessity of proclaiming some spindle-shanked, timorous puppet of doubtful mental capacity as "the high and mighty prince"; but that doesn't relieve us of the necessity of proclaiming some wizened, weasel-brained pettifogger as a model of all rustic virtues, or some millionaire stock-salesman as the archetype of the rugged pioneer, or some blue-blooded aristocrat, carefully groomed by the most exclusive and expensive schools in the country as a reincarnation of Old Abe, the Rail Splitter— if the subject of the build-up chances to be the head of the ticket. No, there is as much romantic and lyrical lying about a great American politician as there is about any king; and if it is usually easier to discover his actual human qualities, that is due to the fact that he has usually achieved real significance fairly late in life, leaving a record of many years during which it was worth no one's while to erect a false structure about him.

The trouble with Clay is that he became important before he attained his majority, and remained so until his death. Therefore whatever was said about him by his contemporaries—the source from which all subsequent treatments must derive—whether it is good or ill, must be considered in the light of the political situation prevailing at the time, and the speaker's attitude toward it. As political reporters of today would put it, for fifty years everyone who spoke or wrote of Clay had reason either to "build him up," or to "smear him." Hence all the records are unreliable. What makes it possible for a later generation to hope that it may attain an approximation of the truth is the fact that the essentials of political manipulation never change; hence a very small acquaintance with the methods and practice of politicians active today makes the efforts of Clay's friends and enemies alike fairly transparent.

Little attention need be paid then, to the lugubrious accounts of Clay's early struggles—including his own. The chances are that his childhood was as happy as that of the average boy of his acquaintance; and it is certain that he was more fortunately situated than a great many. After a few years his mother married again. Her second husband was Captain Henry Watkins, of Richmond, who seems to have been a man of good sense and amiability. Clay always spoke of him in terms of respect and affection, and he obviously did what he considered his duty by his seven stepchildren, as well as by the other seven that his wife bore him.

But it is clear that Captain Watkins had his troubles. After a few years he apparently arrived at the conviction—perhaps understandably—that Virginia was becoming over-populated and that it would be better for him to strike out for the boundless West; so about 1792 he departed for Kentucky. First, though, he looked after the interests of young Henry. The boy had received such education as was available, that is, reading, writing, and arithmetic, in a school conducted in a one-room log schoolhouse by one Peter Deacon, of whom about all that is known is that he was an Englishman of bibulous tendencies.[7] During intervals of sobriety, however, he contrived to give his pupil enough instruction to qualify him for something better than a manual laborer's job. Before he was fourteen the boy had exhausted Peter Deacon's scanty resources and his stepfather, al-

[7] Schurz, vol. i, p. 4.

ready contemplating the move for Kentucky, got him a job as
clerk in the retail store conducted at Richmond by Richard
Denny. But Captain Watkins was not satisfied with this. Presumably young Henry was already showing signs of capacity
that indicated ability to do something more important than dis-
pensing molasses and calico to the inhabitants. At any rate,
shortly before the departure for Kentucky, Watkins made the
stroke that fairly opened the way to a career for the boy. The
Captain was not without influence. For one thing, he was a close
friend of Colonel Tinsley, a member of the House of Burgesses,
and Peter Tinsley, the Colonel's brother, was clerk of the High
Court of Chancery. Through the Colonel, Captain Watkins prevailed upon Peter Tinsley to appoint Henry a clerk in his office.
More than fifty years later Henry Clay was to make the claim
that he had established himself "without patrons, without the
favor of the great or opulent,"[8] but this is to be understood as
only relatively true.

Right at this point it is advisable to pause and take stock, for
it is beyond doubt that right here is a turning point so important
in this life that if it is neglected, much that follows will be incomprehensible. Clay's biographers, for the most part, have assumed that here is where his life really began, almost ignoring
the fifteen years that preceded it. It is true that when he entered
Peter Tinsley's office, Clay for the first time emerged into the
world of affairs; but comprehension of his conduct there ought
to be much easier and more complete if one understands the
mental and emotional equipment he brought with him.

Unquestionably, the boy was sensitive, alert and mentally
ravenous. Even after one has discounted heavily the campaign
oratory of later years, the fact remains that he did know very
well what poverty means. In any country recently trampled by
battling armies, the graces and amenities of life, or most of them,
are inevitably adjourned while the population solves the stern,
primary problem of getting enough to eat. Music, art, literature,
the fascinating occupation of watching the battle of ideas—these

[8] Speech at Lexington, Ky., June 6, 1842.

things are not for the dwellers in a rural community ravaged by war.

At the same time—and this is plainly of high importance—this boy had not endured that bitter want that warps the mind and poisons the soul. At the same age Andrew Jackson was already a veteran soldier with a ghastly saber scar on his head, pitted with smallpox contracted in a prison camp, orphaned and not merely poor, but absolutely penniless. At fifteen Andrew Jackson was already an embittered man, a hard man who grew harder as the years passed. When he finally emerged into the world of easy and gracious living, he was already incapable of illusion, beyond its field of fascination. Nothing could delude him into the belief that the world is, after all, a very pleasant place in which good fellows can always come to an understanding comfortable for all concerned. It is possible that this steely core at the center of Old Hickory's being explains the curious fact that whenever he came into collision with the Great Triumvirate, Clay, Webster and Calhoun, it was the Triumvirate that went down, and the uncouth Jackson who triumphed.

In the office of the clerk of the court Henry Clay came into contact for the first time with young men who were sharply aware of the existence of a great world beyond the horizon, young men whose minds ranged beyond the problems that occupy hard-working farmers' sons—the crops, the weather, the relative merits of hunting dogs and the prospects for the next country dance. It was not that Tinsley's boys were geniuses. Their names, except that of Clay, are now forgotten. But Richmond was the capital of the State, and the High Court of Chancery its chief judicial tribunal. The clerks in the office were inevitably brought into contact with ideas of all sorts. The fact that the contact was not without effect is evidenced by the existence among them of a debating society, where all sorts of matters were discussed. Clay attended, and he used to tell with amusement how, when he first had opportunity to address the assemblage, stage-fright betrayed him into beginning his address by stuttering, "Gentlemen of the jury"; the roar of laughter that greeted this all but extinguished him, but it is significant of his resolution that he kept his feet, and in the end made a speech that was received with applause.[9]

The lad blossomed in this atmosphere. Proof of it, if any were needed, is to be found in the fact that, after he had been in the office only a few months, he was chosen out of all the clerks by a keen judge of men. George Wythe, Chancellor of Virginia, was in need of a confidential clerk, so he borrowed Clay from Peter Tinsley and kept him for four years.

This was the making of Clay, intellectually and professionally. No doubt it is characteristic of the unreal formalism of much of our thinking that men should say that Clay was badly educated, and, in the next breath, admit that he spent four years in intimate companionship with Chancellor Wythe and under his tutelage. For this was one of Virginia's really great men and, as a preceptor, perhaps her greatest. He had signed the Declaration of Independence. He had sat in the convention that framed the Federal Constitution and had much to do with the campaign that secured its ratification by Virginia. He had remodeled the code of Virginia and since 1786 had held her highest judicial office. He was a great lawyer and a great patriot, but it was as a teacher that he attained the highest eminence—not on account of his service as professor of law at the College of William and Mary, but by reason of the succession of brilliant men he had sent out into the world from his office, as well as from his classroom. He had taught, and to the end of their lives he had the veneration of Thomas Jefferson, John Marshall and James Monroe, among many who were less celebrated, but still eminent men. "If anyone would know how and where Henry Clay laid the foundation of his greatness and fame," exclaims one of his biographers, "he is answered in the fact that he was for years the pupil and companion of Chancellor Wythe."[10]

It is certainly true that this instruction was highly informal, and it is probably true that an intellectual discipline of a more austere and rigid type would have improved him as a practicing

[9] George D. Prentice, *Biography of Henry Clay*, p. 9.
[10] Calvin Colton, *Life and Times of Henry Clay*, vol. i, p. 23. (Hereafter cited as Colton.)

attorney; but to say, as Schurz does, that "he could thus, at best, have acquired only a slender equipment for the tasks before him"[11] is deliberately to ignore the plain record. For in later years this man was not only well-nigh irresistible before a jury, but Daniel Webster was afraid of him when they met as opponents before the Supreme Court of the United States; and at least once he induced that tribunal to reverse one of its own rulings.[12] A lawyer who can arouse the apprehension of the acknowledged leader of the American bar, and convince the Supreme Court in the teeth of its own precedents, is hardly to be described as an attorney of "slender equipment."

What Shurz had in mind was the fact that Clay engaged in the formal study of law for one year only, in the office of Robert Brooke, Attorney-General of Virginia. Wythe sent him there, but only after Clay had been under his own tutelage for four years. Clay was educated in the law before he went to Brooke, and doubtless the Chancellor knew it. That final year's formal study was merely a polishing-off process.

But before he left that wise old man he had learned much besides the fundamental principles of the law. Wythe knew history, literature and men, as well as the statutes and the rules of procedure; and all the riches of his powerful mind were put at the service of his pupil.[13] Given on the part of the pupil a swift intelligence and a genuine thirst for knowledge, the result was bound to be an education of substantial proportions, an education far more genuine than that gained by many a student after four years of gentlemanly loafing in a university.

One thing, however, it did not confer upon him, and that was a genuine love of books. This John Quincy Adams, in later years, was never able to understand. It seems not to have occurred to the New Englander, reared in the Harvard tradition, that the

---

[11] Schurz, vol. i, p. 10.
[12] In the case of the Commonwealth Bank, 1820. See Peters' Reports, XI, 257.
[13] "The Chancellor's society and guidance were to him at the same time a school of the classics, of Belles-lettres, of law, of history, and of every useful department of learning to which the taste and ambition of his young friend were inclined; and the habitual connexion between them was as that of father and son, of master and pupil." Colton, vol. i, p. 22.

proper study of mankind is man, except as man is revealed in written records. Here was a man who obviously knew much, yet it was a rare occurrence for him to open a book; it was beyond Adams, so the most he could admit was that Clay was "half educated."

Wythe did make available, however, the sort of text that Clay studied avidly. In Richmond the Chancellor's confidential secretary, although a mere boy, had a certain distinction by reason of his position; and it was easy for him to make the acquaintance of men of eminence. With Clay an introduction was sufficient. The deepest impression he made upon his time was imprinted by his power of winning friendship and usually affection from men of the most diverse types. In Richmond, while yet in his teens, he came into contact with all of Wythe's circle, which included some first-rate men.[14] He knew John Marshall. He knew Edmund Pendleton, who had figured prominently in the Revolution and in the making of the Constitution and who, as a jurist, was Wythe's only serious rival in the estimation of Virginians. He knew Bushrod Washington, nephew of George, and man of letters as well as of the law, who was to precede Marshall to the Supreme Court bench. He knew Spencer Roane, Call, Copeland, Wickham—all gentlemen and all men of genuine intellectual power.

It was inevitable that these contacts should have opened to the country boy of no particular social standing and without money a "brave new world" and that he should have been fascinated by it. It is no proof of inferiority, but rather of Clay's good sense, that it should have been so, for these were fascinating men—cultivated, wise, honorable and, above all, accustomed to the exercise of authority. They were aristocrats of the best type, rulers by virtue, not of birth, but of character and ability.

It is probably essential to any adequate understanding of Clay's later life to bear in mind the fact that he was thrown with these men when he was between the ages of fifteen and twenty, a highly impressionable age, and then abruptly removed from their society and the society of others like them, for nearly ten

[14] Colton, vol. ii, p. 26.

years. This experience doubtless set up in his mind a standard of comparison which, perhaps unconsciously, he carried with him for the rest of his life. Could it have been otherwise? A brilliant youth, thrown for some years into close contact with a group of brilliant men, and then withdrawn from among them, would be a strange human being indeed if he did not refer subsequent experience to this and tend to judge all other society by the standards of the golden period of his life.

After a year in the office of Brooke, Clay received his license to practice law, but instead of settling in Richmond, he determined to follow the example of his stepfather and go to the far West, at this time represented by Kentucky, where the chances for a young man were infinitely better. Captain Watkins had settled near Lexington, in the bluegrass country, and thither young Clay went.

It is difficult for the twentieth century to realize what that meant, for it is the plain fact that today there is no region of the earth as remote from Richmond, Virginia, as Lexington, Kentucky, was in 1797. Singapore is almost exactly on the opposite side of the globe from Richmond, but by use of the commercial air routes a man may reach Singapore in less time, and with vastly less physical effort than were expended in going to Lexington a hundred and forty years ago. A young Virginian who should decide to settle in Alaska today would regard himself as definitely pulling up stakes; but at that, he would be closer to home than Clay was when he entered the frontier town where he hoped to make his fortune.

Kentucky, just admitted to statehood,[15] was the wild and woolly West of the time, and it was probably wilder and woollier than anything Owen Wister's Virginian ever saw in Wyoming. Kentucky, perhaps, was not as tough as either Tennessee, to the south, or Ohio, to the north, because it was the first state of the great valley to become populous, but it was the frontier and, like all the rest of the frontier, it was violent and litigious; therefore it was a happy hunting ground for lawyers. Curiously little attention has been paid by historians to the frontiersman as a liti-

[15] June 1, 1792.

gant; yet this characteristic had an important bearing on the careers of most of the pioneers who have become eminent statesmen. Your frontiersman was perhaps happiest when he was engaged in physical combat; but, failing that, his next great delight was engaging in a lawsuit. Personal affronts, indeed, he rarely took into the courts of law; they were to be settled by *force majeure* or, in the more sophisticated atmosphere of such places as Lexington, on "the field of honor." But disputes of all other sorts were subjects of litigation, which was frequently brought on the most frivolous pretexts. The result was that lawyers flourished exceedingly in the most lawless part of the country.

In this environment Clay's success was prompt and impressive. Later in life he liked to make the world believe that it was a hard struggle, but that was for political effect. "I established myself in Lexington, in 1797, without patrons, without the favor or countenance of the great or opulent, without the means of paying my weekly board," he said.[16] "I remember how comfortable I thought I should be if I could make one hundred pounds, Virginia money, per year, and with what delight I received the first fifteen shillings fee." But as a matter of fact, he did have patrons, he did have the countenance of the great. They were not Kentuckians, but something better—famous men, far away, who loomed tremendously in the minds of Kentuckians. A young lawyer, a pupil of Chancellor Wythe, who came fresh from familiar intercourse with John Marshall, Bushrod Washington, Edmund Pendleton, had the most powerful of patrons. In a frontier community such a man could be sure of attentive consideration and, if he possessed any merit of his own, the road to success was open before him.

This young man unquestionably had merit and Lexington received him gladly. He was far from handsome, but he had something much more valuable than the face and figure of Adonis— he had an air. In fact, his very ugliness was of the type that disarms male jealousy even as it arouses female sympathy. His nose was too long, his ears were too big, his mouth was too wide for the most suspicious husband or lover to feel any twinge of alarm at his first sight of a face like that; while women, glancing at him

[16] In the Lexington speech of June 6, 1842.

indifferently at first, soon noted the liveliness of the keen, blue eyes and the charm of the smile that could light up and transform the whole face. Clay was tall and rangy, a loose-jointed youth, rather knobby as to knuckles and wrists, sandy-haired and sinewy. He was one hundred per cent masculine, and the frontier liked that. Yet, for all his lack of classical beauty, he had been familiar with the best society of Richmond, and he had the stamp of old Virginia on him. In spite of his ungainly frame, he could move with a charming, courtly grace; for a woman he could turn a compliment neatly; for a man he could exhibit an easy, yet polished courtesy quite beyond the capacity of most frontiersmen. Withal he was obviously a youngster avid of life and experience, good-humored, light-hearted, yet with a shrewd and penetrating intelligence and an astonishingly fluent tongue. How could Lexington resist him?

It could not. It promptly surrendered, and in truth for nearly sixty years it lay under the spell that this youth cast upon it before the nineteenth century began. In the very speech in which he complained of his lack of patronage, Clay himself admitted that he fell at once into a lucrative practice. His hope to make one hundred pounds, Virginia money—some $400, a year—was soon fulfilled, and more than fulfilled. Indeed, within a decade his practice was one of the richest in the West.

His clients got their money's worth, too. Kentucky had never seen a more successful advocate. The assertion that he knew little law is hardly justified by the facts, and his severest critics are compelled to admit that he knew all there was to know about Kentucky juries. The early biographies are full of stories of his brilliant coups, most of which owed more to histrionics than to jurisprudence. Like most young lawyers in small southern towns even today, he made his first reputation in criminal cases; there he was irresistible. He was so good, in fact, that it is easy to believe he was a curse to the State of Kentucky. It is said that no client of Henry Clay's was ever hanged,[17] which is testimony

---

[17] Prentice, p. 18. The six preceding pages are given up to stories of Clay's triumphs in the courtroom, most of them pretty doubtful from the standpoint of abstract justice.

to the ability of the lawyer, no doubt, but not necessarily proof that his activity was of service to the State. He seems to have entertained some doubts on this point himself; there is a story that on one occasion he encountered a client whom he had successfully defended on a murder charge. The man, full of Bourbon and gratitude, broke out in noisy welcome: to "Mr. Clay, who saved my life."

"Yes," observed Clay, acidly, "I fear I have cheated the gallows of too many like you, who ought to be hanged."[18]

He has the questionable distinction of being the first American lawyer to plead emotional insanity in answer to a charge of murder. A certain Mrs. Phelps had blown her sister-in-law into eternity with a shotgun. It was done in the presence of Phelps himself, and of other witnesses, so there was no question as to the facts. Everything depended upon the argument of counsel for the defense, and Clay's speech was such a masterpiece of sentimentality that the flustered jury brought in a verdict of manslaughter. It was the one verdict that was patently impossible; but it saved the life of his client, which was all Clay hoped to achieve.[19] Incidentally, it gave criminal lawyers a new weapon, which they have employed assiduously ever since.

His most astounding performance, however, was in the case of one Willis, also accused of murder. The facts were so clear, and the killing was so extraordinarily atrocious that Clay's most prodigious efforts when the case was first tried could achieve no more than a hung jury and a mistrial. Then when the case came up the second time, Clay astonished bench and bar by pleading double jeopardy. This man, he asserted, had already been tried, and the Constitution specifically forbids trying a man twice for the same offense. The court, of course, summarily dismissed the plea, whereupon Clay, with a great show of indignation, proclaimed that if he were not allowed to defend his client, he must withdraw from the case; and he marched out of the courtroom. So great was his prestige by this time that the judge apparently lost his head; he sent a messenger after the irate lawyer, assur-

[18] Colton, vol. i, p. 96.
[19] Prentice, p. 13.

ing him that if he would return he would be permitted to finish his argument in his own way. This he graciously condescended to do, and this jury, also completely bemused, returned a verdict of acquittal.[20]

This went beyond mere sharp practice. Clay took advantage of the presence on the bench of a weak judge to argue to the jury of laymen that the law was something that he knew very well it was not. No completely honest man would have done it. But then Clay never was completely honest. He was a statesman, which is to say, a politician, which is to say, according to Lincoln, "at least one long step removed from honest men."

Condemn him, if you will, but bear in mind that when a man is gifted with any extraordinary power it is all but impossible for him to refrain from using it. It is but human for him to do so, and Clay was, above all, intensely human. He knew that the average jury in his hands was as malleable as potter's clay, so it must have been difficult in the extreme for him to deny himself the pleasure of twisting it to suit his fancy.

He did it once too often, however, for his own peace of mind. During an interregnum he was persuaded to act for a short time as prosecuting attorney. Apparently he had no taste for the job, and took it only to hold the place for a friend whose immediate appointment was impracticable. While he was in the office a Negro slave was brought to trial for killing a white overseer. Had Clay been appearing for the defense, the case would have delighted him, for the evidence showed plenty of extenuation. The overseer was a notorious brute, and there was ample testimony that he set upon the slave with murderous frenzy. A verdict of justifiable homicide should have been easy, and one of manslaughter was predicted by most observers as the extremity of the law. But the man was weakly defended, and the old temptation to exercise his power over a jury was too much for Clay; he prosecuted with utter ruthlessness and with fatal skill. The result was that a man was sent unjustly to the gallows, and to the end of his days Clay lamented his connection with that case.[21]

[20] Prentice, pp. 16ff.
[21] Prentice, p. 18.

He accepted the easy morality of the profession that holds a lawyer's duty to be discharged when he has done his utmost for the client he represents; the sterner code, holding that an attorney, as an officer of the court, shares the court's duty of seeing that justice is done, was beyond his reach.

However, he was no merchant of the law, interested exclusively in selling his services to the highest bidder. Time and again he rejected fat fees because the case was obviously foul; and even more frequently he fought furiously, exhausting all his resources of skill and energy, for a client who had not a cent for his fee. One type of case, in particular, he was never known to refuse; that was the case of a slave suing for his freedom. He seldom lost one of these cases, but it was even more infrequent for him to be paid for trying them.

The big money, though, came from his civil practice. At this time Kentucky was filling up with settlers rapidly, the early land offices were magnificently inefficient, competent surveyors were scarce, and sharpers were plentiful. The result was that land titles and boundaries were in a state of almost incredible confusion. Add the typical frontiersman's delight in litigation and it is at once apparent that the State was a wonderful place for lawyers. Clay got his full share of business, and prospered exceedingly. Had he been an avaricious man, it would have been easy for him to become a millionaire at a time when millionaires were all but unknown in the country; as it was, he became a substantial citizen and was soon able to purchase an estate, then in open country, but now on the edge of Lexington. Six hundred acres of the richest land in Kentucky, which is to say, some of the best farming land in the world, were comprised in this place, which he called Ashland. There he set up as a gentleman farmer, and it remained his home until the end.

Sharing it with him was a woman to whom Clay's biographers have paid too little attention. Lucretia Hart was born in Hagerstown, Maryland, in 1781,[22] but her family had removed to Kentucky some time before Clay's arrival, and her father, Colonel Thomas Hart, was a man of substance and prestige, not only in

[22] Colton, vol. i, p. 31.

Kentucky, but, through his widespread family connections, in Virginia, North Carolina, and Tennessee, as well. One of the Colonel's grandnephews, named for him, was to play an important part in the life of his son-in-law; this was Thomas Hart Benton, born in North Carolina, raised in Tennessee, and the first statesman of Missouri.

For a brilliant, but impulsive and somewhat erratic husband, Lucretia Hart was almost the perfect mate. To such a scintillant personality as Mrs. Gaillard Hunt Smith she seemed dull,[23] an admirable housewife and still a more admirable mother to her swarm of children, devoted to her brilliant husband, but without much understanding of him and still less of the situation in which he was involved. Mrs. Smith's testimony is that of an eye-witness and therefore ought to be good; yet clever women have been known to under-estimate the qualities of those whose abilities lie somewhat under the surface. There is an anecdote told of Mrs. Clay that hints at a quality Mrs. Smith did not perceive. Another woman, "a demure New Englander" according to Bradford, once remarked to Mrs. Clay, "Isn't it a pity your husband gambles so much?" to which she quietly replied, "Oh, I don't know. He usually wins."[24] This story fascinated Bradford, but only "because it so clearly marks the difference of climates and manners." Apparently it never occurred to him that it might mark also a terrific capacity in Lucretia Clay to wither the maker of an impertinent inquiry. Just to keep the record clear, it should be noted here that the meticulous Rogers adds, "This story is denied."

At any rate, in April, 1799, Clay formed an alliance with this woman, and all his life long he never regretted it for a moment. A warm-hearted, gregarious being, avid of life and experience, and during the greater part of his career one of the most cele-

[23] See *The First Forty Years of Washington Society* (Letters of Mrs. Samuel Harrison Smith). It should be noted, though, that Mrs. Smith, who was capable of being extremely catty at times, not only held Mrs. Clay in genuine affection, but as the years passed sought out her society more and more. This is pretty good evidence that, even to an exceptionally clever woman, Lucretia Clay was not a tiresome bore.

[24] Gamaliel Bradford, *As God Made Them*, p. 62. Rogers, p. 163.

brated men in the nation, he was naturally a fascinating figure to
women of all degrees. Some of his more enthusiastic biographers
would have us believe that through all this he remained the perfect model of propriety, which is a pretty severe strain on credulity; but there is ample evidence to support the belief that, however his fancy may have wandered momentarily, to the day of
his death only one woman really counted in Henry Clay's life,
and that woman was Lucretia. During some of the more bitter
campaigns in which he was engaged, appalling stories were told
of the looseness of Clay's morals, even going so far as to mention a Negro mistress at Ashland. These were straight-out campaign lies. Whatever his faults, Clay was a gentleman, and if he
stepped aside from the strait path of rectitude occasionally, he
never allowed these incidents to involve his home.

All this Lucretia apparently understood perfectly. Washington
might gossip, scavengers of the press might lie until they were
black in the face, but she knew in her heart that Henry was her
man, and that no other woman, however predatory, had the re-
motest chance of carrying him off; therefore she went placidly
about her business, letting "the heathen rage and the people
imagine a vain thing." She won renown as the best farmer in
Kentucky, her husband admittedly being the second best. She
bore him eleven children. With the immemorial wisdom of
women, she tolerated his visions and dreams, whether she shared
them or not. She stayed at home and handled the estate, while
he was raging around the world, engaging in incomprehensible
projects with incomprehensible people—with Aaron Burr, with
the British plenipotentiaries at Ghent, with the French, with
Miranda, the South American revolutionist, with Nicholas Biddle, the banker, with Webster and Calhoun, with God knows
who not. When he triumphed, she applauded, but without removing her keen, supervisory eye from the Negroes, the fields
and the string of race horses at Ashland. When he came home to
her whipped, she salved the wounds to his self-esteem and re-
doubled her efforts to make Ashland the finest estate in Kentucky.
If he lost eight thousand dollars in a single night at brag, the
precursor of poker, she never complained aloud, nor even when

he indorsed a note for some so-called friend and then had to pay it. Only when the strain of political combat threatened his physical strength did she intervene to urge him to withdraw. In other words, Lucretia, satisfied that Clay was her own, whatever the world might think, contentedly shouldered the inglorious routine, uncomplainingly and apparently happily did the dirty work, while he shone in the eyes of the world and collected the garlands and the applause.

From one point of view, this would seem to indicate that Lucretia was little better than half-witted; but the world knows, and especially women know, that just such a woman is behind many of the great careers that have dazzled mankind. Perhaps only a woman can understand Lucretia Clay; for mysterious as it is to men, a woman seems to know how it is that no fatigue is too great, no anxiety too rasping, no pain too sharp to be borne gladly, if only, when all the flowers have been heaped up and the roar of cheering dies away, the hero, flushed and smiling, always turns at last to her.

The observant but unimaginative Colton doubtless thought he was paying tribute to Clay when he wrote, "During his long public career, himself the observed of all observers, few, away from Lexington and the neighborhood, have ever heard anything of his family, simply because everything there was as it should be. It has been a quiet history, because it has been without fault and without ostentation."[25] But a good half of the credit in any such observation belongs to the man's wife.

In connection with his marriage there is another fact, however, that should be borne in mind, because it is possible that it has had a far-reaching effect on American history. This is the fact that Colonel Thomas Hart was not only a grower of hemp, but a manufacturer of rope and cordage. A dozen years later this industry, with transportation to the Atlantic coast slow and expensive, was suffering sharply from European competition. It was one of the first for which Clay secured tariff protection; and its prompt revival under this stimulus was undoubtedly an im-

[25] Colton, vol. i, p. 32.

pressive object lesson that confirmed him in his adherence to what he chose to call the American System.

Such matters were far in the future, though, when he and Lucretia were married in 1799. Immediately at hand was the question of a new constitution for Kentucky. A convention to frame one had been called and certain idealists were advocating the inclusion in it of a clause abolishing slavery within the State. On this issue Clay took the unpopular side and made a resounding campaign in support of the clause. "Highly honorable to him," observes Schurz,[26] and so it was; but here was old Virginia speaking again. Clay was the last representative of the school of thought whose philosophical objections to slavery had evoked denunciations of the "peculiar institution" from Patrick Henry, Jefferson, Madison, Marshall, even John Randolph— from nearly every one of the great Virginians who flourished at the turn of the century. Philosophical subtleties, however, were not for the frontier; the practical advantage, real or fancied, of slavery swept Clay and his friends to defeat.[27] Nevertheless, although he lost, he never ceased to take pride in this campaign; and, indeed, it was invaluable to him in later years when he needed a reply to accusations that he was a tool of the slave power.

This was his first active participation in politics. If it was an unlucky beginning in that it got him in bad odor with his neighbors at the start, that effect was swiftly eradicated by an even more resounding campaign against the Alien and Sedition Laws, whose unpopularity in Kentucky surpassed that of abolition. In this campaign Clay stepped out as a Jeffersonian not merely ardent, but extremely eloquent and persuasive; and certain political leaders began to think that this young man might be made an asset of considerable value to the party.

However, it was not until 1803 that he entered definitely into what was to be his life work and then his emergence seems to have been effected without his knowledge or consent. While he was enjoying a vacation at a popular resort his name was put

[26] Schurz, vol. i, p. 27.
[27] Schurz, vol. i, p. 30.

before the voters as a candidate for the legislature from Fayette County (Lexington), and he swept the field.[28] It is interesting to observe that from this time until his death Henry Clay never ran for any office whatsoever without receiving the vote of Fayette County.

The session that followed was not particularly significant in itself, but it was significant for Clay in that it brought him into contact with the leaders of Kentucky politics and built him up from a county notable into a man of statewide prominence.[29] His personal charm and oratorical power now began to count indeed; it is said that the Senate benches were swiftly emptied when he began to speak in the House.

The proof of the impression he made upon the party leaders during his service in the legislature does not, however, rest upon any inferential evidence. It is to be found in the fact that in 1806, when Senator Adair, of Kentucky, resigned his seat, Henry Clay was chosen to fill out the unexpired term, regardless of the fact that he had not yet reached the constitutional age for a Senator of the United States. He was not thirty years old until April 12, 1807; but it seems to have occurred to nobody to raise the point, and he took his seat without opposition on December 29, 1806.

[28] Prentice, p. 25.
[29] Schurz, vol. i, p. 33.

CHAPTER III

CAROLINIAN INTERLUDE

A device for getting the second member of the Triumvirate introduced and properly on the stage

I T WAS in the year 1782 that a son was born to Patrick Calhoun and his wife, Martha Caldwell, at their home near Abbeville, South Carolina. John Caldwell they called him, after his mother's brother who had been murdered by Tories in Virginia the year before his birth.[1]

His paternal grandfather, James Calhoun, had come from Donegal, and after a short stay in Pennsylvania, and then in Virginia, went finally to South Carolina.[2] He, like the Caldwells, was of the Scotch-Irish breed. It is a race possessed of many virtues, but not conspicuously endowed with beauty, physical or spiritual. The Scotch-Irish are able, dangerous and dour. They furnish fine commanders and still better troops. They furnish merchants and industrialists of great shrewdness and frequently of downright fanatical honesty, but as hard as business men ever get to be. They furnish clergymen who as hell-fire evangelists have no superiors, no, not even among the true Scots. They furnish hanging judges, whose probity is beyond the shadow of a suspicion and whose ruthlessness would make Torquemada shudder. They furnish politicians who are often astute and sometimes wise and whose capacity for hard hitting is surpassed only by their capacity to absorb, over and over again, punishment that would knock out men not gifted with their racial toughness.

They usually command respect, and they sometimes evoke

[1] Gaillard Hunt, *John C. Calhoun*, p. 9.
[2] H. von Holst, *John C. Calhoun*, p. 8.

fervent, deep-seated and lasting loyalty, but God knows they are not lovely.

The toughest, the ugliest and the greatest of this racial strain in America came from the same general region. It is less than a hundred and twenty-five miles from Abbeville to the Waxhaws, on the boundary line between the two Carolinas, where Andrew Jackson had been born fifteen years earlier. But if Jackson is the first of the Carolinian Scotch-Irish, John C. Calhoun certainly ranks second. He and Jackson were so much alike, physically, that there is some reason to believe Sartain, the steel engraver, mistook a picture of Jackson for that of Calhoun. One of his famous plates portrays Webster, Clay and Jackson. There is no imaginable reason for such a grouping unless the artist set out to make a plate of the Triumvirate, Webster, Clay and Calhoun, and inadvertently picked up a picture of Jackson, instead of one of Calhoun.[3]

Temperamentally, the likeness is as striking as the physical resemblance. They were both men of principle, men without doubts. They were both incapable of recognizing any opposition as high-minded. They were both persuaded that God had given them a monopoly of rectitude. When they came into collision, therefore, the enmity between them was no superficial matter; it went down to the very foundations of their being.

Like Jackson, and like Clay, Calhoun was orphaned early in life. One of his biographers[4] makes the curious assertion that his mother was left in straitened circumstances, and that the boy had next to no education, yet in the next breath admits that he entered the junior class at Yale and graduated with high honors in 1804. This is obviously contradictory evidence. The fact seems to be that his means were narrow, but that he received assistance from his older brothers, William and James,[5] both of whom were moderately prosperous, in addition to some income from his father's estate.

[3] See Rogers, p. 57.
[4] von Holst, *op. cit.*
[5] William M. Meigs, *The Life of John Caldwell Calhoun*, vol. i, p. 88. (Hereafter cited as Meigs.)

His primary education, as a matter of fact, was the work of a great genius. The Rev. Dr. Moses Waddel (Hunt had it Waddell, but the other spelling seems to be preferred) had married Catherine Calhoun, sister of John, and although she died in 1796, Dr. Waddel maintained an interest in his young brother-in-law, and it was at his school in Columbia County, Georgia, and later just across the Savannah river at Willington, South Carolina, that Calhoun was prepared for college. Waddel was an extraordinarily gifted teacher,[6] and his establishment was one of the most celebrated in the South at the time. To say that Calhoun was ill-prepared for college, therefore, is about the equivalent of saying that a boy who has been through Groton or Lawrenceville is ill-prepared to enter Yale today. In the United States of 1800, Calhoun couldn't have had better preparation.

Yale was his own choice[7] among all the institutions of learning in the country, and it may be argued with a certain plausibility that it was the worst possible choice for this particular youth. Yale at this time was under the presidency of the brilliant, but arrogant and opinionated, Timothy Dwight. A worse preceptor for John C. Calhoun is hard to imagine. They were too much alike. Dwight, also, was one of those men whom a sardonic Providence has deprived of the capacity to doubt. Quite capable of going to the stake for his beliefs, he was equally capable of sending others to the stake for theirs.

He had opposed Jefferson in the election of 1800 and never for a moment did he accept the arbitrament of the polls. Unable to defeat the President at the ballot box he was, at the moment when Calhoun came under his tutelage, busily engaged in fomenting treason in New England with a view to splitting the country apart and destroying the Union he could not control.

---

[6] "Among his pupils were many who became jurists, congressmen, governors, educators, and clergymen of wide repute. Waddel was a tireless and devoted student and teacher of the classics. It is said that the dull boys of his classes would prepare more than one hundred lines of Virgil for a single recitation, and some of the brightest boys as many as a thousand lines. The school was large at times, often having an enrollment of two hundred." Edgar W. Knight, *Public Education in the South*, p. 84.

[7] Gaillard Hunt, *John C. Calhoun*, p. 14.

President Dwight would have been described, a century and a quarter later, as a Fascist of the most violent type.

If this formidable pedagogue had developed a bitter hatred of young Calhoun, the effect upon the youth might have been salutary, but nothing of the sort happened. The South Carolinian, although a Jeffersonian, was obviously a man of parts and, whatever his faults, Dwight took genuine delight in an intelligent youth. It charmed him to prod Calhoun by making outrageous remarks about the Administration just to see the young Southerner rise to the bait. Sometimes—at least such is the legend—they engaged in battles so furious that they forgot the passage of time and consumed the whole lesson period, doubtless with the high approbation of the rest of the class, who thereby escaped an hour's labor. Whether Dwight actually said that this young man was likely some day to become President is open to doubt; but that he took an exceptional interest in Calhoun is pretty well established.

Bradford remarks that "The effects of late education are manifest in Calhoun. His mind had taken its natural mould and bent before outside mental discipline was extensively applied."[8] It may be so; but it is arguable that the type of mental discipline applied by Timothy Dwight was precisely the kind to confirm and fix him in his "natural mould and bent." Consider that here was an intelligent young man of Scotch-Irish extraction, which is to say, with fanaticism in his blood, brought into contact with a man generally admitted to be one of the first scholars in the country, and finding in that man, along with an intellectual brilliance he was bound to admire, an arrogant certainty of the correctness of his own beliefs. Calhoun was already all too certain of the righteousness of his attitudes, anyhow; when he found in the undeniably able Dwight the same certainty, how could he have failed to gather the impression that this moral arrogance is the mark of a superior man?

He found, too, the president of Yale College, a minister of the gospel, and a citizen of such intense respectability that his participation would have given the odor of sanctity to a raid on

[8] Gamaliel Bradford, *As God Made Them*, p. 91.

a hen-house, proclaiming, not merely the right, but the high duty of secession as a method of protesting undesirable national policies. If Calhoun had ever been inclined to suspect a taint of treason in dissolution of the Union—which he never was—the imprimatur of the Reverend Doctor Timothy Dwight upon it would have erased his scruples. It would be distinctly unfair and probably untrue to imply that Yale made Calhoun a secessionist; but it certainly did nothing to reduce his estimate of the moral grandeur of the idea.

Nor was he done with New England when he had fought his last fight with the uproarious president of Yale and had received his degree. He proceeded to what was perhaps the best law school in the United States at the period, the one conducted at Litchfield, Connecticut, by Tapping Reeve and James Gould. Here, if the atmosphere remained the same, he proceeded from abstract principle to its concrete application. That same year, 1804, Judge Reeves had been writing Senator Uriah Tracy, of Connecticut, father-in-law of his partner, Gould, urging, not merely the principle that Dwight argued, but the act of secession.[9] As Reeve lectured on constitutional law, it is easy to guess what sort of principles his students imbibed.

After a year and a half at Litchfield, Calhoun returned to South Carolina and completed his legal studies in the office of Chancellor De Saussure, being admitted to practice at Abbeville in 1807.

He was, however, no lawyer. All he desired of the law was "to acquire by means of it independence and then return to a planter's life."[10] Calhoun probably was an intellectual snob. He was highly argumentative. He was authoritarian. He was somewhat pedantic. He was severely logical. All of these qualities should have strengthened him as a legal consultant, but at this time the corporation lawyer, as we know him, had not yet appeared on the American scene. In 1807 all lawyers were trial lawyers, and a man who was ineffective before a jury might as

[9] Gaillard Hunt, *John C. Calhoun*, p. 15. Hunt confused the partners, however, and charged "Judge" Gould with writing the letter. See Meigs, vol. i, p. 89.
[10] Hunt, p. 16.

well withdraw from the profession. The rough-and-tumble of courtroom practice may have been what disgusted Calhoun with the law. At that, he was not unsuccessful during the three years he remained in active practice; yet daily contests with men who were not his intellectual equals, trying to persuade ignorant juries, and being, perforce, polite to judges for whose mental attainments he had profound contempt probably galled him unspeakably.

Moreover, in South Carolina at that time the life of a planter was the only life of a gentleman. Even the great merchants of Charleston nearly all possessed estates to which they expected eventually to retire. It is interesting to observe that Calhoun expected to acquire a competence by the practice of the law and then, but not before, become a planter. There seemed to be nothing incongruous, to him, in the assumption that the owner must expect to support the plantation, not to be supported by it.[11] This is significant of the trend of thought that was to lead South Carolina further and further away from reality, until in the end she was capable of supplanting reason with the suicidal frenzy of 1861. When the land begins to be regarded, not as the primary source of wealth, but as the plaything of gentlemen already rich, the economy of the country is in questionable, if not dangerous condition. England, to be sure, has survived in spite of that attitude; but only by becoming the workshop of the world, which South Carolina never attempted to do; and even England today is in a situation that gives her economists plenty of cause to worry.

The year after Clay entered the United States Senate, Calhoun entered the legislature of South Carolina, where he served three years so successfully that at the end of that time his constituents promoted him. He was elected to the national House of Representatives.

His position was now such that a prudent young man might entertain serious thoughts of matrimony and Calhoun accord-

[11] This was, in fact, what he did. His account books "reveal a moving story of a losing venture" according to the Beards. *The Rise of American Civilization*, vol. i, p. 668.

ingly contracted an alliance admirable from every standpoint. During his senior year at Yale he had been seriously ill—in fact, he was prevented from attending the graduation exercises of his class on that account. A relative by marriage invited him to complete his convalescence at Newport in the summer of 1804; and thither he went.

This relative was the widow of his first cousin, John Ewing Colhoun who had been Senator from South Carolina from 1801 until his death in 1802.[12] The difference in the spelling of the name is accounted for by the fact that efforts had been made to induce the Senator to change it back to the ancient Scottish spelling of Colquhoun; he was unwilling to go that far, but he did change the "a" to an "o." He had married "a woman of wealth,"[13] Floride Bonneau, of a Huguenot family high in the social scale in tidewater South Carolina. It was Floride Bonneau Colhoun, who, hearing of the illness of her late husband's young cousin, invited him to her summer home at Newport, where he met her daughter, Floride, then twelve years old.

Seven years later Calhoun, in scrupulously correct and even somewhat stilted fashion, was suing for the hand of this daughter. It was an arrangement that appealed to the French good sense of Floride *mère*; true, Calhoun had not been born in Charleston, between Broad Street and the Battery, and therefore could never be regarded as quite the real thing in South Carolina aristocracy. However, he had all the other characteristics of a gentleman, and there was nothing in the least decadent about him, as there was about many of the Charleston aristocrats. As for money, Floride had plenty. Here was a virile, well-bred and highly intelligent young man who was already making a name for himself in the State legislature and who gave promise of going much further; to Mrs. Colhoun this seemed a better match for her daughter than an alliance which would have involved nothing beyond money and social position, neither of which the Colhouns needed. More than that, she was genuinely fond of the young man, so she gave his suit her enthusiastic approval.

[12] Hunt, p. 18; Meigs, vol. i, p. 70.
[13] Hunt, p. 18.

So did Floride and the marriage was accordingly celebrated January 8, 1811.

It was a success, too, which is the best possible evidence that the affair was not altogether cold-blooded. If, in addition to money, "the marriage brought him social position in lower Carolina, and in this way was, beyond a doubt, a material aid to him in his political career,"[14] it also brought him a beautiful and charming woman, who made him a faithful and devoted wife. Floride Colhoun apparently did not, like Lucretia Hart, retire almost entirely into the background and occupy herself exclusively with domestic affairs. She bore her husband nine children, but she also figured in Washington society. She had a mind of her own, and when the Eaton affair came up, it was the French aristocrat who laid down the inexorable law that eventually disrupted the Cabinet.[15] In every respect, she was a wife to do credit to a statesman, and there is plenty of evidence that her husband was proud of her and had no small respect for her judgment.

A more complete contrast to Henry Clay could hardly be imagined than this man, who was to be Clay's great opponent for the next forty years. If there is a single word that can be applied to almost every aspect of Calhoun's life and career it is the word "correct." At this moment he was in the most literal sense a model young man. No one ever accused him of cheating the gallows and turning murderers loose on society. No one ever accused him of violating, not merely professional ethics, but common honesty, by bulldozing the court. He never sat around a gaming table all night absorbed in brag, that early, three-card form of poker. He never got beautifully tight with questionable companions in the taverns. He never threw away his money by indorsing notes for merry and amiable, but unreliable, friends.

Six feet two, gaunt even in youth but erect, thin-faced with a high forehead surmounted by bushy brown hair, blue-gray eyes of startling brilliancy set deep in their sockets and shad-

14 Meigs, vol. i, p. 101.
15 See Claude G. Bowers, *Party Battles of the Jackson Period*, p. 120.

owed by heavy brown eyebrows, he was physically, as well as temperamentally, the typical Ulsterman, startlingly similar not only to his compatriot and contemporary, Jackson, but also to another portentous Scotch-Irishman of another century, Woodrow Wilson. He was the very incarnation of the wrath of God.

As to the quality of his mind, Hunt says that some youthful verses of his have been found, each stanza of which begins with the word "whereas." After that, it is scarcely necessary to add that he was completely humorless, or that "he takes life seriously and his nature is serious." But it is of high importance to note carefully the next remark of one of his biographers: "He has scattered no wild oats, and has needed the forgiveness of neither man nor woman."[16] The writer intended that to be a high tribute, but in reality it is a terrible indictment; the man doesn't live of whom it is true, but some are not conscious of the need; and when a man is not conscious that he needs forgiveness either of man or woman, he is in a perilous state. He may, as Calhoun did, give formal assent to the doctrine that he needs forgiveness of God, but it is likely that in his heart he doesn't really believe that, either; and a man firmly convinced of his own righteousness is a man splendidly equipped to lead a nation to ruin.

The bent of his mind is admirably illustrated by his remark on Charleston in a letter to Floride Bonneau Colhoun, written in 1807 when "stranger's fever," doubtless aestivo-autumnal malaria, was ravaging the place: "Every paper from there brings a long catalogue of deaths. This is in part no doubt to be attributed to the nature of the climate; but a much greater part is owing to the misconduct of the inhabitants; and may be considered as a curse for their intemperance and debaucheries."[17]

It is interesting to observe that whereas the deplorable Mr. Clay was adored by women, the admirable Mr. Calhoun was handled pretty sharply by them. "The cast-iron man, who looks as if he had never been born,"[18] and "a mental and moral ab-

[16] Hunt, p. 19.
[17] Quoted by Meigs, vol. i, p. 83.
[18] Harriet Martineau, *Retrospect of Western Travel*, vol. i, p. 243.

straction,"[19] are two of the famous descriptions of Calhoun contributed by women; and neither of them suggests that the man was one to kindle any burning enthusiasm in the feminine heart.

But it was a highly significant day in the history of the United States when he took his seat in the House of Representatives on November 4, 1811.

[19] Varina Howell Davis, *Jefferson Davis*, vol. i, p. 210.

CHAPTER IV

ON THE BELLIGERENCE OF A PACIFIST AND THE UNRIGHTEOUSNESS OF THE UPRIGHT

How Mr. Clay frequented the Senate in a holiday mood and how he and Mr. Calhoun made war to no apparent purpose

HENRY CLAY had a really astonishing capacity for doing the wrong thing or, when he did the right thing, for doing it in the wrong way, from the standpoint of the conventional moralist. Taking a seat in the United States Senate was certainly not discreditable, but what is a biographer to say of a man of twenty-nine who accepted that high commission with a candid and joyous announcement that he regarded it as "a vacation," and who went to Washington frankly intent upon having a good time?

As a matter of fact, though, he was justified in not taking his position too seriously. As a Senator he was more a political accident than the deliberate choice of the State of Kentucky. Adair's term had only one session still to run, and to the local politicians it probably mattered little who finished it. The full term, to be captured in the election of 1808, was the important thing, not this brief tenure. Here was a bright young fellow who was doing fine work for the party in the legislature and who deserved some form of approbation. Why not let him have it?

He had it, and swept into Washington like a fresh westerly breeze, to the great enjoyment of that city, now grown somewhat stuffy. He, too, thoroughly enjoyed his "vacation," for he stepped back into something of the old society in which he had delighted in Virginia, ten years earlier. Mr. Jefferson was President and Mr. Madison, Secretary of State; Mr. Marshall was Chief Justice, and Mr. Bushrod Washington, an Associate Jus-

[48]

tice of the Supreme Court; Mr. Randolph, although no longer leader of the majority, was still prominent in the House. There were many other friends of the old days in the town, along with interesting people from other sections of the country. Clay had a good time.

Only one thing gave him cause for disturbance and for some secret mortification. The previous year he had become involved with Aaron Burr.

History long ago acquitted Clay of any knowledge of treasonable activity or intent on Burr's part. It may be that Burr really intended to make himself Emperor of Mexico, if opportunity presented. It was exactly the sort of scheme that would appeal to him. It may be that he intended to do more than that—he may have contemplated becoming Emperor of the Mississippi, as well, taking over part of Mr. Jefferson's late purchase for his personal domain. This would have been treasonable, but a man contemplating setting up an empire is not likely to allow himself to be hampered by any such consideration. On the other hand, it is not beyond the bounds of possibility that Mr. Burr was telling the truth when he came over the mountains into the great valley, gathering men, money, boats and supplies; he may have been intending merely to establish a settlement on the banks of the Ouachita. Enterprises of that sort were much in favor with energetic men of the period; and establishment of a settlement far out in the West would have been a logical first step toward later establishment of an empire.

It is possible to believe any of these explanations. What is impossible is to believe that Burr, assuming that he harbored treasonable schemes, proceeded to confide them to his lawyer. The late Vice-President found himself in difficulties with the Federal authorities as represented by the local Federal district attorney, one Joseph Hamilton Daviess, who proceeded to demand his indictment for treason. Burr asked Clay to defend him, and the young lawyer accepted without hesitation. Who would not? Here was a glittering case, the case of the century. Burr was a former Vice-President of the United States. He had just killed Alexander Hamilton, which exploit was regarded in the dueling and ardently Jeffersonian West as a pardonable error of a high-spirited gentleman; for while Kentuckians, at that time, would not go so far as to say that men ought to kill on the field of honor, still most of them believed that if Mr. Burr had to kill anyone, he made an admirable choice in selecting Alexander Hamilton for that attention.

Under these circumstances, any lawyer in Kentucky would have considered it a professional triumph to be asked to take the case; and so did Clay. He did ask, and receive, from his client a formal assertion of his innocence of the charges; and with that he proceeded happily, for while he knew little about Burr, he knew a great deal about the explosive and ebullient Daviess. Among other things, he knew him for a jackass, who was entirely capable of rushing into court without preparing his case. This is precisely what Daviess had done. When the matter finally came before the Grand Jury, the prosecution had no evidence, and Daviess himself had to make the motion to discharge the jury.[1]

This was all very well in Kentucky, but in Washington Henry Clay found, to his intense chagrin, that he owed his victory to the folly of Daviess, not to the justice of his cause. In the hands of the government there was only too much evidence; but the impetuosity of Daviess, by serving warning on Burr, hampered, instead of helped, the government's case. At that, in the subsequent trial, in spite of the extraordinary maneuvering of the Chief Justice, who so far forgot his dignity as to dine with the defendant during the course of the trial, the utmost the jury would do was to render a Scotch verdict of "not proven."

It was all very embarrassing for Mr. Clay, but he had one consolation—with a lordly gesture, he had refused the fee offered by Burr. He had preferred to take the attitude that he was appearing less in the role of counsel for the defense, than in that of a Kentucky gentleman intent upon vindicating the hospitality

---

[1] Even McMaster, the Federalist historian, although he insinuates that the presiding judge was crooked and the jury packed, is compelled to admit the fact that the prosecution went into court without the necessary evidence. John Bach McMaster, *History of the People of the United States*, vol. iii, p. 66.

of the State in the case of a distinguished visitor being perse-
cuted by political enemies. Therefore he loftily refused money
for his services. It was a fortunate act, for it cleared him of any
suspicion of being mixed up in Burr's schemes for profit. So
while the scandal had Clay squirming for awhile, he was never
very seriously involved; even political enemies could not do
much with a lawyer who never got a cent for his services.

But aside from this blushful business, the young Kentuckian
had a grand time in Washington. He was not a candidate for
re-election, therefore he was untroubled by the necessity of keeping his political fences in order. His clients in Kentucky had
given him three thousand dollars—or at least so William Plumer,
the Federalist Senator from New Hampshire wrote in his diary[2]
—to look after their litigation before the Supreme Court, so he
was not bothered by money troubles. The somewhat acrid
Plumer doubtless drew a fair picture of him at this time in a
celebrated passage from the diary:

"Henry Clay is a man of pleasure; fond of amusements. He
is a great favorite with the ladies; is in all parties of pleasure;
out almost every evening; reads but little; indeed, he said he
meant this session should be a tour of pleasure. He is a man of
talents; is eloquent; but not nice or accurate in his distinctions.
He declaims more than he reasons. He is a gentlemanly and
pleasant companion; a man of honor and integrity."

He made a rousing speech in favor of the immediate erection
of a bridge across the Potomac at the expense of the Federal
government—worthy of mention as his first blow for the policy
of internal improvements. Then the session was over and he
went home.

Back in Kentucky he was promptly sent to the legislature to
represent his county, and in Frankfort he was elected Speaker
of the House. It was not a remarkable session, but it gave Clay
experience in presiding which was to be invaluable a little later.
But it was marked by one incident that is worth passing notice.
Jefferson was struggling with the embargo, and Clay introduced
a resolution expressing confidence in the President and com-

[2] Quoted by Schurz, vol. i, p. 47.

mending his policy. This was gall and wormwood to Federalists, including Humphrey Marshall, a member of the legislature and a former United States Senator, who made a bitter speech denouncing the resolution, but could command only one vote, his own, against it. Clay followed it with another resolution, pledging all members to wear only homespun clothes as long as the embargo was in effect; and Marshall, stung to insensate fury by this, denounced it as the claptrap of a demagogue. If Clay had accepted this in silence he would have lost caste in Kentucky; he retorted in kind, and the outcome was a duel in which both he and Marshall were slightly wounded. Henry Clay was too intelligent not to understand the folly of dueling, but he was also too much the conformist, too much the man of the world, not to do what custom required of a gentleman, even at risk of his life.

This is a point that should be noted carefully, for it throws a light on his character that helps explain much in his subsequent career. Clay had none of the fanatic in his make-up unless, indeed, he might be considered fanatical in his opposition to ordinary fanaticisms. Apparently he never quite believed in the divine inspiration of Mr. Clay. This was his weakness when he came into collision with such frenetic messiahs as Andrew Jackson and John C. Calhoun; but at the same time it accounts for a large part of his value to the country. Cherishing always at least a trace of doubt that Mr. Clay was right, he was hesitant about setting up the opinions of Mr. Clay as the law of the Medes and Persians, which altereth not; and he was eager to demonstrate that Mr. Clay was essentially a sound citizen, at heart one of the boys and willing to go along with the gang. So he resolutely went out and shot Humphrey Marshall in the stomach, letting Marshall shoot him in the leg at the same time, knowing perfectly well that the whole performance was idiotic, but also knowing that it was what the times expected of a gentleman. Henry Clay was one of whom it might be said in sober truth that he would rather be dead than out of the fashion, since on at least two occasions he actually risked his life rather than defy the prevailing opinion; and this is the man whose best-remembered utterance was, "I would rather be right than President."

He was heartily glad that his pistol ball, instead of penetrating, merely ripped the skin across Marshall's abdomen. His own wound laid him up for a few days only, and he was soon back in Kentucky—they had, according to custom, slipped across the river into Ohio for the ceremonies—limping, but with his reputation as a thorough gentleman well established on the frontier. Everyone agreed that the affair had had the happiest possible outcome, no one being killed, and all concerned having acquired much credit.

One of the curious characteristics of the early history of the republic was the incomprehensible passion for resigning exhibited by United States Senators. As a matter of fact the Senate, at this time, had not yet risen even to the dignity of being the first gentlemen's club in the United States. That distinction belonged to the House of Representatives, which was the real arena of political activity, while the Senate was regarded merely as a sort of proving-ground for aspiring young politicians, on the one hand, and on the other, a place of dignified retirement for worn-out party hacks—the sort of thing that later acquired the irreverent label of "Lame Ducks' Roost." Members, therefore, were by no means so passionately determined to retain their seats as they became a few years later, and in 1809 Buckner Thurston, representing Kentucky, imitated Adair by tendering his resignation. Once more Clay was offered the unexpired term, and once more he accepted.

But this time he regarded his visit to the national capital as a great deal more than merely a pleasant vacation. During his previous term Clay had found Washington fascinating, and it is clear that he returned in the winter of 1809–10 determined to make a record that would win him something better than merely a seat among the callow youths and ancient dodos who then constituted the United States Senate. He was playing for a seat in the House, and he won it, but at a price that turned out to be, twenty years later, extremely high.

The question of rechartering the Bank of the United States came up in the spring of 1811. This was the first bank, and, as national banks went in those days, it was not a bad institution. But it did fall under the objection common to all such institutions—it did put the fiscal affairs of the government in private hands, giving its managers an undesirable and dangerous power to manipulate the currency. A large proportion of the stock of the bank was held in England—a sinister fact in view of the relations then existing between the harried American republic and the Mistress of the Seas, engaged in a grapple with Napoleon in the course of which both were trampling ruthlessly upon the rights of all neutrals.

All this Clay perceived with great clarity, and he brought it out in a speech on the floor of the Senate, in which he opposed rechartering the bank. The speech was effective. The proposed renewal of the charter was killed by the deciding vote of the Vice-President. The opposition was made up of heterogeneous elements, including some of the shabbiest demagogues in the country; one particularly evil element was the group that opposed it because Albert Gallatin, Secretary of the Treasury, favored it. This gang opposed anything and everything that Gallatin favored, regardless of the fact that he was a man of sturdy integrity and great ability, because he had been born in Switzerland. Even in 1811 the country was already infected with that poisonous hatred and suspicion of foreigners that have plagued it at intervals ever since. But in the tumult of nonsensical opposition to the bank, Clay spoke up temperately and reasonably, ignoring the silly clatter of the ignorant and prejudiced and confining his arguments to those that carried real weight. His speech made it possible for an honest and sensible man to vote against the bank; and there is little room for doubt that some did on the strength of that speech.

But it accomplished more. The speech was published widely, and read by much larger numbers than heard it. It was read by a certain Tennesseean whose mind, up to that date, had been filled with uncertainty about the bank, when he gave it any attention at all, which was not often. After reading Clay's argument, however, this man was convinced that a national bank was an evil *per se*; and while he did nothing about it for many years and sometimes, indeed, seemed disposed to tolerate the evil, in a crisis twenty years later he found in this speech ample reason to set his face like flint against a national bank. This convert to the anti-bank cause, made a convert by Clay, bore the name of Andrew Jackson.

None of this, however, could have troubled the mind of the young Senator as he returned blithely to Kentucky to demand, and receive, the reward of his brilliant work, namely, promotion to the really significant and important branch of Congress, the House of Representatives. It was granted freely and promptly. In a by-election in 1811 the Lexington district of Kentucky chose as its representative in the Twelfth Congress, the Honorable Henry Clay.

A very plausible argument can be built to support the thesis that the country which we know as the United States dates, not from July 4, 1776, but from November 4, 1811, the day Henry Clay took his seat in the House of Representatives. That seat was none other than the Speaker's chair. No other member has ever attained the extraordinary honor of being elevated to the Speakership of the House on the first day he entered it; but rarely, if ever, has there been a House in a mood more revolutionary.

Revolution, indeed, was called for. In the Tenth and Eleventh Congresses the parliamentary system of the United States had reached its nadir of feebleness and futility. James Madison, the diminutive President, had many admirable qualities; he had had more to do than any other individual with writing the Constitution of the United States; on various diplomatic missions and as Secretary of State, he had proved himself a great administrator; his writings, including his collaboration with Alexander Hamilton in producing *The Federalist* as well as his state papers, show that as a political philosopher he was mong the wisest the country has ever produced. He was honest, he was patriotic, he was highly intelligent, he was neither a time-server nor a self-server.

He had many of the elements of greatness, indeed, he was a great man; but as a party leader he was hopelessly incompetent. He was so bad, in fact, that he permitted the Eleventh Congress to stall completely, and it was only by frantic efforts that the appropriation bills, necessary to keep the government departments running, were passed at the last minute.

Mr. Madison furnished the first demonstration, but, unfortunately, not the last, that honesty, industry and intelligence are not qualifications enough for a man who is to hold the office of President of the United States. He must also be a shrewd and not too scrupulous political manipulator. One earlier President, John Adams, had failed, it is true, but the reason for his failure was patent; his whole philosophy of government, as well as his administrative and legislative policy, was detested by many of the ablest men in the country, headed by the most formidable American politician of the time, Thomas Jefferson. Adams was a strong man, but it was his misfortune to come into violent collision with stronger ones, so his collapse needed no explanation.

Nobody of importance opposed Madison in the way that Jefferson opposed Adams. In New England there was, to be sure, a sour remnant of the Federalist party bent upon ruining the country they could no longer rule, and they heaped upon Madison abuse more vitriolic than the Republicans had used against Adams; but they amounted to little, and even in New England each successive election saw their small influence diminish. Instead of becoming more formidable, they were moving steadily toward the suicidal Hartford Convention that was to ruin their party so completely that its very name became an opprobrious epithet. Even as early as 1811, in most parts of the country, to call a man a Federalist was very much like calling him a Communist a century and a quarter later—that is to say, it was not often seriously intended to describe him, but merely to insult him.

So in spite of the efforts of Timothy Pickering and his friends, it is fair to say that Madison began his first administration with no able, convinced, resolute opposition. Perhaps he would have done better had there been some Jefferson in the field against him, some opposition conducted clearly and intelligently, for Madison knew how to deal with strong men. But his opponent was sheer inertia, apathy, lack of ideas, except the idea of petty scrambling for petty personal advantage. Achilles could deal with Hector, but Paris got him at last. Madison had not hesitated to enter the lists against Hamilton and Marshall and John Adams, nor had he suffered disaster at the hands of these Titans; but he had no idea of how to handle George Clinton and the rabble of nonentities in the two houses of Congress. He could acquit himself well in combat with any sort of an idea; but when he faced men with no ideas at all, he was bewildered and disarmed.

So the Ship of State ran into the doldrums and hung there, motionless.

It was the interval between two epochs. The Revolution was over, and the great men of the Revolution were dead, or stricken in years. They had been a precocious generation. Jefferson's Declaration of Independence had made him immortal at thirty-three, Hamilton had led the country at thirty, Madison himself in writing the Constitution had touched what was perhaps the apogee of his career at thirty-six. For twenty-four years they had been busy with the establishment of the country and they had worked admirably. But the work was done. The battles had been fought, the new paths had been broken; thenceforth the task was not organization, but administration and this task called for different qualities from those displayed by the revolutionaries. A generation had grown up that had never known a king, and to rule the new Americans, born and bred citizens of a republic, it was necessary to devise methods different from those that had served with revolted colonists.

Yet affairs were still largely in the hands of old revolutionists. The trouble was that as the great ones died off, small ones took their places. The Vice-Presidency, once occupied by John Adams and Thomas Jefferson, had come down to Aaron Burr and George Clinton. Congress, once led by Madison, Macon, Monroe and the erratic, but able, John Randolph, now was led by nobody in particular. The terrific, driving energy that had fought the Revolution and set up the republic was utterly gone, largely because the old leaders were gone and those who assumed to lead tried to imitate them when a new type of leadership was required.

Madison himself had been one of the great political philosophers of the Golden Age. He had been a daring speculator, an iconoclast, a breaker of new paths in political thought. He was a successful leader of men in revolt against the old traditions, but in 1811 the call was not for that. The new generation had traditions with which it was well satisfied. It desired, not to break new paths, but to proceed along the old, well-trodden ways, and for this sort of leadership the man who had written the Constitution was not prepared.

To Madison, and to all his generation, the republic was still an experiment, almost miraculously established and most precariously maintained. Madison had been born a subject and remained one until he was twenty-five years old; not by right of birth, but by his own efforts had he become a citizen. It is nothing uncommon for men to continue revising their intellectual attitudes into extreme old age, but a man's emotional attitudes are usually fixed long before he is twenty-five. To that order of society into which he is born a boy attributes an authority and a legitimacy greater than he can ascribe to any order subsequently established; his reason may tell him that the new order is right, and he may act all his life according to the dictates of his reason, but his emotional side will always cherish secret doubts, which may hinder and hamper his action.

There is no question that James Madison, intellectually, was convinced that the republic was the only just government of the United States. Intellectually, he repudiated the notion that the King of England possessed any sort of claim to the allegiance of the people of America. Nevertheless, he knew that he and his contemporaries had made the republic, and he had been taught in his youth that God made the King. He had only too clear a conception of the frailty of the republic; he knew—because he had been there—how laboriously it had been set up, and with what difficulty it had been maintained. So had his predecessors, Jefferson, Adams and Washington. Each of them had been painfully aware of the flimsiness of the fabric they had created, and each feared above all else the effect of collision with some more firmly established government. Washington's last official utterance had been a warning against that danger so earnest that it has reverberated in the memories of Americans for a century and a half. Adams firmly believed that he had committed political suicide rather than risk a collision with France; the fact that history has attributed the suicide to a different reason doesn't alter his belief. Jefferson, in his effort to keep the country clear, for eight years wove a course so tortuous that to this day historians are not able to agree on the direction of all its sinuosities.

But the first three Presidents all dealt with a country dominated, and largely inhabited, by men who were familiar, through personal experience, with the horrors and dangers of war against a powerful enemy. Madison was the first to face a different population, a people who were born freemen and emotionally conditioned to regard the republic, not as a strange and doubtful experiment, but as part of the natural order of things. They knew nothing else, and only by a deliberate effort could they imagine anything else. It never occurred to them that the United States of America existed, so to speak, only by sufferance and that it could be expected to survive only as long as it carefully avoided the shock of battle. Faith in the republic was not, with them, an intellectual proposition, based on carefully reasoned argument, and on that alone. It was also an emotional condition, not consciously learned, but absorbed from birth; therefore it was brighter and more serene than that of the revolutionary generation could possibly be.

The first of these new Americans to attain a position of conspicuous national leadership was Henry Clay, of Kentucky. One shrewd observer[3] has noted that Clay had been only two weeks a Senator when he introduced a new note into American politics in a speech with rhetorical references to the Union and the Fathers. Up to this time Washington and his contemporaries

[3] Henry Adams, *History of the United States*, vol. v, p. 189.

had been referred to as "those great men," sometimes as "venerable heroes" or in similar terms. Clay was the first to raise them from the status of eminent citizens to something not easily distinguishable from tutelary deities of the republic.

He also crashed headlong into what had been the basic principle of American foreign policy ever since the inauguration of Washington, to wit, the avoidance of war. "Sir, is the time never to arrive when we may manage our own affairs without fear of insulting his Britannic Majesty?" he inquired, scornfully, in December, 1810. "Is the rod of British power to be forever suspended over our heads? . . . Whether we assert our rights by sea, or attempt their maintenance by land—whithersoever we turn ourselves, this phantom incessantly pursues us. Already it has had too much influence on the councils of the nation."

The importance of this speech, and of many others like it, is its emotional, not its logical, content. In truth, there was very little sense in it, as Madison, and especially as Albert Gallatin, his Secretary of the Treasury, knew all too well. The United States was not prepared to fight anybody. Its policy of neutrality had been growing increasingly difficult ever since the beginning of the Napoleonic wars, but it had been pursued resolutely and with immense profit. In thirty years its population had jumped from less than four to seven and a quarter millions, and its wealth had increased in even greater proportion. The Jeffersonian embargo and nonintercourse policies, while they were hard on the South and West, stimulated the industrial development of New England enormously. The howl against them that was raised there was based more on politics than on actual economic losses. The twisting and squirming necessary to keep the United States out of war had not been heroic, but the policy had paid tremendous returns.

This Gallatin understood thoroughly and Madison well enough to make him a sincere opponent of war. More than that the nation was even worse prepared morally to wage war than it was from the military standpoint. The resolute determination to keep the peace had been accompanied, not merely by neglect, but by actual demolition of the armed forces. A navy was then regarded as purely an aggressive weapon and as it was the steadfast determination of the United States not to fight, the navy had been practically abolished. The policy toward the army was influenced by pre-Revolutionary thinking. In all history, up to that time, a standing army had been the main support of autocratic government. Autocratic government was now abolished, and democratic control substituted, but it was an experiment without precedent and few had much confidence in its success, even among the chief experimenters. Elementary prudence, then, dictated the elimination of the chief support of the old system, as far as possible. So the army was reduced to a small police force to guard against Indian depredations. Reliance for defense against invasion was placed in the militia.

Paradoxically, the worst feature of this policy was its success. The country had not been invaded. On the contrary, the sole apparent effects of the almost complete abolition of armed forces were release from a heavy burden of taxation and a sense of security that could and did exalt itself into cockiness. The new generation of Americans grew up not only without fear, but without even a wholesome respect for the power of a trained army. The Westerners, in particular, were filled with a quite irrational confidence. The East, after all, had had plenty of experience with the cruisers of the French and British navies. While England and France were locked in the death grapple the American merchant marine had prospered prodigiously, but not without losses. The number of American ships sunk or seized had mounted to an immense total, so the East retained a healthy respect for the power of a broadside. Moreover, it would be exposed to the first assault from the sea, whereas the West could not be reached except after a march so long and difficult as to make Napoleon's invasion of Russia seem trifling by comparison.

Thus Mr. Clay's fulminations against the British aroused but wan enthusiasm in the breast of Mr. Madison, and none at all in that of Mr. Gallatin, one of the most complete realists in the history of American politics. In New England, that section of the country that had prospered most under Jefferson's policy, and that hated him most virulently, the noisy Westerner was denounced with unbridled fury.

But even in New England the spirit of the time was against the old order. Even in New England the opposition to the dominant party was small, and at each successive election it grew smaller. This was not clearly realized at the time, and has not been fully realized since, because the opposition included most of the literate and articulate in New England, and the noise they made was out of proportion to their real numbers. Timothy Pickering, Fisher Ames and the group included in the Essex Junto perhaps never represented a majority of the people of New England, but they did represent the political machine, and so potent was their organization that they carried local elections when a true expression of the will of the majority would probably have defeated them. Even so, every election since 1800 had reduced their power, not merely in the nation, but in New England itself, and it is certainly reasonable to assume that desperation in the face of this relentless disintegration of their strength had at least as much effect as partiality for England in driving them to the suicidal expedient of the Hartford Convention in 1814.

The case of New England between 1800 and 1814 is, indeed, a whole textbook for the political pathologist. It is the classical instance of one of the most curious factors in American political history, to wit, the ignorance of the educated. New England leaders professed immense admiration for Old England, but they proved by their course that they had not the faintest conception of the real significance of such Englishmen as Charles James Fox, Edmund Burke and the younger Pitt. These were among the earlier examples of that new type of British statesmanship which was to make the Empire, within the brief space of a single century, the largest, the wealthiest, the most powerful and, in some respects, the happiest, the world has ever seen. In these very years the British ruling class was developing that extraordinary intellectual capacity by which it raised statesmanship from the simian to the ophidian level, abandoning the tactics of the gorilla in favor of those of the serpent, rejecting brutality for craft.

In England such men as Pickering and Ames, after two or three smashing defeats, would have realized the truth and come into camp. In New England a few of their ablest men—John Quincy Adams, for example, and Plumer, of New Hampshire—did so, and remained powerful, if not dominant, figures to the end of their active lives; but for the most part the intellectual elite of New England chose, instead, to wage a futile, increasingly bitter, and increasingly silly fight against the stars in their courses. In so doing, they set an evil precedent that has plagued the country ever since. To this day the educationally, economically and socially privileged classes in the United States have never learned the immense difference between being consistent and being bullheaded. In no great popular movement since the revolution of 1776 have they, as a class, taken any position except one of frantic and usually blind opposition. In the very year when the British aristocracy was deftly and quietly absorbing, and thereby hamstringing, the once dangerous Ramsay Mac-Donald, the analogous class in this country was driving a man possessed of the same sort of magic control of the masses, Huey Long, of Louisiana, into fantastic excesses that probably would never have occurred to him had he not been goaded into them by blind opposition.

It seems to have occurred to none of these people seriously to examine the proposals of the young men who invaded the Twelfth Congress in a veritable flood. Like the scriptural demon who, being cast out, promptly returned with seven others, young Mr. Clay disappeared from the Senate of the Eleventh Congress only to reappear in the House of the Twelfth backed by a whole platoon of brawling boys some of them noisier than he. Out of one hundred and forty-two members of the previous House, no less than sixty-one had been replaced by new men, most of them young men as age is counted among politicians. Clay, sitting in the Speaker's chair at thirty-four, looked down upon the two South Carolinians, Langdon Cheves, thirty-five, and John Caldwell Calhoun, twenty-nine; upon his new colleague from Kentucky, Richard Mentor Johnson, thirty; upon the Tennesseean, Felix Grundy, thirty-four; upon the Georgian, George M.

Troup, thirty-one. To the veterans of the Revolution, even Cheves was a mere stripling; but to the horde of even younger men who had invaded the House after the last election these leaders were old enough and they commanded the votes and the loyalty of youth.

In such circumstances something was bound to happen, and Madison, Gallatin and all their generation knew it. But they were helpless before the rush of the new generation, and so the country swung dizzily into a war whose records still make historians gasp.

The War of 1812, viewed from the standpoint of either the soldier or the statesman, is certainly one of the most incredible incidents in the history of this country. It may with a certain plausibility be described as a war without cause and without effect—without cause, because diplomatic negotiations, assisted by the good offices of Russia and Sweden, were apparently on the point of winning substantially all that this country demanded; and without effect, because when the Peace of Ghent ended it, none of the objects for which we had ostensibly fought was so much as mentioned. This leaves the affair incomprehensible from the standpoint of the statesman.

From the standpoint of the soldier it is equally incomprehensible. A country with neither an army nor a navy attacked one whose army was commanded by Wellington and whose navy had been trained by Nelson; yet it did not suffer swift and obliterating defeat. It chose for one of the chief commands a doddering old gentleman whose idea of campaigning was to take his wife and much of his household goods along, and to send his orders, including the plan of campaign, far ahead to be picked up by a gratified, but astonished, enemy. Naturally, that commander and his army were lost; yet the country was not over-whelmed. The capital was raided with ridiculous ease and the public buildings burned; yet at the end of three years Wellington advised Castlereagh to make peace on the best terms he could get, abandoning territorial demands, "for the state of your military operations does not entitle you to demand any." In short, it is a war that cannot be explained on any rational diplomatic or strategical theory.

Yet it is possible that the War of 1812 came as near to being a really inevitable conflict as any military adventure in which this country has engaged. It was not an economic necessity. On the contrary, New England, in spite of heavy losses to shipping, had prospered greatly under the peace-at-any-price policy of Jefferson; and the South and West, much more seriously damaged by embargo and nonintercourse, had nevertheless survived and had steadily increased in wealth and population. It was not a military necessity, for we were far removed from the struggles convulsing Europe. The urge to war was psychological, but none the less compelling for being immaterial.

Historians have spent incalculable time and energy tracing the complexities of the course of events that led to war. Yet somehow their explanations fail to explain. Henry Adams, for example, fifty years ago unraveled all the tangled diplomatic negotiations and set them out in the light of his extraordinarily lucid prose; yet when one has gone through the hundreds of pages he devoted to the subject,[4] although it is perfectly clear what each negotiator did, and, usually, why, it is still undetermined why the war was fought. McMaster labored with equal diligence to prove that it was the embargo that drove us into war, despite the obvious fact that as long as it lasted we stayed out. Others have undertaken to lay it to disarmament, ignoring the fact that the war was eventually declared by the United States. New England has sometimes been blamed, despite the frantic opposition, skirting the borders of treason, of her leaders.

Of course, it is clear enough that the war was made by the young War Hawks in Congress, of whom Henry Clay was chief. But why? These men were not enemies of the human race. On the contrary, most of them were uncommonly amiable young fellows and their leader is frequently described as the best-loved man who ever figured prominently in American politics. They were not overburdened with wisdom at this time, but in later years many of them developed into very wise men indeed, so it

[4] In his *History of the United States*, vols. vi and vii.

is impossible that they could have been complete fools, even on the sunny side of forty. The leading War Hawk of 1811 was to go down in history with the label of the "Great Pacificator"; what strange compulsion made him blood-thirsty at the beginning of his career?

Clearly part of the explanation is to be found in the fact that sixty-one new men, most of them young, were injected into a House with a total membership of one hundred and forty-two at a single election. At one swoop the government was turned over to the boys. They had a mandate. They had to produce. Undoubtedly their responsibility lay heavily upon them. Naturally, therefore, they looked at the government that had been passed along to them and, naturally, they found it in deplorable shape—not economically, but politically. The people had no confidence in Congress and, what was worse, Congress had no confidence in itself. Never before, except at the moment when the Articles of Confederation were supplanted by the Constitution, had the reputation of the national government been at so low an ebb. It was clearly the business of these young men to restore it and of course they examined the record of the old gang to discover, if they could, what had dragged down the central government to so low a level.

What, then, had been the policy of the older men? Why, prudence and peace. Obviously, a new group could not afford to follow the old lines, and the most obvious means of making clear the break with the old government was a resort to recklessness and war.

A foolish policy? Well, yes, from the standpoint of the statesman and the soldier. However, the proof of the pudding is the chewing of the bag; the test of statecraft is empirical. No policy is to be condemned if it succeeds. By all known rules, whether the rules of statecraft, of logic, or of economics, the policy adopted by Henry Clay and his confreres in 1811 should have resulted in the ruin of the United States. But it did not. On the contrary, it re-established the confidence of the nation in itself and it introduced the United States into the society of nations as an independent power, henceforth to be reckoned with in all diplomatic negotiations affecting the Atlantic ocean.

It is of first importance to remember, in reading the history of these years, that the men at the head of the government were still emotionally colonials. Their belief in the democratic experiment was intellectual and the terror that haunted their minds was that of collision with the mother country. They had, indeed, won one war against England, but only by dint of seven years of fearful strife and the intervention of France. The breaks had been in their favor, and they knew it. Little Jimmy Madison was not the man to tempt Providence by attacking England a second time and, from his standpoint, he was right. But Madison was ending his days. He had attained the summit of political ambition, and his point of view could not possibly be that of men who stood at the threshold of their political careers. Madison was a candidate for re-election in 1812, but he knew he must appeal to the people on the basis of the preceding four years; he certainly could not feel that he had a mandate to alter, much less to reverse, that record.

The War Hawks did feel precisely this. The country was heartily sick of old men afraid of their shadows. It was not ill treatment to which the country objected most violently; it was fear. When Clay, Calhoun, William Lowndes and others began to thunder in the House, the opposition asked again and again why they chose England as their foe, seeing that France had violated our rights quite as flagrantly and had imposed upon us hardships quite as onerous. None of the orators made a satisfactory answer to this query and for a very good reason—they were not representing a popular rising against England, as they pretended. There was a rising, all right, but it was not against England, it was against the politics of terror. As far as diplomacy and international law were concerned, there was as much reason to fight France as to fight England. Napoleon had been every whit as contemptuous of our rights as had been the British ministry. But England, not France, was the predestined foe for the very reason that England was regarded in America as the most formidable power in the world. If you must fight someone, not to right a specific wrong, but merely to vindicate your self-respect, then that objective is certainly to be gained more readily by smiting the heavyweight champion than by attacking anyone else. Logically, there was little to choose between the two oppressive powers; but psychologically it was impossible to fight anyone but England.

Even so, it was not easy to drag the administration into a war. Again and again Madison's negotiations almost succeeded, in spite of the fact that distance and the extreme slowness of communication made intelligent negotiation almost impossible. Events were moving at high speed in Europe, the situation frequently changing overnight. An American minister, ill informed as to what was going on in Europe, and not informed at all of what was going on at home, in order to keep the situation well in hand must have been equipped with prophetic insight, intelligence and audacity surpassing Talleyrand's. The Americans, William Pinkney in London and Joel Barlow in Paris, were good men, but they were not that good. They blundered again and again. Yet even their stumbling diplomacy came close, more than once, to a peaceful settlement. At home James Monroe, Secretary of State, arrogant, obstinate and conceited, was nevertheless firmly resolved to keep the peace, if he could. He was handicapped, like the ministers, by lack of true and exact information, and dropped the egg basket more than once for that reason. Even so, he came close to success. Albert Gallatin, Secretary of the Treasury, drenched the firebrands in Congress with cold water more than once simply by proposing various taxes to finance the war; for the young politicians were as violently against taxes as they were against peace. All Gallatin accomplished, however, was to make himself even more disliked than before. The answer to his protests against fighting without financing was cheap, nasty, and curiously modern. It was, in effect, "If you don't like this country, why don't you go back where you came from?" The fact that he had been born in Switzerland, far from heightening the gratitude of this country for the great services he rendered it, only gave every demagogue a weapon to use against him.

JOHN C. CALHOUN

" . . . the profound frivolity of human existence
was utterly beyond his comprehension."

ALBERT GALLATIN

". . . far more valuable was the twinkle in his eye."

On the Belligerence of a Pacifist

In the end it was all fruitless. Nothing availed to stop the collision. Nor is this as strange as it seems if one takes into consideration that none of the many efforts to avert the conflict bore on the real issue, which was not the military situation, nor the offenses of France and Great Britain, but the young men's necessity to prove themselves. A man who has been through a war and has borne himself creditably, thereafter may speak softly and walk prudently without any doubt of his motives in his own mind or in the minds of others. His courage has been proved. The fact is of record and the factor of cowardice is canceled out of all future calculations of his course. But a man who has never fought is ever under suspicion if he is too strongly for peace. Disregarding the opinions of others, he cannot be any too sure of his own motives. Therefore he is prone to truculence to stifle the small voices that in his own heart raise the question of his bravery.

Nor should it be inferred that this spirit was the monopoly of the young men in Congress. Clay and Calhoun, Cheves and Lowndes, Grundy and Troup, were not engaged in a personal adventure. They were faithfully and accurately representing a spirit that was abroad in the land. They were not merely individual young men, they were spokesmen of a young generation that was thoroughly sick of the feebleness and ineptitude of the old men and that heartily preferred war to any more doddering. This was especially true of the new West, a country vastly different from the original thirteen States and further removed from the relative stability and order of old England. Kentucky and Tennessee were the Wild West of those days—wilder by far than Arizona and Wyoming were in later days when Theodore Roosevelt was riding the ranges. Violence was accepted as part of the established order in the West—violence against Indians, against Spaniards and, especially, against personal enemies. So completely un-English was this region that Clay had had to fight vigorously to prevent Kentucky from formally and explicitly repudiating the English common law as the basis of the administration of justice. Pacifism in the West was unheard-

[69]

of, nor was there any respect in that region for any sort of bond, spiritual or political, uniting us with the mother country.

Doubtless the war was inevitable. The new generation had to signalize its accession to power in some dramatic fashion, and it would have required a more powerful social imagination than had then been developed—has it, indeed, been developed yet?— to devise some better method of accomplishing this than to set trumpets to shrilling and drums to rolling while troops fell in line for what a prince a century later still had the temerity to describe as "fresh and glorious war."

CHAPTER V

NEW ENGLAND INTERLUDE

For the purpose of getting Mr. Daniel Webster introduced and appropriately placed in this chronicle

B UT the war that the young men had been demanding so loudly proved to be, when they got it, anything but fresh and glorious; on the contrary, it was about as stale and unprofitable a war, in the beginning, as any nation ever fought. Poor old Hull, completely befuddled, marched to Detroit, crossed into Canada, sat down awhile, and then, apparently being able to think of nothing else to do, retreated to Detroit and surrendered. Van Rensselaer marched to the border, but there half his army balked, refusing to cross the line, and the British fell upon the other half, beat it and captured it, while the rest looked on apathetically. Smyth came roaring up, denouncing Van Rensselaer and promising to plant the standard in Canada instantly; twice he rushed to the border and twice retreated; then he went home. Dearborn didn't march at all.

Ah, it had been anything but glorious when the month of May, 1813, arrived, and with it came yet another young man to the youthful House of Representatives.

Daniel Webster, of New Hampshire, was thirty-one when he took his seat, and in taking it completed the Triumvirate that was to dominate the political thinking of this country for forty years and to leave behind it an extraordinary body of myth and tradition such as attaches to no comparable group in the nation's history. The three never dominated the country's action, but only its imagination. No one of the group ever attained the chief position in the republic. Nor were they in any sense a political unit. Washington, Jefferson and Hamilton were officially related in the first administration, but these three men were never bound by official ties and when they worked together, which was not often, it was a fortuitous and brief combination. Yet their names are inseparable. In the North it may be Webster, Clay and Calhoun, in the South, Calhoun, Clay and Webster, in the West, Clay, Webster and Calhoun, but in every section of the country their names are linked, and they are the first that come to the mind of the average American when the word "statesmanship" is uttered.

Of the three, Webster was by far the most complex character, and therefore the most troublesome to biographers. He cannot be characterized in a phrase, yet he was the sort of man whom everyone tries to label. He has been called everything from "the Divine Daniel" to "the fallen Lucifer," and there is some justification for every name that has been applied to him. There are those who hold him to be the first man in the Triumvirate, and there are those who would deny him any of the elements of greatness. Webster is difficult, and any unqualified pronouncement upon him is bound to be hazardous. However, there is one label which, if constantly kept in mind, elucidates a great deal of his career. He was the Contented Debtor.

Throughout his life, Daniel Webster owed everybody. This is, in itself, not especially significant, for it is a condition common enough in both public and private life. What lends it high significance in Webster's case is the fact that it did not trouble him in the least. In this one respect he had something of the amorality of Richard Wagner. It is true that Webster sometimes paid; in fact, he always paid if it were convenient to pay. Unfortunately, he sometimes paid in the wrong coin—not in legal tender, but in the confidence that the people reposed in him. This was the quality, rather than political ingratitude, that came nearest to justifying the terrific observation of the younger Adams: "Such is human nature, in the gigantic intellect, the envious temper, the ravenous ambition, and the rotten heart of Daniel Webster."[1]

That is, however, a typical Adams outburst, which means that

[1] John Quincy Adams, *Diary*, September 17, 1841.

while it is not to be dismissed altogether, it must be heavily discounted. "Rotten heart" is altogether too violent a term to describe a certain bluntness of moral perception which rendered the man incapable of feeling that debt is slavery. Webster was not, as Adams thought, incapable of gratitude; but his towering egotism frequently led him to accept favors not as gifts but as services rightly due him and therefore affording no occasion for gratitude. Modesty, not gratitude, was what he was incapable of feeling; but on numerous occasions it worked out to the same result in the estimation of his contemporaries, and sometimes in the estimation of later generations as well.

His first debt, and by long odds the greatest he ever contracted, he owed to his own family. Ebenezer Webster, his father, and Ezekiel, his brother, were both men of a moral stature overtopping that of Daniel. Ebenezer, descendant of a long line of New England Puritans, scratched a scant living out of a stony New Hampshire farm. He bore the title of Captain, not by courtesy, but because it was honestly and arduously won on the battlefields of the Revolution under Washington; and late in his life his neighbors elected him to the position of county judge, sufficient testimony to his probity. Daniel was the weakling in his flock of ten children, or so it seemed at first, and from the very beginning of his life was outrageously spoiled by a doting family. In the schools that were available he proved himself a brilliant student and an omnivorous reader; so as soon as Captain Ebenezer secured the judgeship, which meant an addition to his income of three or four hundred dollars a year, he determined that this boy should have the educational advantages lack of which had hampered his father. He therefore sent him to Exeter Academy and after that to Dartmouth College which meant that he received about as good an education as was procurable in America at that time.

The burden of Daniel's support during these years was not borne by his father alone. His brother, Ezekiel, also contributed consistently and heavily. At this point it is pleasant, as well as only just, to record and to underscore the fact that for once in his life Daniel Webster exhibited gratitude and paid a debt. His wish, from the beginning, was to enter the practice of law; but that meant a long "starving time" when he would be lucky to keep himself alive and would certainly have no money for any other purpose. So, for once, he resolutely thrust aside his ambition and for several years slaved at a hard and distasteful teaching job in order that Ezekiel, in his turn, might have an education. In later years Daniel worried not a whit about what was due Mr. Nicholas Biddle, the great banker; but his debt to Ezekiel Webster he paid honestly, and paid in full. Not even John Quincy Adams could call that a rotten heart.

Released at last from this obligation, Webster went to Portsmouth and hung out his shingle. His success was rapid. Between 1807, when he opened his office, and 1813, when he went to Washington, he had shouldered his way to the front rank of his profession in New Hampshire. He was a born advocate, unquestionably one of the greatest trial lawyers this country has ever produced. What concealed vein in his apparently stark New England heritage produced it is a mystery of heredity, but from some source he derived an opulent imagination. Gorgeous imagery, comparisons as happy as unexpected, sonorous and musical phrases came to him effortlessly and, as it seemed, inevitably. Webster was the poet of the Triumvirate.

Henry Cabot Lodge, his biographer, says that this richness of imagination was saved from wasting itself in mere efflorescence by a stroke of luck that seemed anything but lucky at the time. When he first set up in Portsmouth, Webster found as his principal opponent at the bar one of the toughest of New Englanders in Jeremiah Mason, a lawyer famous throughout the region, first because he was six feet and seven inches tall and, second, because his gift of profanity was the admiration and envy of all the teamsters, lumberjacks and seafaring men in the country. What made him difficult for the young attorney, however, was neither of these, but his capacity to give his arguments to a jury an air of hard, dry, common sense that few Yankees could resist. Time and again, when they met in the courtroom, after Webster had fired at the jury a learned, polished and eloquent oration, he saw Jeremiah Mason, instead of replying in kind, wander over to the jury box, bend his great length to lean upon the rail, and address the jurors in a conversational, confidential tone—and win the case.[2]

The real ability of Daniel Webster is revealed by the fact that this mortification, instead of crippling him, was absorbed, assessed correctly, and turned to good account. He drew the right inference, to wit, that eloquence, while valuable, is not enough. He did not abandon it. On the contrary, he studied assiduously to polish and refine it; but he pruned it, sharply and ruthlessly. In the Portsmouth courtroom he learned that eloquence is gunpowder that, burned in free air, gives only a fizz and a spark, not becoming destructive until confined within the iron bonds of clarity, logic and reason. As the years passed the well-turned phrase became constantly better turned, the musical period became more musical, the flowery metaphor became more gorgeous and intricate; but at the same time the argument became clearer and clearer until it approached the limpidity of a dewdrop. The word was still chosen in part because it fell pleasantly upon the ear, but primarily because it conveyed the exact shade of meaning desired. Webster became more, rather than less eloquent but, under the hammering of his knotty opponent, he became comprehensible even to the dullest juror; and when this was attained, he found that he could blast even Jeremiah Mason out of his way. Incidentally, that worthy became one of his greatest admirers, and in later years repeatedly admitted that young Webster was too much for him.

Grace Fletcher was the daughter of the minister at Hopkinton, a few miles from Concord—"the" minister, in 1808, meaning, of course, the Congregationalist. It was an exalted social position in a New England town, but even at that time the economic level of a minister's household rarely corresponded to its social prestige. Grace Fletcher had had plenty of training in how to keep up appearances on pretty slender financial resources. Without doubt she had had, too, as a New England minister's daughter, plenty of parental warnings against setting her heart on the

[2] See Lodge, *Daniel Webster*, pp. 37 *et seq.*

vanities of this world, and plenty of instruction as to what are the solid values of life.

It was excellent training for a girl who was to marry Daniel Webster. Plenty of witnesses have testified that she was both charming and intelligent, some have given her credit for wit, and nearly all agree in attributing to her good humor and a quiet gaiety that made the Webster home a delightful place to visit. It is annoying that the records of her are so fragmentary, for the glimpses we do have indicate that she was an unusually attractive woman. However, it may be that the very obscurity that shrouds her is more significant than anything that contemporaries might have written. During twenty years in which Webster was maturing his powers, she was his companion. They were critical years, the time during which an unwise, or even an unsympathetic woman might have done incalculable damage to a personality as complex and as delicately balanced as this one. If Grace Fletcher Webster was, as her contemporaries aver, gifted with humor and intelligence, there must have been more than one occasion when she was tempted to repeat the error of Michal who, when she saw the young king dancing, laughed. No less than David, Daniel Webster had his moments of absurdity; but if Grace observed them, no one was ever the wiser.

They had been married five years when, in 1813, Webster came down to Washington to play the role of a young man opposed to the war. His, however, was a new kind of opposition in that it was intelligent. Not the least striking evidence of the moral and intellectual bankruptcy of the period that was closing is that it took a man of the rising generation to supply temperate and reasoned opposition, while the old men gave themselves over to passion, to prejudice and spleen. No suspicion of harboring treasonable designs attaches to Webster, yet his opposition to the war was every whit as firm and clear as that of Timothy Pickering, or any of the others who were conspiring for the dissolution of the Union and giving to the enemy moral encouragement if not physical support.

In a Fourth of July oration at Portsmouth in 1812 he had made his position clear. "Resistance and insurrection form no

part of our creed," he said. "The disciples of Washington are
neither tyrants in power nor rebels out. If we are taxed to carry
on this war we shall disregard certain distinguished examples
and shall pay. If our personal services are required, we shall
yield them to the precise extent of our constitutional liability.
At the same time the world may be assured that we know our
rights and shall exercise them. We shall express our opinions
on this, as on every measure of the government,—I trust without passion, I am certain without fear. By the exercise of our
constitutional right of suffrage, by the peaceable remedy of
election, we shall seek to restore wisdom to our councils, and
peace to our country."

It is true that if Daniel Webster had made that speech in 1917
he might reasonably have expected to join Eugene Debs in the
penitentiary; but in 1812 the republic was still blithe and bold,
and a brave man could speak out in a brave country with relative
immunity. Besides, when Timothy Pickering was writing to the
Governor of Massachusetts urging him to seize the national
revenues in that State "for our protection against the foreign
enemy and the still greater evil in prospect,—domestic tyranny,"
a man who merely urged the electorate to vote against the war
party was a very archetype of mildness.

Webster was no traitor, but he was no fool, either. In a private citizen who never emerges from private life, it may be incongruous to link loyalty and intelligence as if they were on the
same level; but in a statesman, who has to do with framing the
policies of a country, they are on the same level. In a statesman
disloyalty may be the most hateful of vices, but folly may be
vastly more disastrous to his country. There is on record no instance of a silly statesman's bringing anything but damage upon
his people, while there are numerous instances of thoroughpaced
scoundrels who made excellent rulers. Nobody in his right mind
would argue that Talleyrand, for instance, was guiltless of mul-
tiple treasons; yet there is no doubt that he rendered France
services far more valuable than those of many an honest man.

In any event Webster, from the moment he arrived in Washington, was not only a marked man, but one who held the good

opinion of both parties. A Federalist, and in the opposition, he nevertheless spoke moderately and recognized the necessities of the situation; therefore even the War Hawks could not pump up any violent objection to him personally. As for New England, a large section, even of the Federalists, gagged at the poisonous dose the Essex Junto was compounding for them to swallow. Therefore a leader who knew how to oppose the war without opposing the country was very much to their taste and they hailed him with tremendous enthusiasm. Mr. Webster was in an exceedingly enviable position. Perhaps it was a little too enviable for the good of Mr. Webster's soul; perhaps a little more difficulty at the start, some Washington experience analogous to his Portsmouth encounter with Jeremiah Mason, might have had the effect of eliminating some of the soft spots in his character that were to become dreadfully conspicuous in later years. But who knows? Difficulty at this period might have broken him.

At any rate, with his appearance the stage was set for the drama that was to last forty years, the drama of the making of a new nation, in which three men were to play conspicuous and vitally important parts. Many other actors were to appear on that crowded stage, some of them to play, for a time, parts overshadowing those of any of the Triumvirate; but none remained so prominent for so long. All three were beaten repeatedly by other champions; but no man was strong enough to destroy any of them.

"Individualities may form communities," observed Disraeli, "but it is institutions alone that can create a nation."

The organization that went into the War of 1812 was the creation of individualities. Washington, Jefferson, Hamilton, Franklin, John and Samuel Adams, Patrick Henry, Paine, Madison—all those whom we call the Founding Fathers, were still individualities, remembered in the flesh by many men. The republic was in the situation of Russia a century and a quarter later—a nation with political principles, but without a political history, therefore without institutions. Those principles were, for the most part, derived from experience with English institutions, hence there was as yet no sharp psychological differentiation between this country and England. Any Midlands squire could have followed the debates in Congress, if not with approval, at least with complete understanding of the arguments and of the point of view.

But the nation that went into the Civil War was not England and not English. In the intervening years the principles enunciated by the Fathers had been debated, construed, extended, applied, sometimes tortured to suit contrary purposes, and slowly embodied in institutions. Long before the outbreak of the war, when Hayne and Webster thundered at each other across the Senate chamber, the debate was largely incomprehensible to Englishmen. Throughout this process of erecting the superstructure on the foundation the Fathers had laid, three men were in the minds of the public. No matter who held the center of the stage, Webster, Clay and Calhoun were always about. No matter who projected a policy, it was modified somewhat by Clay, Webster and Calhoun. No matter what party was in power, its activities had to be planned with a view to the opinions of Calhoun, Webster and Clay.

In a sense, they were sectional figures, all three. Webster was the North, Calhoun the South, Clay the new West. None ever quite attained, in popular estimation, the nationalism of Andrew Jackson, not to mention that of Jefferson or Washington; but together they were the nation. All of them were denied the Presidency, which was frequently, indeed, usually, given to lesser men; but a dozen Presidents have been forgotten by a generation that easily remembers these three.

Their faults are not far to seek, which is, no doubt, one reason why they are so interesting. At least this is true as regards Clay and Webster. Calhoun was a little inhuman in his unwavering correctness, but the average man, observing the other two, perceives that in some respects they were no better than he is and usually discovers in common frailty a common bond; or, perhaps, he sees that they succumbed to weaknesses against which he is proof, which affords him the soothing experience of being able to view a great man from a point of superiority. In any case, all three men were in some measure frustrated, and certainly any rational human being who has reached life's noon must have a pretty clear understanding of the feeling of a defeated man. Laurels and acclaim may go to the perpetually successful, but the keen curiosity of mankind, and frequently its affection, clings to the world's great failures, sometimes more glamorous than most successes.

But in the year 1813, when Daniel Webster joined the other young men in the House of Representatives, no shadow of personal failure had as yet darkened the path of any of them. The failure that threatened them at the moment was the failure of the nation, for the war had demonstrated with appalling clarity how far was the United States from being a nation in the real sense of the word. The military defeats were bad enough in themselves; but far worse was the fact that they had been caused, not by the superior power and skill of the enemy, but by stupidity, irresolution and disunion on our own side. The conquest of Canada, so fervently promised by Clay, had been, in the beginning, entirely feasible. The military forces the United States put into the field were probably adequate, in point of size, had there been vigor and determination in the high command and discipline in the ranks. But the American armies fell to pieces, not under the hammering of the British, but out of sheer lack of cohesion. Indeed, on several occasions, once the enemy was actually engaged,[3] they fought creditably, sometimes, perhaps, brilliantly; the impossibility was not to make the American soldiers fight, but to bring them into action at all. Lack of organization and lack of competent commanders were made vastly more serious by lack of confidence, sedulously fostered by the New England Federalists, not in the national leaders only but also in the very idea of nationality. The repeated refusals of the militia to cross the boundary line into Canada, for example, are eloquent of the vagueness of allegiance to the United States that prevailed everywhere.

It was a hard lesson for the War Hawks, but a salutary one, at least for Clay. It cured him forever of his tendency to indulge in militaristic bombast, and it showed him the magnitude of the

[3] As, for example, at Fort George and Sackett's Harbor.

task that lay ahead in welding this congeries of States into a nation. But the immediate task was to fight, and each of the three, in his own way, devoted himself to the task of making the nation efficient. Even Webster, the formal opponent of the war, accepted the necessity of prosecuting it and sedulously avoided involvement in the treasonable enterprises of Timothy Pickering, Governor Strong, of Massachusetts, and the other Federalists who permitted the bitterness of their partisanship so to blind them to their duty as Americans that they omitted no effort to give aid and comfort to their country's enemies.

At that, by the end of 1813 everyone, including the quondam War Hawks, was heartily sick of the war. Napoleon had been disastrously beaten at Leipzig in October, which seemed to mean that Great Britain's hands would be freed to turn the full power of her arms on this country. So when, on December 30, a note arrived from Lord Castlereagh, the British Foreign Secretary, offering to negotiate, the offer was accepted with almost ludicrous haste. Americans already in Europe were named as American negotiators, with the addition of Henry Clay, who resigned the Speakership January 19, 1814, and started at once for Europe.

The period of confusion and futility that followed the close of the Golden Age of the republic was over; the Silver Age was about to begin.

CHAPTER VI

ON THE METHOD OF WINNING A LOST WAR

*Explaining how Mr. J. Q. Adams' austerity and Mr. Henry Clay's
frivolity worked together for good at a peace conference in Ghent*

THE ancient city of Ghent had brooded over the Low Countries for a thousand years before Henry Clay saw it, but if
the history of the city meant anything to him the records do not
indicate it. Mr. Clay was in Ghent on business, and business he
attended to, assiduously. Old man Gallatin, his colleague, might
feel differently about it, might spend a large part of his time
writing letters to the Marquis de Lafayette and Madame de
Staël, might employ his all too-abundant leisure in wandering
about the city and in encounters with such odd fish as David, the
painter, Humboldt, the philosopher and other persons of negligible political importance; but that was not for Mr. Clay. There
is no reason to believe that he thought any the less of Gallatin
for his interest in outside affairs, but he did not share it. After
all, Albert Gallatin was a foreigner, a European, and it was
natural for him to exhibit an un-American interest in the past.

But what were the old Counts of Flanders or the medieval
guilds, or the cloth markets, or the hundred sieges of Ghent to
a man from Kentucky with difficult business to negotiate? Mr.
Clay was in Europe for the purpose of winning back a lost war,
and that was certainly no business to be dispatched in a casual
and off-hand fashion. More than that, Mr. Clay was to be assisted in the affair by a group of colleagues on whom it was but
natural for him to look with a somewhat rueful countenance.
Jonathan Russell was all right, as he could generally be counted
on to support anything proposed by Mr. Clay; but James A.
Bayard was, to begin with, a Federalist, although not one of the

[82]

Hartford Convention stripe, being a Senator from Delaware and a loyal supporter of the war; and he was not only a Federalist but a vigorous and somewhat stiff-necked individual, whom Mr. Clay had found hard to handle in the Senate. Then there was old Gallatin—politically unexceptionable, honest, able, and high in the confidence not of President Madison only, but also in that of Jefferson himself. Young Mr. Clay had to respect Gallatin, partly because Gallatin's prestige was immense and Clay's as yet was small, but largely because of the inescapable fact that the old Swiss was a wiser man than the young Kentuckian. Clay was not blind to Gallatin's superiority, and he admitted it with a readiness that does him credit; but for all that, Albert Gallatin was not the partner he would have chosen to adventure with him on a desperate gamble.

Worst of all, though, from the Kentuckian's standpoint, was that dreadful fellow Adams. Except in the points of financial honesty and political ability, Henry Clay and John Quincy Adams were as antithetical as any two men in American public life. An accurate description of either would serve, by simple reversal, to produce an accurate description of the other in everything save honesty and ability; and, inevitably, at this time neither regarded the other as either honest or able. Careful, painstaking, a model of industry, odiously moral, Adams was incessantly racked by anxiety as to both his body and his soul; he went to bed promptly at ten o'clock, unless dragged out to attend some official festivity, which he regarded as a species of martyrdom, and got up in what Clay regarded as the middle of the night to put in three or four hours of labor at his desk before breakfast. He has described the spirit in which he approached the convention in words so lugubrious that they would have paralyzed Clay with horror could he have heard them: "The weight of the trust committed, though but in part, to me, the difficulties, to all human appearance insuperable, which forbid the hope of success, the universal gloom of the prospect before me, would depress a mind of more sanguine complexion than mine. On the providence of God alone is my reliance. The prayer for light and vigilance, and presence of mind and fortitude and resignation, in fine, for strength proportioned to my trial, is incessant upon my heart. The welfare of my family and country, with the interests of humanity, are staked upon the event. To Heaven alone it must be committed."[1] Fortunately, Adams committed this outburst of despair to his Diary, and not to his ebullient colleague from the West, or Clay might have packed up and gone home before the negotiations began.

As a matter of fact, Clay's estimate of the commission, while probably the only one possible to him, was wrong in almost every particular. A wisdom unparalleled in his career, at least since the day when he drafted the Constitution of the United States, seems to have guided James Madison in the selection of its personnel. True, he fumbled it, as he fumbled everything while he was President. Instead of naming Albert Gallatin as its chief, a position clearly belonging to him both by virtue of his ability and by the rule of political seniority, Madison added him to the group after all the other negotiators had been named. This left Adams the titular chief; but that position was promptly corrected by a revolt of the other members. "Father finds great difficulty with his own colleagues," wrote James Gallatin, then a boy of seventeen serving his father as secretary. "The accident which placed him at the foot of the commission placed Mr. Adams at the head of it. Messrs. Clay, Bayard, and Russell let Mr. Adams plainly know that, though he might be the nominal mouthpiece, Gallatin was their leader. Clay uses strong language to Adams, and Adams returns the compliment. Father looks calmly on with a twinkle in his eye."[2] This situation, however, added another to the already heavy load of burdens the old Swiss was forced to bear.

Otherwise, however, the composition of the commission was admirable. Russell, perhaps, might have been spared, but the particular qualifications of every other member were essential either to its balance or to its strength. Bayard, for example, had

[1] John Quincy Adams, *Diary*, entry for April 28, 1814.

[2] James Gallatin, *Diary*, entry for August 10, 1814. Young James was an ardent partisan of his father, of course, but he was no fool, and his observations of the course of the negotiations have been astonishingly well supported by the researches of later historians.

BIRTH-PLACE OF HENRY CLAY

CALHOUN'S RESIDENCE AND OFFICE, "FORT HILL," ABBEVILLE CO., S. C.

the power of incisive argument coupled with a suavity in dealing
with men of the world that proved invaluable in actual contact
with the British negotiators. The discussions were intricate and
involved, decision of many points resting upon the interpreta-
tion of ancient treaties, old and inaccurate maps, and documents
whose phrasing was equivocal. Here the learning and tireless
industry of Adams meant the difference between success and
failure. The British negotiators, and Lord Castlereagh, the Foreign Minister, apparently entered the conference blithely assuming that they had to deal with a cowed and dispirited opposition;
here the fiery resolution and superb confidence, not seldom rising
into arrogance of Clay, upset their calculations and disconcerted
them woefully. The plain truth, though, as the grandson of J. Q.
Adams acknowledges, is that the triumph of Ghent was the
triumph of Albert Gallatin. His supreme value was not so much
in the actual conversations with the British—although he drafted
a great many of the interminable notes that passed back and
forth through six weary months—as in the council room where
the Americans made their own plans. He was the charioteer
driving four spirited and powerful, but only half-broken horses.
He negotiated skillfully in the presence of the British; but far
more valuable was the twinkle in his eye when Clay used strong
language to Adams and Adams returned the compliment. His
"Gentlemen, gentlemen, we must remain united, or we will
fail," counted for more toward success than many notes.

The story of Albert Gallatin is one that fair-minded Americans read without much satisfaction. No American has ever devoted himself to promotion of the public good with less self-
interest than this immigrant; and few men have been worse
rewarded. In 1814 America already was afflicted with that spirit
which Charles Dickens in 1830 satirized mercilessly in "Martin
Chuzzlewit." One of the unloveliest features of our national
history has been xenophobia of a peculiarly cheap and witless
kind. Doubtless it is true that every nation dislikes and distrusts
the alien; but the United States, whose whole population is alien
or descended from aliens within a few generations has contrived
to achieve a bad eminence in this respect which was hardly chal-

lenged until Hitler inaugurated his campaign against the Jews, the universal aliens. Within the last decade we have had a Cabinet officer who actually proposed to solve the crime problem by wholesale deportation of aliens; and a hundred years earlier Albert Gallatin, one of the greatest Americans, was the victim of a nagging persecution that drove him at last earnestly to advise his children to abandon the country and return to Europe. The Alien and Sedition Laws were frank retaliation for his effective criticism of Federalist fiscal policy. He was accused of cherishing foreign allegiance when he opposed the War of 1812, and he was blamed for the unprepared condition of the country when it came, although Congress had refused to levy the taxes which he recommended for its prosecution. He was continually attacked by the lower forms of life in his own party; any demagogue could win a little cheap applause by denouncing the man with the thick German accent who was at the head of the Treasury. His humiliating position at the tail, instead of at the head of the peace commission was due to Congressional carpers who pretended to regard it as a violation of the Constitution that the Secretary of the Treasury should accept membership on such a commission, although in Washington's administration Chief Justice Jay had done so without objection.

Even on the commission itself, men had this prejudice in the backs of their minds and occasionally let it be perceived. When the British first agreed to negotiate, they mentioned London as the place. Gallatin was not unwilling, but Clay and Adams wrote to him flatly refusing to go to London on the ground that there they would be snubbed and treated as colonists, adding, "You are a foreigner, which places you on an entirely different footing."[3] It is all the more to the credit of Albert Gallatin that his patience and good humor never failed for a moment in spite of these incessant pinpricks; but reading of them does much to deflate the pride of an American.

Robert Stewart, Viscount Castlereagh, is usually accounted one of England's really great Foreign Secretaries. What imp of perversity possessed him when he was selecting his envoys to

[3] James Gallatin, *Diary*, entry for April 26, 1814.

the conference at Ghent has never been satisfactorily determined by historians. They were James, Lord Gambier, a peer of no particular distinction in any line; Henry Goulburn, a member of Parliament holding an under-secretaryship of state—not even a man of Cabinet size; and William Adams, who had received the degree of Doctor of Civil Law, but who apparently was not otherwise distinguished in any way. Gallatin was dismayed when he saw the list. He took it as evidence that Castlereagh had no intention of making peace, for he could not believe that an able minister would enter into serious negotiations represented by an array of stuffed shirts. "Father feels that he is quite capable of dealing with them,"[4] wrote son James, but that wasn't the point; father dared not hope that they would be permitted to deal at all.

Two other members of the American delegation also were quite capable of dealing with the British non-entities. These were John Quincy Adams and Henry Clay. Adams' capacity, the thing that made him invaluable to the commission, was demonstrated right at the start. The first act of the British commissioners, on August 7, was to send their secretary to Bayard, the first American he happened to find, with a formal notification that the British were in town, accompanied by a lordly intimation that they would be pleased to receive the Americans at their hotel at one o'clock the following afternoon.

This was a gross discourtesy, although it is quite conceivable that the British commissioners didn't know it. Throughout the negotiations they displayed an astonishing unfamiliarity with the usages of international law, and this may have been the first display of that ignorance. In any event, it assumed dense ignorance on the part of the Americans. Possibly as regards Clay and Bayard the assumption was justified, but hardly as regards Gallatin and most certainly not as regards Adams. He had not been studying three hours before breakfast every morning for nothing. "I referred my colleagues to Martens, book vii, chap.

[4] He fears negotiations will soon come to an end and has but little hope; he does not think the British Government wish to make peace or they would have sent more powerful delegates.—James Gallatin, *Diary*, entry for August 12, 1814.

iv, section 3, of his Summary"[5] he wrote in his diary of that date,
"where the course now taken by the British Commissioners ap-
pears to be precisely that stated there to be the usage from
Ambassadors to Ministers of an inferior order." Clay and Bayard
sputtered with indignation, perceiving the insult clearly enough,
but it was Adams who could cite, not the work only, but the
book, the chapter and the section to prove it to all the world. His
precise information left the British not a leg to stand on. They
stood convicted, right at the start, either of grossly bad manners,
or of inexcusable ignorance. They were on the defensive before
the formal negotiations began.

But by his own very different methods Henry Clay was almost as swift in arriving at a correct estimation of the British.
By August 19 the worst fears of Adams and Gallatin apparently
had been justified. The British had presented a series of demands
that were preposterous. They included the cession of part of
Maine, the erection of an Indian puppet state south of the Great
Lakes, practical control of the Mississippi by the British and the
ejection of Americans from all fishing rights in British waters.
Gallatin despondently drew the inference that his first suspicion
had been right—that the sardonic Castlereagh had been merely
playing with him in sending the delegation to Ghent, and Adams
saw no possible course other than to pack up and go home. But
he wrote in his diary that day, "Mr. Clay has an inconceivable
idea, that they will finish by receding from the ground that they
have taken."

If Adams had realized how Clay came by that idea, he would
probably have regarded "inconceivable" as all too weak a word.
As a matter of fact, Clay, himself, would have been hard put to
it to explain how he knew; but know he did, beyond peradventure. He had not found out by reading the British notes. He had
not found out by reading Martens by candlelight at five o'clock
in the morning. He had not found out by study of history, by
ratiocination, by any of the conventional and praiseworthy meth-

[5] He referred to Georg Friedrich von Martens, German writer on international law, whose *Précis du droit des gens modernes de l'Europe* was accepted as
authoritative in all countries.

ods through which students learn and which are commended to youth by all right-thinking persons. He had read, not books and documents, but the faces of the British negotiators, sitting across the conference table. This sort of reading was an exercise which Clay had practiced assiduously for many years, and in which he was expert, but it was learning acquired by means which John Quincy Adams could in no wise approve.

There was currently popular—deplorably popular in the estimation of Mr. Adams and men of his type—a diversion called brag. It was the ancestor of modern draw poker but, played with three cards instead of five, it was even faster and the technique then called "bragging" and later "bluffing" was even more important. Mr. Adams was aware of the existence of this form of amusement, as he was aware of the existence of burglary, arson and mayhem; but he would have resented the imputation that he was expert in its practice as he would have resented the imputation that he could pick a lock. The idea that anything useful to a statesman could be learned by playing brag was one of that rather numerous class of concepts to which Mr. Adams' mind was completely impervious. Henry Clay, however, standing on the lower, or Kentucky-Virginia, level of morality, found in brag unfailing fascination and delight. The only disgrace attached to it, in his mind, was the disgrace of being out-bragged, and so losing to a player whose hand was in fact worse than his own. Many and many a night he had sat until dawn crept in to dim the candles, alert to avoid this disgrace, intensely, albeit subconsciously, aware of the quiver of an eyelash, the slightest twitching of a muscle, the faintest fleeting change of expression in the face of the man across the table and instantly making his own play conform to the information these tiny indications conveyed. "There was another card-party in Mr. Clay's chamber last night," wrote Adams in one of a number of such entries in his diary, "and I heard Mr. Bentzon retiring from it after I had risen this morning." Adams was filled with cold disgust; it was impossible for him to imagine that, no less than himself, Mr. Clay was learning by candlelight things that would be useful in the conferences held by day.

But so it was. When the British threw on the table their appalling demands, Mr. Clay, thoughtfully considering, not the documents on the board, but the faces of the men who put them there, felt an old familiar tingle run through his nerves. He had seen this sort of thing before. This was the first time in his life he had ever sat in a peace conference, yet somewhere he had seen this sort of thing before, not once only, but many times. Despite their surface plausibility, and the jaunty assurance with which they were presented, there was something not quite right, something that didn't ring true about these proposals. Mr. Clay began to generate an idea that Mr. Adams correctly described as inconceivable—inconceivable, that is, by a grave and right-thinking New Englander engaged in serious business with men whom he supposed to be of like mind, but not at all inconceivable by a frivolous Kentuckian, who regarded all life as a gamble and thought it by no means impossible for a sophisticated and cynical Foreign Minister to play a little poker with islands, and nations, and continents as the chips. Mr. Clay conceived the idea that these Britishers were trying to out-brag him, were running a gigantic bluff, and at the thought all his gambling blood began to sing in his veins. Here was something that he knew. Here was something he could handle, something, as the vernacular of a later day has it, right down his alley, and he rose to meet it with an alacrity that puzzled and rather irritated his colleagues.

That day, August 19, 1814, even Gallatin gave up hope. "The position is untenable; I am preparing for departure. Our negotiations may be considered at an end,"[6] he reported to his official superior. Even Bayard had come away from the conference seething with hopeless, helpless wrath, and Adams was extracting what melancholy satisfaction he could from seeing his most pessimistic predictions come true. This was the moment the unaccountable Mr. Clay chose to be jaunty and almost gay. He had seen somehow the flicker of an eyelash, the twitching of a muscle, that had gone unperceived by the others; doubtless he did not know himself what made him so sure, and certainly he could not explain it to the rest. Can any gambler explain to non-

[6] Gallatin to Monroe, August 20, 1814.

gamblers how he knows that his opponent is bluffing? Nevertheless, there is little doubt that Clay's buoyant assurance was the
strongest single factor in preventing the Americans from summarily ending the parley and prolonging the war for months or
years. Clay's morally dubious experience at the game of brag
served the country as well at this crisis as Adams' precise knowledge had served it at the opening session. The inference that it
is sometimes well for a statesman to be learned in the ways of
the wicked is one that the New Englander never drew and could
not draw; but for all that it seems to be plain.

The event proved that Clay was right, although the surface
appearance of things indicated that it was impossible. The Americans had not distinguished themselves on land, and although
their little navy had done some brilliant work, the utmost it
could accomplish was to sting, not to stab, the Mistress of the
Seas. The long, desperate struggle against Napoleon was drawing to a triumphant close; even then the allies were mustering
for the descent upon Leipzig, where the bloody drama was to
end, save for the momentary flash of the Hundred Days. It was
clear that England's full power would shortly be released, and
already three fearful blows against the American republic were
about to be delivered. On the surface, England had every right
to claim a dictated peace.

But things were by no means as rosy, from the British point
of view, as surface appearances indicated. First of all, and most
important of all, Great Britain had been fighting almost constantly for twenty years and the people were utterly sick of war.
The struggle against Napoleon they understood, or thought
they understood, and they were doggedly determined to carry
it through; but the average Englishman had no very clear understanding of why the American campaign had been begun in the
first place. More than that, as wars went in those days, it was
proving to be frightfully expensive. Maintaining a large ex-
peditionary force at a distance of three thousand miles is tremendously difficult today, and it was much more difficult a century and a quarter ago; co-ordinating the efforts of several such
forces operating at such a distance is next to impossible today,

even with swift transportation and instantaneous communication, and proved quite impossible to the British in 1814.

It was true that the coming defeat of Napoleon would release large British forces, but Castlereagh well knew that it was doubtful that they would be released for service in America. Soldiers, as well as civilians, were tired of war. When Napoleon was beaten, they would consider their duty done; and the government that would proceed to ship them across the Atlantic, to serve in a fresh war whose causes nobody clearly understood, would be more than inviting, would be insisting upon, mutiny in the ranks and riots in the streets at home. Castlereagh's position, therefore, formidable as it seemed to be, in reality was precarious.

His logical play, in the circumstances, was to rush the Americans into signing a treaty before they had time to discover the true values of the situation. This he understood with great clarity; what he did not understand was that to accomplish it he should have sent to Ghent the British equivalent of the three best poker players in the kingdom; instead he sent three gentlemen of lives so blameless that they knew no more about really big gambling than they did about the psychology of the Hottentots. A man who knew what it was to lose $8,000 in an evening —taking into consideration the changing value of money, that would be more like $25,000 today—and then win most of it back again, was not to be deceived by this trio.

Moreover, as time passed, the situation, from Castlereagh's viewpoint, grew steadily worse. The grand strategy against the Americans was intelligent enough in its original conception, but it was far from intelligently executed, and it failed calamitously. It involved three blows, which should have been synchronized perfectly and all delivered with great power. One was to smash down through the Hudson Valley. Another was to smash up through the Mississippi Valley. The third was to cut the republic in two by driving westward from Baltimore and interrupting north-and-south communication. The first and the third were well synchronized, but neither was delivered with enough power; the battle of Plattsburg, on September 11, stopped the invasion down the Hudson Valley and the next day the attempt to seize Baltimore failed. All that was accomplished was a raid on Washington and the burning of the public buildings; but this was a mere diversion—valuable psychologically, but insignificant as far as military objectives were concerned. The real objective, the effort to employ the Chesapeake Bay country as a wedge to split the republic, was lost. The third blow, that aimed at New Orleans, was not delivered until it was all over; which was well for Castlereagh, since it failed more disastrously than either of the others.

If the Foreign Minister did not perceive the true situation himself, he was yet in no doubt about it, for it was pointed out to him in blunt words by the greatest British soldier of the times, none other than the Duke of Wellington himself. As regarding the haggling at Ghent he wrote: "In regard to your present negotiations, I confess that I think you have no right, from the state of the war, to demand any concession of territory from America. . . . You have not been able to carry it into the enemy's territory, notwithstanding your military success and now undoubted military superiority, and have not even cleared your own territory on point of attack. You cannot on any principle of equality in negotiation claim a cession of territory excepting in exchange for other advantages which you have in your power. . . . Then, if this reasoning be true, why stipulate for the *uti possidetis*? You can get no territory; indeed, the state of your military operations, however creditable, does not entitle you to demand any."[7]

The Iron Duke was in possession of complete information. Castlereagh had asked him if he were willing to assume the American command, which he agreed to do "though I don't promise myself much success there." Clay, on the other hand, was completely ignorant of most of the facts; yet he was as certain that the British position was a weak one as was the well-informed Wellington.

However, if this uncanny ability to read the mind of his oppo-

[7] Wellington to Castlereagh, November 9, 1814. Quoted by Adams, vol. ix, pp. 41–42.

nent enabled Clay to save the conference in August, it was not that which won honorable peace in December. Clay, given his head, would probably have driven the British to a rupture. He declared, in fact, for three years more of war. Even Bayard, who was not unacquainted with the game of brag, was appalled. "Mr. Clay is for bragging a million against a cent," he said to Adams. But the wise old foreigner with the twinkle in his eye was always there to check his exuberance when it went too far, and to restrain Adams from goading Clay, and perhaps even Bayard, into actual physical violence. What Gallatin must have endured is beyond estimation. As Clay had predicted, the British gradually abandoned one point after another, each of which they had originally presented as a *sine qua non*. Eventually it became apparent that a treaty could be negotiated were it not for two vexed questions, the fisheries and the navigation of the Mississippi. Clay frankly cared not twopence about the fisheries, which were important mainly to New England; but Adams stood ready to defend them to the death. Adams cared no more about the British right to free navigation of the Mississippi than Clay did about the fisheries; but Clay knew that to go back to Kentucky after having surrendered the river would be political, and perhaps physical, suicide. All agreed that by yielding one point, they could seal the bargain; but each man felt that to yield his particular point would be to betray his section.

Adams had one trick that could be relied on to drive Clay wild. It was his habit of dragging God into the debate on his side. When he had exhausted all the political arguments in favor of his point, he would begin to argue on lofty moral grounds, and at that juncture Clay would erupt. As touching the British right to navigate the Mississippi, for instance, he professed to discover a guarantee of that right in the Treaty of 1783. True, the right was mentioned under the misapprehension that the Mississippi extended into Canada, but there it was, and Mr. Adams expressed grave doubt that the American commissioners had a sound moral right to question it; whereupon Mr. Clay discoursed sarcastically on the morality of a government that would persistently sacrifice the interest of its best friends to preserve those of its bitterest enemies. In view of the fact that New England was even then howling for secession, the remark was envenomed, and Gallatin had to step into the breach again.

Any question that Gallatin was a statesman, not a politician, must be settled by the fact that his wisdom was deep enough to perceive that the very qualities that made these two hate each other so were, in their several ways, elements of the strength of his commission. For these wrangles were scrupulously kept within the walls of the Hotel d'Alcantara, where the delegation was lodged. In the presence of the British, Adams supported Clay, and Clay supported Adams with a vigor and skill that were too much for the bewildered gentlemen who represented London. In private they might, and they very nearly did, drive Gallatin over the verge of insanity with their rows; but in public they made a magnificent team, and the man who held the reins was willing to risk their tearing him asunder in private if only they would help him bring about the peace which he was determined to have if human power could accomplish it. At this time in their careers both Adams and Clay were little more than strong men; but Albert Gallatin was great.

The peace treaty that they finally signed on Christmas Eve, 1814, was, of course, a logical absurdity and it has been the target of acidulous jesting ever since. It granted not one of the demands made by either party. It settled not one of the disputes that precipitated the war. After three murderous years England and the United States agreed, in effect, simply to ignore the whole thing. The impressment of seamen, the rights of neutrals, the Indians, the fisheries, the Mississippi—all the "sacred" causes for which men had died, ships had gone down in the sea and towns had gone up in flames, were referred for settlement by subsequent negotiation. Eventually they were settled by that method, and with such satisfaction to both sides that neither country has raised any question about them for a hundred and twenty-five years. Viewed in this light, the Treaty of Ghent stands as one of the most blistering commentaries ever written on the futility and stupidity of war.

An uneasy sense of the fundamental absurdity of their position was responsible, at least in part, for the last terrific row between Clay and Adams. It was over the custody of the papers relating to the conference. Clay, who was proceeding to America at once, wished to take them with him to be deposited with the State Department, alleging, not unreasonably, that he might have pressing need to consult them when he undertook to defend the treaty in Congress. But Adams, although he was not proceeding home directly, asserted his right as titular head of the delegation to keep them; and nothing could budge him. Moreover, he pointed out that the negotiations were not yet concluded; there was a treaty of commerce yet to be drawn, and there might be need to consult the papers in the course of that business. Apparently Gallatin let them fight. There was no longer any necessity of presenting a solid front to the British, and he must have been extremely tired of suppressing silly squabbles. The New Englander, though, had nine points of the law on his side; the papers were actually in his hands, and they were not surrendered.

So Clay came home, more than a little uncertain of the sort of reception his labors were to receive, because he was none too proud of them himself. But he had no cause to worry. News of the peace was received with wild delight, partly because General Andrew Jackson, at New Orleans, had just retrieved the country's self-respect by strewing Pakenham's British army for miles along the Mississippi levee. The treaty might be as empty as a bass drum as regards everything else, but it ended the fighting without any humiliating conditions. This was enough for the country.

More than that, it has proved to be one of the most durable treaties of peace ever signed, and one may argue plausibly that the very emptiness that makes it seem absurd also made it permanent. It represented a peace without victory; but because the treaty was empty, there was nothing in it which either nation felt called upon to revenge. The war, however, had had at least the result of proving to each nation that the other could, and on sufficient provocation would, hit hard. The British seemed to have overlooked the fact that since 1783 the United States had collected a population of eight millions, approximately two-thirds as many people as Great Britain had. The Americans had conveniently forgotten that in the Revolution the colonists had the assistance of a very powerful ally, who did far more for them than Napoleon could. Reason and justice are noble ideals, but a healthy respect for the fighting power of an opponent always was, and still is, the most powerful of all inducements to keep the peace.

But as far as this country is concerned one of the important results of the War of 1812 was its ornithological effect; miraculously, it transmuted a War Hawk into what Bottom might have called a sucking dove. The Honorable Henry Clay left Ghent completely immunized against reinfection with war fever. As he fought desperately on the diplomatic field to retrieve what the country had lost on the battlefield, it must have caused him acute discomfort to remember the day when he had cockily announced that a brigade of Kentucky riflemen would be force enough to subdue Canada. He was to make plenty of mistakes in the years that lay ahead, but he would never be that particular kind of an ass again. He was to join forces with Calhoun more than once thereafter; but never again would he join the South Carolinian, or anyone else, in driving the country toward war.

The War Hawk died at Ghent; the Henry Clay who returned to America bringing what seemed to be a barren peace, and glad to escape with that, was the man who within twenty years was to win the title of the Great Pacificator.

CHAPTER VII

ON GETTING OUT OF A HOLE

Showing how Mr. Clay in 1816 convinced himself that he had been wrong in 1811, but unfortunately failed to convince the most important among those he had convinced in 1811 on the matter of the Bank

Mr. Clay came home a changed man in more than merely his attitude toward war. He was now a statesman of national, and even international, importance. His name had figured, as a member of the peace commission, in half the newspapers of Europe. He had exchanged pleasantries with the Duke of Wellington while Madame de Staël stood by. He was no longer merely a celebrated Kentuckian, but a celebrated American.

This is not to be read as an assertion that he immediately swelled up in his own conceit to an inordinate extent. He was much too intelligent for that. But he was also too intelligent not to appreciate the change in his own status. He had been hitherto the recognized spokesman of the West, but not much more. Henceforth he was to represent a point of view not merely western, but national. It was at this point in his career that Henry Clay began to rise above, or fall below, sectionalism. It was here that he began to be absorbed into the aristocracy.

He had never been in the least a fanatical democrat. The son-in-law of Thomas Hart lived in an environment distinctly frosty to extreme egalitarianism; nor is a brilliantly successful attorney, whose services are eagerly sought by the richest men in his section, likely to become a fire-eating champion of the masses. The frontier, however, is always somewhat democratic, made so by the necessities of its existence. Captain John Smith probably never heard of the rights of man, in Rousseau's definition of the term, but at Jamestown, the extreme frontier of 1607, he compelled the gentlemen to dig, simply because it was dig or die. In Kentucky, two hundred years later, Henry Clay occupied a privileged position, in his own right as a leader of the bar, and again as a son-in-law of a rich man; but at that, Kentucky was still close enough to the wilderness to have small respect for traditional privilege. A man was still valued primarily for what he could do, and any assumption of lordly airs would have been suppressed promptly and brusquely. Jefferson was the idol of the West, and Clay's position and traditions were not such as to make it difficult for him to fall in with the current hero worship. It is doubtful that he had ever, before coming to Washington, made any serious attempt to investigate the basis of Jefferson's philosophy.

In any event, he saw no discrepancy between his professions of Jeffersonianism and the fight he waged to restrict the United States Navy's purchase of cordage to the domestic product. The fact that father-in-law Hart was, among other things, a ropemaker, seemed to him pertinent only to the extent that it directed his attention to the national advantage of encouraging the domestic manufacture of cordage. Today a United States Senator who would fight through the Senate a measure compelling the Navy to purchase a product made by his father-in-law would be subjected to some extremely barbed comment, if nothing worse; but in the early years of the nineteenth century the possibilities of economic exploitation of the government were far from fully explored. Not only did Clay never experience a qualm of conscience in this connection, but neither did his contemporaries see anything questionable in his course.

Nor was the atmosphere of Washington in his case a climate favorable to the development of such democratic tendencies as he possessed. He would have hooted at the idea of establishing an American aristocracy of blood; but he was keenly appreciative of the advantages of an aristocracy of brains and character. Hamilton's phrase, "the rich and well-born," is one that Henry Clay would never have coined. He understood the power of wealth perfectly, but he never exhibited Webster's tendency to attribute virtue to its possessors. As between Nicholas Biddle and John Quincy Adams, for instance, Clay was never in a moment's doubt that the poor man was the mighty man.

But there was nothing in Clay's temperament or training to lead him to doubt that government is safest when it is in the hands of men of experience, training and demonstrated ability; nor was it possible for him to distinguish between the technical operations of government and the power of sovereignty. Not only did he believe that men of superior equipment and ability should occupy the offices of government, but he came to believe more and more strongly that they should control it. Jefferson himself never doubted the first part of the proposition, to wit, that the agencies of government should be in the hands of carefully picked men; he believed in a representative, not a direct, democracy, but at the same time he was filled with a pessimistic certainty that even these picked men would rapidly degenerate, were they removed, or did they fancy themselves removed, ever so little beyond the power of the masses. This was a concept foreign to Clay's habit of thought. He was friendly and intelligent. Around him in Washington he found intelligent people whom he liked. How could he doubt that his friends and associates in the capital knew better how to operate the machinery of government than a horde of semi-literate backwoodsmen in Kentucky? The thing was self-evident; he didn't doubt it. Why, then, was it not the duty of a patriotic man to use every endeavor to effect the retention of these obviously superior people in office with power enough to direct government policy?

This is a question to which many another honest man than Henry Clay was giving the wrong answer, and to which many are giving the wrong answer to this day. The woefully simple answer, the correct answer, is that his apparently "superior" people are not, in fact, superior. Intelligence, education, experience of the ways of the world, are all extremely important on the lower levels of government. They are highly desirable, if not indispensable, in the business of carrying out a settled policy. The cultivated, educated, charming people who fascinated Mr. Clay in Washington were, indeed, the best people in the world for clerks, for bureau and division chiefs, for diplomatic and con-

sular officials, for under-secretaries, for every sort of government functionary short of the policy-determining officers. Unfortunately, though, the "best people," in the very nature of
things, are incapable of grasping the fact that nature designed
them, in most cases, for underlings. Seventy-five years after
Clay's return from Ghent the perfect flower of the "best people,"
Henry Adams, with all his intellectual subtlety, which gave him
understanding of countless things that were hidden from most
of his contemporaries, was never able to understand that understanding, alone, is not enough for a statesman of the first rank.
Adams was the very archetype of government clerks; but as a
statesman he is not to be mentioned in the same breath with
William J. Bryan, a man vastly his inferior, intellectually, but
equipped with a terrific moral energy which Adams lacked.

In 1815, when Clay returned from abroad, the cult of the
"best people" was hardly questioned at Washington. Jefferson's
ideal of a representative democracy, in which the people themselves should put the conduct of public affairs in the hands of the
most competent men, was working out, in practice, into an oli-
garchy. The Federalist party, convicted of treason by the Hartford Convention, was a wreck and its intellectual goods and
chattels were at the mercy of any looter who cared to help himself to them. The most important of them, the very basis of
Federalism and of the Hamiltonian philosophy of government,
was the belief that democracy means the rule of the mob. This
was appropriated by any number of men who called themselves
and, doubtless, sincerely believed themselves to be Jeffersonians. Clay and Calhoun were of the number, and Webster had
been frankly a Federalist from the beginning. None of them, at
least in the beginning, was as brutally frank about it as, say,
Fisher Ames and perhaps Clay never quite admitted it, even to
himself; but from 1815 the statecraft of the three ablest parliamentarians of America was based on the theory that the country
is safe when the determination of its broad policies, as well as
the actual operation of its governmental machinery, is in the
hands of a ruling class.

It is not a theory that can be dismissed with a sneer. On the contrary, it is the theory under which the actual conduct of American affairs has been carried on during much the longer part of the nation's history. Only on rare occasions have the people revolted and snatched the business of the country from the hands of the ruling clique, and usually they have maintained their interest for a short time only. Such a revolt had occurred in 1800, when the Hamiltonians were summarily dismissed; but by 1815 the turmoil had subsided. Shocked and dismayed by the violence of the storm, the more limber politicians had unanimously repudiated all connection with Hamilton and ardently paid lip-service to Jefferson, while the rigid had been relegated to private life. A few, most of them such New Englanders as John Quincy Adams and William Plumer, of New Hampshire, either were genuinely convinced, or acquiesced in what they believed to be the considered decision of the people.

But as the excitement of 1800 died down, the Jeffersonianism of the ordinary sort of politicians died with it. The very word "Federalist," in large areas, was no longer a name, but an epithet, so gentlemen anxious above all to retain their offices naturally did not resume it. All they resumed was the practices and political philosophy of the Federalist party. This is no unfamiliar procedure; it is what the politicians, with charming irony, term "realism" in politics, and it accounts for the fact that the same party can elect, in successive campaigns, Abraham Lincoln and Ulysses S. Grant, and can nominate, in successive campaigns, William J. Bryan and Alton B. Parker. When a politician decides upon a "realistic" policy, he decides to eliminate reality from his political professions and to depend upon the voters' romantic attachment to a party name, or to a dead party leader, or to some other form of symbolism to keep them voting for policies which bear no perceptible relation to the symbol.

As regards Calhoun and Clay, it is a temptation to cite, as a perfect illustration of their swerving toward a cynical political "realism," the chartering of the second Bank of the United States, in 1816. Yet it is rather difficult to establish, on the basis of the existing records, any convincing evidence of disingenuousness in this matter. In 1811 Clay, it is true, had not only voted against rechartering the old bank, but in a speech in the Senate —the speech that convinced Andrew Jackson—stated the fundamental objections to such a bank. "What is a corporation such as the bill contemplated?" he inquired and then damned the bank with the answer to his own question: "It is a splendid association of favored individuals, taken from the mass of society, and invested with exemptions and surrounded by immunities and privileges." A few minutes later he observed, "The power of a nation is said to consist in the sword and the purse. Perhaps at last all power is resolvable into that of the purse, for with it you may command almost everything else. The specie circulation of the United States is estimated by some calculators at ten millions of dollars, and if it be no more, one moiety is in the vaults of this bank. May not the time arrive when the concentration of such a vast portion of the circulating medium of the country in the hands of any corporation will be dangerous to our liberties? By whom is this immense power wielded? By a body who, in derogation of the great principles of all our institutions, responsibility to the people, is amenable only to a few stockholders, and they chiefly foreigners."

These were vital objections. They were the objections on which, twenty years later, the bank was destroyed, and which have prevented its resuscitation since. They were not dependent upon any construction of the Constitution; they had nothing to do with constitutionality, but bore directly upon policy, irrespective of the Constitution, and no sort of establishment of the constitutionality of the bank would have removed them.

Yet justice to Henry Clay in 1816 demands notice that in 1811 these passages did not constitute the main part of his argument. He threw them in as mere make-weights. The body of his speech was devoted to a long, if rather exiguous, constitutional dissertation. He was interested in an analysis of the doctrine of implied powers and his principal effort was to show that it could not reasonably be extended to cover the rechartering of the bank. Undoubtedly, in 1816 he remembered that speech of 1811 as a speech on the doctrine of implied powers, and it is not beyond belief that he had forgotten the real objections to the bank, which he had touched in passing and which, evidently, never had interested him much. In 1816 he descended from the Speaker's chair in order to make a public retraction of the speech of 1811; but what he retracted was the constitutional argument, and the childish xenophobia that had led him to denounce, as one of the gravest evils of the bank, the fact that Englishmen held much of its stock. The solid objections he could not retract; he could only ignore them, and he did.

If the whole question of the bank had hinged upon the matter of implied powers it would have been, as he thought it was, quite defensible; for statesmen of 1816, as they pondered the question of reviving the bank, might have anticipated the remark Grover Cleveland was to make seventy years later: "It is a condition which confronts us, not a theory." Moreover, that condition was acutely distressing. The fiscal affairs of the country were in appalling confusion. Part of the trouble, if not all of it, was due to the folly of the young War Hawks, Clay among them, in rejecting the prudent, if bitter, advice of old Gallatin, who had urged them at the outbreak of hostilities to levy taxes ruthlessly. They had not done it, and now the country was paying the penalty in financial distress accompanied, and intensified, by currency derangement that amounted almost to chaos.

In 1816 the stock answer to any problem connected with the currency was a national bank. The objections to such an institution were already becoming apparent, but the thinking, even of the ablest men, had not proceeded far beyond noting the objections. Other means of establishing reasonable control of the currency had not yet been worked out—but why say "had not" rather than "have not"? In nearly a century and a quarter we have managed to get rid of the national bank obsession, but one who would say that we have arrived at a satisfactory solution of the currency problem is certainly little acquainted with the uproars that harass Washington today. To sneer at Clay, Calhoun and their colleagues because, confronted with a situation that demanded instant, vigorous action, they could think of no expedient better than a revival of the bank would be to sneer at them for not being at least a century ahead of their time.

In 1816 the former Jeffersonians voted to commit the power of the purse to private hands. Tested by the only true standard of Jeffersonianism "equal rights for all, special privileges for none," it was poisonously anti-Jeffersonian; but it does not follow that this is definitely the point at which they deliberately turned their backs on the philosophy of the Sage of Monticello. There is, indeed, no such point in the careers of two of the three great men who dominated the political scene so long and the third, Webster, had never been a follower of Jefferson. As for Clay and Calhoun, the latter died still regarding himself as the true exponent of the Jeffersonian philosophy, while Clay would have repudiated the suggestion that he ever voluntarily abandoned Jefferson; his belief was that Jefferson's theories failed in certain crises, so he was forced to adopt other ideas.

At the same time, the chartering of the second Bank of the United States is a convenient point at which to date the beginning of the Silver Age of American politics. There had been an interregnum. The Golden Age had definitely expired with the election of the Eleventh Congress, or, rather, during the term of the Tenth, those bodies so impotent and futile that the government itself all but broke down because Congress was unable to pass any bill, even the necessary appropriation bills. Then came the war, and the development of our political institutions had to be adjourned while the military situation absorbed the country's energies.

Now the emergency was over, and the minds of men were released to struggle with the problem of making what they could out of the republic that Washington and his colleagues had founded, and that Madison, the last of that great group, had defended, not brilliantly, but successfully. The revolutionists were through; the administrators were on the scene, and the administrative mind was to dominate henceforth.

The change is illuminated by the manner in which the new group attacked the currency problem. The Golden Age had been the age of brilliant improvisation, rising at times to inspiration.

The Declaration of American Independence had no model.[1] "To place before mankind the common sense of the subject, in terms so plain and firm as to command their assent" is the way Jefferson described his effort. "Neither aiming at originality of principles or sentiments, nor yet copied from any previous writing, it was intended to be an expression of the American mind."[2] But the expression of the American mind was in itself a venture of high originality. The Constitution of the United States, in turn, has no model except to the extent that it repeated ideas expressed in the Declaration. Here, again, an army of historians has traced back almost to the beginning of history certain ideas, and even certain expressions, embodied in the document; but the thing as a whole was unprecedented. Washington's First Inaugural owes astonishingly little to previous models of statecraft. Hamilton, conservative as he was, in many of the *Federalist* papers, relied on nothing but "the common sense of the subject," regardless of precedents, and so broke new ground. Franklin, John and Samuel Adams, George Mason, Patrick Henry, even, to some extent, John Jay, all were keenly aware of the novelty of their position and cherished no hope of finding useful precedents for their guidance. But the heroes of the Revolution were superbly self-confident; lack of guidance, instead of paralyzing, stimulated them. Where there was no precedent they blithely made one and, because the average level of their common sense was astonishingly high, it was usually a good precedent. The result was statecraft of a brilliance unmatched in our history, and not often rivaled anywhere.

But in 1816 the Golden Age was over. The Revolutionists had become the Founding Fathers. Their startling, if sometimes inspired, innovations had become the political equivalent of "the faith as it was delivered unto the saints." Rule and formula were coming into their own, and where Jefferson's only hope had been

[1] This is substantially true, notwithstanding the fact that Becker and others have demonstrated how Jefferson picked up an idea here and a phrase there until the derivation of almost every line in the document has been traced back, sometimes for centuries. But the whole document as a political instrument, has no predecessor.

[2] Letter to Lee, 1825.

to convince the public that he was acting like a man of sense, the politician of 1816 could do very well by convincing the public that he was acting in accordance with Jefferson's rules. The Golden Age had no shibboleth; the Silver Age made one out of the teachings of the previous generation. The statecraft of the Silver Age was no longer a frank, unfettered "expression of the American mind." It was an attempt to apply to changing conditions the Jeffersonian, Hamiltonian, Washingtonian expression. It was derivative, therefore shackled.

Precisely for that reason, however, it deserves the close attention of anyone who would understand the country that we live in today. Conditions that faced the Revolutionists have never been repeated and it is hard to imagine that they can ever be duplicated in the future. Conditions that faced the men of 1816 have not only been repeated, in their essentials, but are being repeated constantly. Therefore, while the actual deeds of Jefferson, Hamilton, Madison and the others constitute the basis of our national history, interest in their methods is somewhat academic, since those methods are hardly likely to be useful again unless the conditions that made them valid are reproduced, which seems impossible. On the contrary, much of the work accomplished by Clay, Webster and Calhoun has already been undone; but their methods and especially their habits of thought, are pretty much the methods and habits of thought of American politicians to this day.

Thus when they attacked the currency problem, they undertook to hew no new paths. They did not even explore possibilities that had already been pointed out. The essentials of the sub-treasury scheme were already in men's minds—Gallatin was one of several who had advanced the idea tentatively—but the new leaders were no such intellectual pioneers as the old ones had been. As far as Webster was concerned, of course, the question did not arise. His Federalism presented no philosophical obstacles. He had always been a bank man, so he had nothing to retract and his sole interest was in making the new bank the right kind of an institution—that is to say, right from the Federalist viewpoint. He therefore showed up much better in the

debate than did Calhoun and Clay. The question presented itself
to them as largely an exercise in dialectic. Some sort of fiscal
agency was obviously necessary, and they could think of nothing
but a bank. To the men who made the Constitution, this would
have been enough; but Clay and Calhoun had not made it, they
had inherited it, and already the Constitution had crystallized.
Their problem was more than simply an exposition of the necessity for a fiscal agent, "the common sense of the subject"; it
was, from their point of view, also necessary to make their
present conviction square with the deliverances of the Fathers
on the subject. Statecraft was no longer merely a matter of "expression of the American mind." The factor of orthodoxy had
entered and politicians began to develop more and more the
theologians' subtlety of reasoning. The speeches of Calhoun and
Clay on the bank bill are full of it.

It was not so with Webster. The New Englander's Federalism had never been of the poisonous type. He had opposed the
Hartford Convention, and his influence had kept New Hampshire pretty well clear of that foolish disloyalty. Hartford, indeed, was not the product of Federalism, but of the overweening
egotism of certain Federalist leaders whose real grievance was
that they were excluded from any share in control of the government. To do them justice, it was probably something a little
higher than mere lust for office that motivated them; it was
probably lust for power, combined with a childlike faith that
they were the only people in the country possessed of intelligence enough to handle public affairs. It is a phenomenon familiar to every generation and it was made manifest with unusual clarity in the years after 1932, when many supporters of
the old regime were perfectly honest in the belief that the country was doomed to destruction because they and their friends
were no longer handling its affairs.

Webster, with all his faults, was too big a man to deceive
himself in that fashion. He never wavered in his belief that the
Jeffersonian dictum, "Equal rights for all and special privileges
for none" was fundamentally nonsensical; but he would have no
hand in an effort to destroy the union to prove his belief right.

Having kept clear of Hartford, therefore, he retained the respect of loyal men even among his opponents and was able to wield a powerful influence in the fight to re-establish the bank.

Nor did he have to waste time in fine-spun arguments devised to show that his position was essentially that of Jefferson. He wasn't a Jeffersonian and had no desire to be considered one. He was able, therefore, to proceed directly to the question of the soundness of the fiscal structure provided in the various bills then before Congress. His idea of a sound bank, of course, was one sound from the viewpoint of a banker. He wanted a bank that would, first of all, remain solvent, one that would meet every obligation on the day it was due, and in which men with money could deposit their funds with quiet minds. He framed a bill admirably designed to meet these requirements and stuck to it through thick and thin. The social implications of his sort of bank worried him not at all. The fact that it would confer immense power over the lives of all the people upon a favored group of individuals seemed to him only right and proper; financial affairs, he argued, ought to be handled by men who know how, and he fought bitterly every attempt to hold the financiers responsible to any public authority. In the end, he voted against his own bill because it had been amended so as to give the government a very slight degree of control over the operations of the bank. Webster's position was not merely undemocratic, but actively antidemocratic, but it had the immense advantages of being simple and comprehensible and his speeches, by comparison with the tortuous constitutional arguments of his colleagues, struck many of his hearers as being full of hard, common sense. In the end, it was his bank that was established, with some rather slight modifications.

It proved to be a good bank, too, in the sense that it did what he expected it to do. The fact that it also did what his opponents expected it to do, that is to say, it created an immense, centralized and autocratic financial power, seemed to him a trifling objection. Of the three great parliamentary leaders who dominated American politics in this formative period, Daniel Webster was by far the most successful, because his political philosophy was the simplest, most direct, most consistent, most completely integrated in the group. His character was complex, but not his ideas. He was frankly the servant of big business, but he served it excellently, and there is no conclusive evidence that there was any conscious hypocrisy in his course. Why should there be? Democracy, in the Jeffersonian sense, never has been universally accepted in this country, even in theory. Equal rights for all and special privileges for none is not even the ideal of a great many people who are no doubt as honest as Jefferson. The fact that a man has money is still accepted as *prima facie* evidence that he is virtuous by a great many people other than Ed Howe, the Kansas philosopher, although in the twentieth century few have Howe's courage to proclaim the belief. If this belief is still accepted in some quarters today, there was much more evidence to justify it in Webster's time. In 1816 money actually was the reward of industry, frugality and sobriety much more frequently than it is now.

This is not to be construed as an assertion that Daniel Webster was a thoroughly honest man. Twenty years later, in connection with this same bank, he resorted to thinly disguised blackmail; and even his elastic conscience could hardly have been stretched to cover that sort of thing. It was a question, however, of personal finances, not political principles; in standing frankly as the representative of property, Webster, far from suffering qualms of conscience, felt that he deserved the commendation of all decent men.

But the dullness of Webster's social perception, while it makes him the easiest of the three to understand, also makes him the least interesting. He captured the imagination of the country and attained a long fame by an ability that had nothing to do with his character and not much with his mentality. It was his histrionic talent, powerfully reinforced by a musician's ear for rhythm and sonority. The sense in Webster's speeches frequently breaks down, vaporizes and vanishes under analysis, but their sound is always superb. "Liberty and union, now and forever, one and inseparable" considered as any sort of statement of policy or principle is sheer jargon; but its merit as elocution has preserved it for a century. Add to its mellifluousness Webster's fine voice and splendid bearing and it becomes formidable. One might easily believe that this man could have reproduced Macklin's feat of bringing tears to the eyes of his hearers by reciting the multiplication table. The twentieth century was presented with evidence of how tremendous this gift may become in the case of William J. Bryan, the Webster of our time; for while their social sympathies were diametrically opposed, the two men won power by the same qualities.

Henry Clay and John C. Calhoun were much more complex, and therefore more difficult to understand and more fascinating to study. Webster's simple faith in the creed of the Holy Dividends could not satisfy them; but neither were they able to repose implicit confidence in Jefferson's theory of human rights above property rights. For one thing, they had before their eyes evidence that Jefferson himself had never been able to translate that theory into government policy. Jefferson had carefully outlined a set of policies which he deemed necessary to achieve his ultimate goal of equal rights for all and special privileges for none.[3] These included economy in government, reduction of the national debt and what we should now call less interference by the government in business; yet, as President, Jefferson had increased expenses, shot the national debt up enormously, the Louisiana Purchase contributing one large item, and by the adoption of the Embargo and Nonintercourse Acts had made the government interfere in every man's business and throttle that of the shipping interests. The Napoleonic wars, of course, were the reason; but the plain fact remained that the Jeffersonian methods had been abandoned and practical politicians have much more respect for facts than for theories.

There is no reason to doubt that both Clay and Calhoun accepted "in principle," as the diplomatic negotiators say, the Jeffersonian thesis of equal rights for all and special privileges

---

[3] An exceptionally clear distinction between Jefferson's aims and the methods he advocated to secure the aims is drawn by Herbert Agar in *The Pursuit of Happiness*, published in 1938. It is a distinction frequently missed, but absolutely necessary to any comprehension of Jefferson as a statesman.

for none. There is no reason—perhaps it would be better to say, no sufficient reason—to doubt that at this time both were sincerely desirous of finding the best method of achieving that end. But they had both seen Jefferson's methods fail. They were young, able and ardent. Such men are traditionally impatient of demonstrated failures. The fact that they swung away from the Jeffersonian methods, far from being to their discredit, is the best of evidence that they were possessed of intelligence and energy. Unfortunately, in setting up the sort of bank they established, that is, in restoring the power of the purse to private hands with almost no governmental control over those hands, they did more than turn away from Jefferson's methods—they turned away from his objective, also. Equal rights for all and special privileges for none is an ideal inconsistent with a policy of turning over to a favored group, control of the money of all the people.

They should have been wiser, without doubt; but, equally without doubt, that is a charge that can be leveled with justice against every man of that generation and likewise of this one. Who shouldn't be wiser than he actually is? There is this to be said for Calhoun and Clay: the currency problem when they faced it was acute, so critical that some answer had to be found without delay; they found an answer; it was not ideal, but it served. The agency they set up as an answer to their problem actually answered it; in the end, of course, the agency itself posed other questions, as grave as the currency problem, but for twelve or fifteen years the second Bank of the United States worked admirably. Judged by any reasonable standard, this is no bad statecraft. The politician who can meet any problem of comparable gravity and settle it in such fashion that it will stay settled even for a decade is no fool. Indeed, as politicians go, he is something of a wonder, for there are not many who can do it.

Establishment of the second bank, however, affected more than the fiscal and political history of the United States. It had, also, a psychological effect on the leaders mainly responsible for its establishment. Viewed with regard solely to its immediate effect upon the welfare of the country the bank bill shows up well; a better bill might have been written, of course, but a fair-minded observer can hardly escape the conclusion that this was pretty good statesmanship.

Its effect upon the men who did it, and especially upon the two who were its conspicuous champions among the Jeffersonians, is quite another story. One must avoid dogmatism in discussing such a point for we are dealing here with impalpable history, unsupported by any documents, unproved by any evidence that would be admitted in a court of law, and whatever assertions one makes with respect to it should be plainly marked as inferences, which the reader may accept or reject as they agree with, or contravene, his own judgment. Subject to this caveat, it may be pointed out that in establishing the bank of 1816, Henry Clay and John C. Calhoun had consciously and deliberately denied equal rights to some and conferred special privileges upon a few.[4] No matter what their motives, this they had done. A man committed to any course of action, especially if he is bitterly assailed for it by opponents whose motives he has small reason to respect, tends to find justifications for that course in odd places and by odd processes of reasoning. Clay and Calhoun were attacked, not only by honest opponents of their policy, but also by a rabble of politicians of the lower grades, some of whom had never had an honest opinion on anything at any time in their lives. What could be more natural, then, than for a project which had first been adopted as a dubious expedient soon to assume the character, in their minds, of a fixed conviction?

One thing is certain, namely, that somewhere in their political careers these men swerved away from Jeffersonianism and worked out political philosophies not merely at variance with it, but in certain points contradictory to it. It is certain, too, that the break was not spectacularly sudden; indeed, it was never frankly admitted, probably not even to themselves. It came by

[4] There were 31,334 subscribers to the stock of the bank, of whom 15,610 subscribed in Baltimore, an indication that the people nearest Washington had a distinct advantage if only in a better understanding of the situation. See McMaster, vol. iv, p. 313.

slow degrees, each step being not only logical but apparently forced by circumstances. If Calhoun and Clay had been plainly recreant, if they had turned their backs upon their old master suddenly and for obviously personal interest, they might have been, perhaps, more dramatic, but they would certainly have been less interesting. It is precisely because their careers include no sudden, spectacular reversals, but represent the slow attrition of a political idea under the stress of forces that are still operative that they are interesting.

After nearly a hundred and twenty-five years it is still no easier than it was in 1816 to keep clear, always, the distinction between ends and means, between ideals and the methods adopted to attain them. When methods fail, men still are prone to decide that the ideal has failed. Yet no really great ideal has ever been completely attained, or is completely attainable; equal rights for all and special privileges for none is an ideal that has never been more than remotely approached by any government on earth; and Clay and Calhoun were far indeed from being the last politicians to give it up in despair. After a century and a quarter great nations are frantically denouncing any effort to attain it as degeneracy.

So the bank was set up, and in the operation Mr. Webster and Mr. Calhoun attained standing as national politicians equivalent to that won by Mr. Clay at Ghent. It was the first achievement of the Triumvirate as a group, the first occasion which the public had to link together the three names that for the next thirty years were to resound as no others did in the halls of Congress and to become the summation, first of politics and, later, of statesmanship, in the minds of many generations.

Yet immediately after the bank fight the group dissolved, for Mr. Webster took no part in the procedure of electing James Monroe to the Presidency. That was a project for Republicans, and he was a Federalist. It was not accomplished without something of a flurry, for the Virginia Dynasty, that had held the Presidency for all but four years of its existence, was arousing jealousy both in the North and in the South. New York wanted a chance at the office, and some Southerners were willing to throw out the Virginians, but their choice was not Tompkins, of New York, but William H. Crawford, of Georgia, and they tried to put him in nomination by calling a snap caucus. The effort was blocked, but the ill-feeling aroused seemed to have caused some perturbation in the mind of Henry Clay. When the caucus finally assembled, he offered a resolution to the effect that it was inexpedient for members of Congress to nominate candidates for the Presidency. Probably all he wanted was a test of sentiment, for he acquiesced calmly enough when his resolution was voted down. It is only in view of what happened four years and again eight years later that the incident is worth remembering.

Monroe was duly nominated by the old caucus method and in due course was triumphantly elected. Calhoun was translated to the Cabinet as Secretary of War, where a little later he was to make the error that, although long undiscovered, was at last to prove politically fatal. Clay remained in the House of Representatives, where he was to make *his* fatal error in connection with the same dangerous and incomprehensible man, a soldier named Andrew Jackson.

The Secretaryship of War had, in fact, been offered to Clay, but he had refused it. There was a Cabinet post that he would have been glad to take, but only one. This was the Secretaryship of State, then regarded as the ante-room to the Presidency. Madison had been Jefferson's Secretary of State and Monroe had been Madison's. Mr. Clay unquestionably would have been glad to be Monroe's; but Monroe couldn't see it. Instead, he gave the post to the grim Puritan of Ghent, John Quincy Adams, and if Clay refrained from using violent language to Adams on this occasion, it was because he was restrained by the proprieties, not for lack of emotion.

The appointment, in the circumstances, was natural, right and proper; but Mr. Clay had already reached the point where he would rather be President than right, and was rapidly proceeding to the point where he would rather be President than anything, even immortal in his country's history.

CHAPTER VIII

ON COMMITTING SUICIDE DEBONAIRLY

An account of how Mr. Calhoun, in the Cabinet, and Mr. Clay, in the House, succeeded in arousing the undying enmity of the one man who could defeat them both

PERHAPS the quality of instruction has improved so that it is no longer true, but thousands of schoolboys of the last generation emerged from their study of United States history with the impression that the period between the War of 1812 and the Civil War was practically a blank. Pinned down, they might admit hearing some mention of the Missouri Compromise, nullification and the debates on slavery, but it was the considered opinion of the youth of the land that during these forty-five years nothing really interesting happened. Nor is this such a reflection on the intelligence of the boys as it seems to be, for it is only recently—that is to say, within the last quarter of a century— that even grave and learned historians have begun to get a clear conception of what did happen.

Today we are beginning to suspect that the judgment of youth was not without some reasonable foundation—that the ordinary school history up to the turn of the century was extraordinarily successful in omitting the happenings of large significance, replacing them with detailed accounts of events of relatively minor importance. Before rushing into denunciation of the writers of textbooks, however, one should have the elementary fairness to examine the handicaps under which they labored. These were formidable. One is the fact that the men who made the history of this period had, for the most part, entirely erroneous ideas of what they were doing and therefore left records that are misleading in practically every particular. Another is the fact that periods of rapid and radical change can never be assessed accurately except in perspective, and usually in long perspective; and this was the period of the most rapid and radical changes in the physical environment of civilization that the world has ever seen. As a matter of fact only now, a century and a quarter from the beginning of the period, are we attaining a perspective that renders judgment fairly easy.

Between the administrations of James Madison and James Buchanan the physical environment in which civilized men lived altered more radically than it had altered between the time of James Madison and the time of Homer. In the time of Madison as in the time of Homer the speed of a running horse was the fastest known mode of transportation, and the speed of sound the fastest mode of communication, ignoring smoke and semaphore signals, which antedate history. In the time of Madison as in the time of Homer, the water wheel and the windmill were the greatest concentrations of power, and the muscular exertions of men and animals furnished by far the larger part of the energy by which all the work of the world was performed. In the time of James Buchanan the locomotive and the electric telegraph were both in common use and the age of steam power was well established.

But the alteration in the physical environment was neither swifter nor more profound than the alteration in the mental outlook and attitude of the American people, and none of these changes could possibly have been foreseen by the founders of the Republic. Washington and his colleagues had devised and established a system of government admirably adapted to a rural, agricultural republic whose population was not only homogeneous, racially, but conspicuously lacking in extreme variations of social and economic position. Washington himself was reputed to be the wealthiest man in that country, but Washington never saw the day when he could have duplicated the feat of Stephen Girard, who, when subscriptions to the stock of the Bank of the United States in 1816 fell short by three million dollars, took the balance himself.[1] Yet Girard was the first of a long line of

[1] McMaster, vol. iv, p. 313.

multimillionaires whose fortunes increased in size with the passage of time. The distance, measured on the economic scale, between Washington and the poorest free man in the country was trifling by comparison with the distance between the richest man and the poorest man in 1860.

The men who established the Constitution observed that the agricultural-pastoral democracy of their day was the result of evolutionary processes that had continued for a hundred and eighty years. Being intelligent, they envisaged, not the possibility only, but the inevitability of change; they assumed, however, that the rate of change would be of the same order as the rate during the preceding two centuries, which was of the order of the rate since the beginning of recorded history. How could they have imagined that the country, during the next century, would change at a speed fifty times that of the changes of the preceding fifty centuries?

It was the task of the men of the Silver Age of American politics to take the work of their predecessors and apply it to conditions that did not exist when their predecessors were alive. They had a Constitution written to govern a simple, static, agricultural country; and they had to make it work in an increasingly complex, increasingly kinetic, increasingly urban country, growing at unprecedented speed, changing at unprecedented speed, and receiving an unprecedented flood of immigration of racial stocks different from those of the original inhabitants. Rarely, if ever, have statesmen been confronted with a more exasperating problem.

First of the complications was, of course, that none of them quite understood what was going on. No man ever quite understands his own times, and if these men had understood theirs they would have exhibited a wisdom putting to shame all philosophy. Even as early as 1816 one might have said with truth that this was not at all the country that Washington and Jefferson had known, but who would have understood the saying? Certainly not the voters, upon whom politicians were dependent for their chance to wield power. Certainly not many politicians. The fact that the Triumvirs did understand, if dimly, that the republic of the Founders was somehow slipping away from them is proof that they were extraordinary men.

As one looks back upon it from the safe distance of a century and a quarter, the amazing thing is not that the statecraft of these years was frequently fumbling and blundering, but that the country was not rent apart by the extraordinary and wholly unforeseen stresses to which it was subjected. Perhaps the major part of the credit is due, as all of it is commonly assigned, to the prescience of the men of the Golden Age. The fabric they created proved to be the most elastic governmental structure erected in human history, with the possible exception of the British monarchy; and even that is a doubtful exception because the monarchy was not encased in a written constitution, as the republic was. But surely not all the praise should go to the wisdom of the Founding Fathers; something remains to be said for the dexterity of the Silver Age.

Dextrous these men undoubtedly were—perhaps too much so, perhaps too often dextrous when wisdom was required, perhaps sometimes enchanted and enthralled by their own dexterity to the neglect of obvious differences between right and wrong. All the same, high skill commands admiration, and it took skill of a very high order to make the Constitution work at all in the years between 1815 and 1860. In the end, of course, it failed. The marvelous juggling could not continue indefinitely and the crash was terrific when it came. But note that it did not come until the Silver Age was over and the great politicians who were its ornaments had died. They were mortal, after all, these Clays, Websters, Calhouns, Jacksons, Bentons, Van Burens, Casses, Livingstons and Clintons who for more than a generation compelled an impossible system to work, forced old laws to fit a new country, found precedents for the unprecedented, swiftly identified the unimagined, evolved formulas for chaos. After they died, the system collapsed; but not until after they died.

The generation that has had charge of national affairs since 1914 is somewhat inclined to self-pity, as being a generation called upon to perform the impossible, called upon to make immutable laws for a shifting, almost a fluid, civilization, called upon to make an ancient Constitution fit conditions that are not only ultramodernistic, but that change more rapidly than laws can be framed. There are not lacking those who have given up in despair, declaring that democracy itself is an outworn concept and that equal rights for all and special privileges for none embodies an ideal that, while it might have applied to a simple, agricultural country, is wildly impossible as applied to a highly industrialized nation, continental in extent, rich beyond all precedent in human history, and ethnologically so complex that it is rivaled only by the polyglot ethnic composition of the Levant.

Defeatists of this type ought to study the period between the War of 1812 and the Civil War. The modern complexity that appalls them is simplicity itself by comparison with the changes that were overwhelming the country in these years; for in addition to all the disturbances that drive us to distraction they had to face at the same time a change vastly more profound and more disturbing than anything that is occurring in our times, to wit, the Industrial Revolution. As a matter of fact, every important phase of our national life was changing faster then than it is now. Heterogeneous races were pouring into the country faster —in proportion to the whole population—than they are now. Urbanization was proceeding faster, in proportion to population, than it is now. The gap between the richest and the poorest was widening faster then than it is now. Every influence that political philosophers cite today as exerting a strain on the democratic ideal was stronger then than it is now. In addition to all this, the very foundations of civilization, not here, only, but in all the world were being wrenched and jarred by the introduction of steam, instead of muscle, as the main source of the energy by which the work of the world was performed. The problems of government under which modern statecraft reels and staggers certainly are no more complex than those that confronted the men of this period; and in view of the fact that there is nothing in our day remotely comparable to the changes introduced by the industrial revolution, one is tempted to assert that modern complexity is hardly more than kindergarten stuff by comparison with the difficulties faced, with a fair measure of success, by American statesmen between 1815 and 1860.

In this group were many who came and went, some who outshone the Triumvirate for a time, many who defeated them at one point or another and at least eight who snatched from their grasp the great prize for which they contended. But part of the lasting interest that clings to these men arises from the very fact that they failed to achieve the greatest office in the republic and time and again saw it pass to men who were not their peers in intellectual capacity, in experience in government, in political skill, or in force of character. When it came to the Presidency, the American people turned their thumbs down on Webster, Clay and Calhoun. By some this consistent denial has been attributed to mere chance, by some to political errors made by the men themselves, and some have seen in it evidence that there is inherent in democracy a tendency to reject the first-rate man and to prefer one of inferior quality.

Not many have had the temerity to suggest that the reason they were rejected was simply that neither Clay, Webster, nor Calhoun was fit to be President. The immediate question that such a suggestion raises is: Was Franklin Pierce, then, better fit for the office than these? Was Millard Fillmore? Was William Henry Harrison? Was John Tyler? The question answers itself when the mere names of these obscure Chief Magistrates are mentioned; but both question and answer are irrelevant. The relevant fact is that only on rare occasions have the American people voted for a President; as a rule, they vote against his opponent. The energy and resourcefulness of politics in this period were exerted, not to elect any nonentity, but to beat Henry Clay, or John C. Calhoun, or Daniel Webster.

Observing this, some political commentators have inferred that political success over a long period generates its own destruction; for conspicuous success inevitably arouses envy and enmity based on it and on a dozen other grounds. Enemies increase with time, so after long-continued success a man collects enemies enough to drag him down. But this reasoning overlooks another paradox of American politics, to wit, the fact that the possession of enemies is not necessarily an element of political weakness. Who collected the most magnificent array of enemies in American history? Unquestionably Andrew Jackson, who has strong claims to be considered the most consistently successful politician the country ever produced. Close after him, whether one measures enemies by their number or by their virulence, comes Thomas Jefferson, who held the Presidency himself for eight years and practically appointed the men who held it for sixteen years more. Possibly the third most violently hated man who ever came to the office was Franklin D. Roosevelt, in 1936; and when the battle was over he had left his opponent just eight electoral votes—the most tremendous victory since the election of 1820, when James Monroe beat John Quincy Adams by 231 to one!

Each member of the Triumvirate did collect enemies by scores and hundreds, and the collections grew as the years passed; but it is doing those enemies too much honor to say that they beat Webster, Clay and Calhoun. When such men are beaten consistently, it is because they beat themselves. In the cases of these three this was not only true, but conspicuously true. More than that, while the circumstances altered, the cause of failure in nearly every case was the same—a curious blindness to things that were perfectly obvious to men of far less powerful intelligence. The history of the Triumvirate strongly suggests that not in religion, only, but in politics, too, some of the most important truths are hidden from the wise and prudent and revealed unto babes.

Clay, for example, never quite got through his head a true realization of where power actually resides in the United States. From the beginning Clay was one of the insiders. He observed at close range the manipulations by which power is used by politicians, financiers, merchants and industrialists. He saw with his own eyes how easily shrewd fellows, in ordinary times, may impose their will upon the country; and he fell into the error, not uncommon among men who occupy an advantageous political, social and economic position, of forgetting that after all the power is borrowed, when, indeed, it is not embezzled, and that the loan may be called at any moment.

He was keenly aware that James Monroe had not been selected for the Presidency by the people of the country, but by a caucus of politicians in Congress. This was true; but Clay overlooked the equally important truth that the people had ratified the selection with an emphasis leaving no doubt that Monroe was actually their choice for the office. When a President is so approved by the country at large, the disposition of the voters is to support him in whatever he may do that is not blatantly unjustifiable. Monroe's choice of J. Q. Adams for Secretary of State certainly was not unjustifiable; the people saw nothing objectionable in it, nor did any important politician, except Henry Clay. Even he could not denounce the appointment publicly, but no sooner did Monroe assume office than Clay began to find fault with practically every act of the administration. This was juggling dynamite, but with the fatuity that sometimes overcomes the greatest politicians, Clay could not see it. Had Monroe actually been the creature and agent of the Congressional caucus, criticism, even carping criticism, of all his acts might have involved small danger to the critic; but he was not; he was the agent of the people and Clay's course was inviting the wrath of the people to descend upon him.

However, as the event proved, it was not his baiting of Monroe that was his dreadful mistake in these years—or, rather, the baiting was only incidental. The time came when Clay saw what he deemed a superb opportunity to hit the President, and in his enthusiasm he assumed that this was an occasion on which the old maxim, "Any stick will do to beat a dog" would apply. Unfortunately, the stick Henry Clay picked up to belabor James Monroe turned out to be no stick at all, but a rattlesnake, very much alive and very peevish. The club Clay selected for his purpose was an army officer named Jackson; and, although no one realized it for many years, that fatal choice doomed Henry Clay.

One of the delights of reading the history of this period is the persistent intrusion of the sardonic element. At this time Henry Clay and John C. Calhoun were two of the most celebrated men

in America; hoots of derision would have followed the suggestion that the destinies of both were to be profoundly affected by
the erratic mental processes of a Congressman from Tennessee
so obscure that his name figures in history only this once.[2] John
Rhea, of Tennessee, inadvertently set in motion a chain of events
of which he was never to see the end—events that were to affect
the careers of many far greater men than he and, in particular,
to balk the personal ambition of both Clay and Calhoun.

It began with the dispatch to the southern frontier—at that
time the Georgia-Florida line—of the ablest commander in the
Federal service, General Andrew Jackson, victor of New Orleans. There was only too much reason for sending him; the
border was aflame. Life in south Georgia was being made hellish
for honest men by raids from Spanish territory of Seminole Indians, who would descend upon outlying settlements, scalp, loot
and burn, and be off and across the border again before organized
pursuit could reach them. Nor were the Indians the only terrors
of the region. Renegade white men, smugglers, fugitives from
justice of all types, every sort of hard character, found sanctuary
in Spanish territory, and what diplomatists primly refer to as
"incidents" were almost of daily occurrence. Protests to the
Spanish governor produced voluble expressions of regret, but
no action beyond shrugs and assertions that the Spanish military
forces were wholly inadequate to keep order.

The Georgians naturally developed a biting skepticism as to
this. They believed, no doubt sincerely, that what was lacking
was not the ability, but the will, to hold down the rogues. They
said, and produced some evidence in support of the assertion,
that the Spanish authorities encouraged the Seminoles, and
white ruffians, too, in their depredations, partly out of dislike
of the Americans and partly for a share in the loot.

The new commander, never conspicuous for his tolerant un-

[2] John Rhea (pronounced "Ray") does have one other claim to fame, but it is
equally dubious. With Robert Wright he shares the distinction of being the subject of a characteristic epigram by the bitter John Randolph of Roanoke. Randolph observed that the House of Representatives exhibited two anomalies:
"A Wright always wrong; and a Ray without light." See William Cabell Bruce,
John Randolph of Roanoke, vol. ii, p. 202.

derstanding of a foreign point of view, shared this belief in Spanish duplicity; but aside from that, he immediately realized, as any competent officer must, that the military problem before him was not to be solved permanently merely by driving the marauders back across the line. The permanent solution was to break up their refuges in Pensacola and other fortified Spanish posts.

But this involved invading the territory of another nation, that is to say, an act of war, and the United States had not declared war against Spain. Andrew Jackson, however, was not the man to hang back on what he regarded as small points of punctilio. He reported the situation to the President, and then appended to his letter a bit of *Realpolitik* that would have commanded the admiration of Otto von Bismarck. He realized that the President had no legal authority to order him to make war on Spain. Only Congress could do that. But, he announced, there would be no necessity of "implicating the government." If the President really wanted Florida seized, let him just say a word to that effect to some trustworthy person, say Congressman John Rhea, who would pass the tip to the commander and "it will be done in sixty days." Then, when Spain was confronted with a *fait accompli*, the diplomatists could unravel the tangle at their leisure.

When this extraordinary communication arrived Monroe happened to be bedridden. He said later that he did not read it through, but only the first few lines, and the cynical proposal was right at the end. But the Secretary of War happened to come in to visit him, and a few minutes later the Secretary of the Treasury; so, to Calhoun first, and afterward to Crawford, the President handed the letter; each returned it with the comment that it was a matter for the President's personal attention, but Monroe laid the letter aside unread and promptly forgot it.[3] This is Monroe's story; but Rhea maintained to the end of his life that the President definitely informed him that the administration approved of the suggestion of General Jackson. The charitable explanation is to assume a mutual misunderstanding;

[3] See Parton, Life of Andrew Jackson, vol. II, p. 435.

it is easy to believe that Rhea may have approached the President, asked if he approved of the General's course, and received an affirmative reply without Monroe's having the least idea of what he was talking about. Such mischances are frequent enough when men undertake political tricks that are a little too smart for straight dealing.

In any event, Rhea gave Jackson the signal to go ahead, and he, never doubting that it came straight from the President, went, with characteristic vigor and terrific effect. Within less than the promised sixty days he had smashed the Indians, seized Florida and set not Madrid, only, but London, too, to raving and raging. Not only did he destroy Seminoles in battle, but whenever he laid hands on one of their chiefs with a particularly bad reputation along the border he instantly hanged him. He captured a number of white renegades, too, and strung them up as ruthlessly. He seized the Spanish governor, which was an act of war, and not content with that flung him into his own *calabozo*, which was harder for the Spaniards to forgive than war. Finally, among the spies he rounded up were two British subjects, Arbuthnot and Ambrister, but this made no difference at all to the American, and the lieges of His Britannic Majesty were hanged as promptly and as high as any Seminole.

Naturally, the uproar in diplomatic circles was prodigious. The howls of the Spanish and British ministers in Washington resounded throughout the country. Monroe and his Cabinet, with one exception, were stunned and, in truth, scared half out of their wits by the hurricane that Rhea had unleashed. Two members of the Cabinet were, however, more directly affected than the others—Calhoun, in whose department the explosion had occurred, and Adams, whose department would have to deal with the results. Calhoun was acutely embarrassed although, if he really knew nothing about the Rhea letter, his embarrassment was excessive. After all, he was not the first War Secretary whose officers had exceeded instructions, and a first-rate man in such circumstances proceeds with great circumspection. In the first place, a good executive of any sort invariably stands behind his men as long as it is humanly possible to do so; and in the second place, a good Secretary of War doesn't worry a great deal about mere technical compliance with orders. His first question is, was the move a reasonable one from the military standpoint? That question Calhoun would have had to answer in Jackson's favor because, viewed strictly from the military standpoint, his campaign was eminently reasonable. The next question in such a case is: Granting that the offending officer did improve the local situation, did he, in doing so, jeopardize more important interests? This question Calhoun would have had to refer to the Secretary of State, for there was no other military strategy to be jeopardized; the only interests involved were diplomatic and not within the province of the Secretary of War. Had Calhoun been a first-rate man for the job he held, he would have supported Jackson at least until Adams demanded that he do otherwise. This is assuming that he knew nothing of the Rhea letter; if he did know of it, then he, like every other member of the administration, was committed to support of the man in the field.

Let him tell in his own words what he actually did. Twelve years later, in a letter to Jackson, he said, "Believing that where orders were transcended, investigation, as a matter of course, ought to follow, as due in justice to the government and the officer, unless there be strong reasons to the contrary, I came to the meeting [of the Cabinet to decide what to do] under the impression that the usual course ought to be pursued in this case, which I supported by presenting fully and freely all the arguments that occurred to me." Bear in mind, that in writing this letter Calhoun was endeavoring to excuse himself to a very wrathful man,[4] and naturally, therefore, was putting the best face possible on the matter. What he refers to smoothly as "investigation" really amounted to throwing Jackson to the wolves, if one may describe so disrespectfully their excellencies the Span-

[4] It was the explanation in writing which Jackson, then President, had demanded of Calhoun, then Vice-President, after the wily Major Lewis had let information of Calhoun's actual stand come to Jackson's notice. Up to that time, the General had been under the impression that Calhoun was his strong defender in this Cabinet meeting.

ish and British ministers. They were thunderously demanding
that Jackson be, first disavowed and then cashiered. Calhoun was
apparently ready to grant their demands, for that is certainly
"the usual course" when an army officer, without orders and on
his own responsibility, has made war on one friendly nation and
hanged the subjects of another.

Mark the logical invulnerability of his position. Here, for the
first time, we meet the essential Calhoun. He is the man of principle, the man whose principles were inviolate, though losses to
the country followed, though injustice to other men followed,
though wrong and evil of staggering proportions followed. Such
men may command a certain austere admiration, but no such
man ought ever to be elected President of the United States.

The Cabinet member who had just cause for indignation
against General Jackson was the man who had to clean up the
mess he had made, the Secretary of State. In the first place, nobody has ever intimated that Adams knew anything about the
Rhea letter. True, Crawford, years later, said that Monroe produced it at this Cabinet meeting; but Monroe and every other
Cabinet member denied it, and in any case, the fat by that time
was already in the fire. Adams had no idea of the storm that was
impending until Jackson burst into Florida and the whole structure of diplomatic amenities came crashing about the Secretary's
ears. Whether Jackson had been right or wrong made no difference in the fact that the Secretary of State had two infuriated
foreign governments to pacify, and it was evident that it was
going to take some fast thinking to do it. If ever a Cabinet
officer had just cause for feeling a sense of grievance, Adams
was the man.

The astonishing thing is that he did not, or at least gave no
public evidence of it, if he did. On the contrary, at this Cabinet
meeting, where every one else was nervous, exasperated, and
most of them frankly scared, the Secretary of State showed up
in a mood that, for Adams, was positively bland. The Puritan
was a patriot before he was a politician; Jackson had put him in
a dreadful hole, but with the same spasm of energy he had

yanked the country out of one. The General had cleaned up the border mess, definitely, completely and permanently. Adams, like every other well-informed man, was convinced that eventually we should have to take Florida. Well, Jackson had taken it at the cost of very few men, but plenty of trouble for the State Department; one can imagine the head of that department totting up the account and viewing the total with a smile of grim appreciation. If the country could expand at no greater price than the sacrifice of the political career of John Quincy Adams, why, to J. Q. Adams it looked like a bargain.

At the meeting, therefore, he astounded his tremulous colleagues by proposing that the United States disavow nothing, apologize for nothing, surrender not a foot of land, and compliment General Jackson on his exploit! Trouble would follow, of course, but leave it to him. What was a State Department for if not to deal with just such trouble? Perhaps the soldier had splintered international law; if so, it was regrettable, but for a government to disavow one of its generals, particularly a highly successful one, would be construed by every chancellery in the world as unprecedented weakness, and aggressions on that country would follow from every direction. Oh, no, Mr. Adams was stoutly and serenely in favor of standing behind Jackson to the last gasp.

To Monroe this counsel was inspiring. That veteran politician understood with great clarity what the country would say of an administration that abandoned a soldier who had just conquered an immense territory for it. Jackson had been a popular hero ever since the battle of New Orleans. Now his prestige was immensely enhanced and for a group of civilian politicians to decree that he should be publicly disgraced would be nothing short of suicidal, for the politicians. Instantly, therefore, he sided with Adams. There would be nothing in the way of public censure for the General, and the question then resolved into a debate upon methods of soothing the foreigners without sacrificing the officer. Adams stood out for no concessions whatever, but he was overborne and the evacuation of the Spanish territory was ordered; and the Secretary of State was instructed to make the best terms he could with London and Madrid on that basis.[5]

It would have been well for Henry Clay had he followed the course of his sometime colleague at Ghent. There is hardly a doubt that Clay could have made himself President of the United States by repeating in the House of Representatives what Adams had said in the Cabinet meeting. It is beyond belief that his failure to do so is attributable solely to conscientious scruples. The War Hawk of 1812 was, indeed, pretty well immunized against further attacks of war fever, but it strains credulity to the breaking point to assume that he had grown so tenderly sensitive about international relations that the Florida campaign shocked him too deeply for him to find an excuse to stand by a soldier who had served the country well. Clay's conscience never grew that tender.

The aspect in which the matter presented itself to him was that of a terrific blunder on the part of an administration for which he had never felt any great admiration. Mr. Monroe had laid himself wide open to the sort of attack that Clay knew well how to deliver. The temptation was too much. Clay attacked.

The fact that he could attack the administration only through the soldier did not halt him. Mr. Clay could see no injustice in that, for Jackson unquestionably had exceeded his orders; and as for there being any great danger in it, Clay believed that the only danger lay in the fact that the man was a popular hero and attacking him might alienate a few votes. This danger he was

[5] By way of rounding out the story it should be pointed out that he did make terms, but in his own way. The note that Adams sent to the aggrieved governments of Spain and England surely must have few parallels, considering the circumstances that inspired it, in all the history of diplomacy. No one could assume from reading it that it was an exculpation addressed to nations seeking redress for grave injuries; on the contrary, it denounced the Spaniards in scathing terms, not only for their temerity in presuming to hold their own territory, but almost for existing at all; while as for London the note just fell short of demanding an indemnity from the British king for the expense the Americans had been put to in seizing and hanging his subjects. The sheer audacity of it seems to have taken the breath of both foreign ministers, and to have confused them badly; at any rate, each moderated his tone immediately, and negotiations proceeded to a fairly satisfactory conclusion involving the purchase of Florida for $5,000,000 paid, not to Spain, but to American citizens holding claims against Spain.

prepared to risk. As for the man himself, it is doubtful that Clay knew much about him. Few people in Washington did, although he had been there for a short time as a Senator. Jackson came from the wild frontier, and frontiersmen were not often well known in Washington. Why should they be? They were seldom effective politicians, and even more rarely effective in the subtle politics that filled Washington.

So Clay undoubtedly felt that he gave the swashbuckling gunman of the backwoods more than his due when he began his speech with a reference to "the illustrious military chieftain" for whom he expressed "profound respect" for although his "acquaintance with him was very limited" yet it had been "of the most amicable kind." At any rate, Mr. Clay then dropped the amenities as regards Jackson and proceeded with a longer and more fulsome expression of his high regard of another "exalted personage," meaning, of course, the President. To this he gave some real attention, obviously regarding it as much more important than the other.

Having thus, after the immemorial custom of orators, expressed his high esteem for his victims, he proceeded to perform the operation described in the expressive language of Kentucky as "nailing their hides to the barn door." His castigation of Monroe was whole-hearted but, as it had little, if any, traceable effect on political history it need not detain us here. What he did to the wild General from the backwoods is the significant and memorable part of the address.

It may be that Clay, in his scorn of the ignorance of the frontiersmen, thought that the General might not catch the full implication of his historical allusions. "Remember that Greece had her Alexander," he thundered, "Rome had her Caesar, England her Cromwell, France her Bonaparte, and that if we would escape the rock on which they split we must avoid their errors." Andrew Jackson's formal education was, indeed, a thing of shreds and patches, but at that it was amply sufficient to give him a strong distaste for being compared with tyrants. If Clay's acquaintance with the man, instead of being "very limited" had been intimate, and if, on the basis of such acquaintance he had studied long to find the form of insult that would sting worst, he could hardly have done better than to accuse this man by implication of being an enemy of his country's liberty. Tom Benton and his brother once engaged in an earnest and very nearly successful effort to blow Jackson into eternity with gunfire; yet in after years the General found no difficulty in forgiving that and in receiving Benton as one of his staunchest friends. Clay's intimation that he was a would-be Caesar, however, was in a different category; and although they frequently met on terms of civility afterward, Jackson always hated him.

The spectacle of a man cutting his own throat, politically, is sufficiently curious to make Henry Clay's address on the Seminole War, delivered to the House in January, 1819, something of a landmark in American oratory. The whole speech is redolent of insincerity. The orator began by expressing opposition to any formal censure of the officer and then proceeded to denounce his conduct from the standpoint of legality, of discipline, of expediency and of common humanity. He spoke of "suffering to be trampled down law, justice, the Constitution and the rights of other people." He spoke of "examples of inhumanity, and cruelty, and ambition." He spoke of the war as "inglorious as regards the laurels and renown won in it"; a war against "a few half-starved, half-clothed, wretched Indians and fugitive slaves." He said that never had a Kentuckian in war "stained his hand by —nothing but my high sense of the distinguished services and exalted merits of General Jackson prevents my using another term—the execution of an unarmed and prostrate captive," which was close enough to saying "murder" for a duller man than Jackson to understand it.

Finally he reached a peroration in which he described this soldier, whom he was opposed to censuring formally, as an appalling menace to the very existence of the country. "Members of the house friendly to the General," he said, in closing, "may bear down all opposition; they may even vote the General the public thanks; they may carry him triumphantly through this House. But, if they do, in my humble judgment, it will be a triumph of the principle of insubordination—a triumph of the

DANIEL WEBSTER

" . . . his respect for plutocracy was profound."

JOHN QUINCY ADAMS

"... careful, painstaking, a model of industry,
odiously moral. . . . incessantly racked by anxiety
as to both body and soul."

military over the civil authority—a triumph over the powers of this House—a triumph over the constitution of the land. And I pray most devoutly to heaven that it may not prove, in its ultimate effects and consequences, a triumph over the liberties of the people."

Now, it stands to reason that if any army officer was half as bad as all this, to let him escape without censure was scandalous. A general guilty of gross insubordination; of invading the territory of a friendly nation; of perpetrating there acts of "inhumanity, cruelty and ambition"; of trampling upon the Constitution; of flouting the authority of Congress; and of hanging, without a shadow of legality, innocent, unarmed men—such a general certainly should have been cashiered and dismissed from the service. In strict justice, such a general should have been shot. When Clay refused to demand even as much as formal censure he showed that he did not believe his own speech.

There is, therefore, a sort of poetic justice in the fact that this speech dynamited his own political career. He asked for it, and he got it. Within less than ten years this outrageous officer was not only President of the United States, but incomparably the most powerful individual in the land. His mere word was enough to install as his successor in the Presidential chair a far smaller man than Henry Clay. But that prodigious influence was always thrown against Clay, always employed to batter him down, and one of the reasons was the undying hatred kindled in the breast of the soldier by this speech of 1819.

So within the same twelve months two members of the Triumvirate contrived to set in motion forces that eventually were to frustrate their ambition. Although the truth became clear only after many years, from this time on neither John C. Calhoun nor Henry Clay had a chance to attain the Presidency. Moreover, each had brought his nemesis upon himself; Calhoun —he whom Harriet Martineau was later to dub the "cast-iron man"—by the steely rigidity that caused him to desert one of his men rather than desert an abstract principle which, after all, didn't apply; Clay by a disingenuous attack made on a soldier because he disliked the commander-in-chief. Moralists may find edification in the tale; but as we observe the long and appalling sequelae that followed upon what seemed at the time rather small deviations from the path of strict rectitude, most of us are likely to reflect upon some incident at some time in our own careers and be inclined rather to wince than to rub our hands.

CHAPTER IX

ON THE MISSOURI COMPROMISE

An examination of the political ideas of the Triumvirate in a chaotic period with some suggestions as to how Mr. Clay, forty years in advance, won a war for the side he opposed

I N THE Speaker's chair, under a huge canopy of crimson silk supported by four posts, Henry Clay sat one December day in 1819, and looked over a gathering of one hundred and eighty-five men, many of them newcomers, who composed the House of Representatives of the Sixteenth Congress.

If the Speaker enjoyed a sense of mild elation on that day, it was justifiable, for the occasion seemed to be an auspicious one. The House was meeting for the first time in the restored Capitol, which the British had burned during the war; the hall in which it met, identified a bit acidulously by McMaster as "the chamber now given up to the most hideous collection of statues ever gathered together in any land,"[1] was looked upon as the finest in America, although the acoustics were terrible and most of the light and air were shut out by great crimson curtains hung, in the vain hope of eliminating echoes, against the windows and between the columns along the semicircular wall.

The restored Capitol was widely regarded as symbolical of a restored nation, not unreasonably. In spite of endemic distress due to wild cat banking and frenzied land speculation, the country was prosperous. The South was growing a little restive under the pinch of a tariff frankly designed to secure the prosperity of manufacturers, but she had not yet attained full realization that this grip was destined to throttle her—indeed, Abbott Lawrence was not to begin for some years yet to rub his hands

[1] McMaster, vol. iv, p. 580.

gleefully over the prospect that the tariff would "keep the South and West in debt to New England the next hundred years." The picture, as a whole, was one of peace and prosperity.

Even in politics, there seemed to be a lull. The re-election of James Monroe was by this time a foregone conclusion, and although it could not have been altogether pleasing to Mr. Clay, he was taking it philosophically. His time would come in 1824, and it was the part of a good politician at the moment to run with the wind. For the rest, things were going pretty much as he would have wished. True, at the last session there had been a little dust-up over the admission of Arkansas as a slave State and things had grown so tense that the bill to admit Missouri had been lost. A good deal of political capital had been made of the issue in the subsequent campaign, especially in the North. The cry that slavery had now crossed the Mississippi had been very effective, and a disquietingly large number of members had been retired by their constituencies. As Mr. Clay looked out from under the red canopy, he saw almost as many new faces as familiar ones.

However, that was all part of the game. One had to be prepared for occasional vagaries on the part of the public, and a sensible man would not permit himself to become unduly exercised over them. After all, the direction of events was still largely in hands that Mr. Clay was disposed to regard as safe— the hands of gentlemen who understood the game as it was played in Washington, gentlemen with whom it was usually possible to come to an understanding and who, in any event, fought with weapons that Clay knew how to handle and according to rules that he was prepared to accept. His own election as Speaker, for example, had passed almost as a matter of routine, and there was little to indicate that the session then opening would be momentous in any way. There was, indeed, the matter of these western States, but agreement had been almost reached at the last session when the arrival of March 4 compelled adjournment. Mr. Clay had little reason to doubt that a satisfactory adjustment would be brought about quickly and smoothly.

As to slavery Mr. Clay, like most of his contemporaries in

public life, held two distinct attitudes, one personal, the other political. As a civilized man and an intelligent Southerner, he regarded the institution as an evil one, almost, if not quite, as detrimental to the white as to the Negro race and ruinous to the land itself. As a politician, he felt even more strongly that the agitation that was beginning to arise was an unmitigated nuisance, diverting attention from matters that, to him, seemed vastly more important and injecting terrific emotional stress into discussions that should have been conducted in a coolly rational spirit. The tariff, for example, should be studied with an eye single to its economic effects; but bitterness arising from the slavery question was rapidly permeating even the debates on the tariff. To Henry Clay this was not only foolish, but irritating. A man racked by emotion is unpredictable. How could the most skillful player at the great chess-board of politics figure in advance a long and complicated series of moves when his opponents, blinded by anger, might at any moment do wholly irrational, and therefore unexpected, things? Mr. Clay was opposed to anything that seemed likely to break up the game; and the rising agitation about slavery threatened to do exactly that.

Fortunately for his peace of mind, Mr. Clay had no idea how right he was. Down in Virginia a wiser man heard the first debates on slavery "like a fire-bell in the night" and quaked. But although Jefferson foresaw part of what was to come, he was already an old man, his political career was over, his resourcefulness had been exhausted in establishing and defending institutions adapted to the rural, agricultural society that was now crumbling before his eyes. Authority and responsibility had passed on to younger men, and his voice was no more effective than Cassandra's.

In 1820 Mr. Clay heard the beginning of the fateful debate with relatively little apprehension, but with much annoyance. Mr. Calhoun, too, from the tranquility of his post in the Cabinet, saw the thing as an intrusion, a deplorable irrelevance, certain to confuse and likely to disrupt the logical development of the country in the new century. Mr. Calhoun at this time was still very much the nationalist. Like Mr. Clay, he was acutely conscious of his status as presidential timber, and a future President of the United States should sedulously avoid fomenting sectionalism.

To attain any comprehension of these men it is essential to bear in mind that they were both, intellectually, in the forefront of their times. They were intensely modern, progressive to a degree that in the opinion of the ancients amounted to wild radicalism. It would be fatuous to suppose that they understood the implications of the changes they saw and felt taking place. No man understood all, or many, of those implications. But men of alert and supple intelligence were aware that gigantic forces were being unleashed, forces that would test all things, and statesmanship in particular.

It was about this time that the factor of scale began to figure in a new way in men's calculations of America. We have been a vast country for so long that it is difficult to imagine the time when we were a small one. Even in colonial times men were acutely aware of the existence of the huge continent behind the narrow strip of settlements along the Atlantic coast, but in those days the wilderness was a threat, rather than a promise. The early Americans schemed not to conquer the wilderness, but to prevent the wilderness from conquering them; theirs was the task to guard the flickering light of civilization against the immense darkness beyond. They regarded the prodigious size of their domain with defiance, rather than with pride.

There were always, of course, a few seers who dared dream of the subjugation of this enormous realm, some time in the far distant future. Jefferson, for example, assumed that it might be a matter of four or five hundred years—a rather short period in view of the fact that it had taken two hundred years to drive the frontier back some two hundred and fifty miles from the coast. But Jefferson was always a visionary and to the average American of his time the back country was far more terrifying than inviting. Long after the Revolution the existence of hostile, or certainly untrustworthy, Indian tribes made it, from the military standpoint, a source of weakness, rather than of strength.

But in 1820 steam power was beginning to be no longer an

experiment of interest mainly to scientists, but a factor of great
and increasing importance in the lives of ordinary men and
women. As long as he was dowered only with the strength of
his own sinews and those of his horses and oxen, the American
clung precariously to the edge of his continent and regarded its
gigantic reaches doubtfully and apprehensively; but when he
acquired this machine with the strength of a thousand giants his
attitude toward the wilderness changed rapidly into exultant
masterfulness. All young men felt this change and rejoiced in it;
Calhoun, at thirty-eight, and Clay, at forty-three, were among
the younger statesmen, and they, too, rejoiced.

Calhoun had been called on, as Secretary of War, to submit
for the information of Congress a list of internal improvements,
especially roads and canals, that would contribute to the national
defense in time of war; and in January he had responded by sub-
mitting a colossal program, one covering all needs of transportation and communication, civil or military. "It is," he pointed
out, "one of the great advantages of our country, enjoying so
many others, that whether we regard its internal improvements
in relation to military, civil, or political purposes, very nearly
the same system, in all its parts, is required." Again and again
he spoke for internal improvements as justifiable in that they
contributed to national unity. It did not occur to him at this
time that anyone would question the value of national unity.

It is easy to believe, therefore, that Calhoun, like Clay, heard
the beginning of the debates on slavery with more exasperation
than profound terror. There was so much to do that expending
time and energy on this question doubtless seemed to him a
shocking waste.

It had begun in 1818 when James Tallmadge, Jr. introduced
an amendment to the bill admitting Missouri to the Union. It
provided that no more slaves be introduced into Missouri and
that children born to slaves already residing in the new State be
given their freedom at the age of twenty-five years. Somewhat
to the surprise of the leaders, the amendment was carried in the
House. The Senate, however, promptly struck it out. The

House, by this time thoroughly aroused, refused to concur, and the outcome was that Missouri was not admitted at all.

The same amendment—proposed in this case by John W. Taylor, of New York—was rejected by the House in the case of Arkansas, which was admitted as a slave State despite the fact that it lay beyond the Mississippi River.

The battle, therefore, was not over the extension of slavery beyond the Mississippi—that was already accomplished—but over its extension into an area in the same latitude with the free soil of Illinois. This was denounced by the anti-slavery group as a projection of slavery into the North. Geographically, the argument was of doubtful validity, as slavery already existed in Maryland and Delaware and the Mason and Dixon line, northern boundary of Maryland, if projected would cut through the extreme northern part of Missouri. But slavery had been excluded from Ohio, Indiana and Illinois, despite the fact that all those States extend well below the latitude of the Mason and Dixon line. Therefore, in spite of geography, the anti-slavery people did have something more than a mere "talking point" in their contention that to permit slavery in Missouri would be a restriction of free soil.

In December, 1819, Speaker Clay had hardly called the House together before Missouri was back again, and it soon became apparent that Congress was going to be deadlocked once more. Taylor was promptly on hand with his amendment, and into the bill it went. In the meantime, a bill admitting Maine had been passed by the House and sent to the Senate, where it was still pending. When the Missouri bill, with the Taylor amendment forbidding the introduction of more slaves and the gradual abolition of slavery, came from the House, the Senate promptly struck out the amendment and then attached the rest of the Missouri bill to that admitting Maine, and passed the Maine bill, thus amended.

It was an impasse; the House refused to concur, and began to debate another Missouri bill of its own. Time wore on. Nothing was accomplished except a steady increase in the bitterness that was riving the country. William Pinkney, of Maryland, made a sensationally popular speech on the slavery side, and Rufus King, of New York, made an equally memorable one on the anti-slavery side, but accretions to the reputations of Messrs. Pinkney and King seemed to Clay but a small return for the almost complete paralysis of Congress as a legislative body. December passed, with nothing accomplished. The new year, 1820, arrived with nothing done. January passed, and the deadlock seemed to be as rigid as ever.

There was no doubt about where the Speaker stood as an individual member. He had made that perfectly clear on the last day of 1819, when he descended from the Speaker's chair and made a speech against the bill to admit Maine. He was quite frank about the grounds of his opposition. "A State in the quarter of the country from which I come asks to be admitted into the Union," he pointed out. "What say the gentlemen who ask the admission of Maine? Why, they will not admit Missouri without a condition that strips her of one essential attribute of sovereignty. What, then, do I say to them? That justice is due to all parts of the Union. Equality is equality, and if it is right to make the restriction of slavery the condition of the admission of Missouri, it is equally just to make the admission of Missouri the condition of that of Maine."

So much for the member from Kentucky. But Henry Clay was also Speaker of the House and, although party organization was in an amorphous state at the moment, as much of a party leader as any man. And why stop with that? The man was more. He was an American. Somewhat dimly, somewhat uncertainly, but nevertheless definitely he apprehended the critical nature of the changes that were transforming the country and appreciated the need of cool, clear-headed statesmanship to deal with them. As for slavery, it was, in his opinion, an evil; but it was an old one, and, as he thought, a decaying one. He did not believe that its extension into Missouri would prolong its life indefinitely, as many of the agitators against it in the North believed; nor is it likely that he thought its exclusion from Missouri would go far toward eliminating it from the country. In brief, he didn't care much, one way or the other, what happened to the slave issue in

Missouri; but he did regard as tremendously important the maintenance of the unity of the country.

Therefore, when Senator Thomas, of Illinois, came forward early in February with a suggestion for breaking the deadlock, Clay was immediately interested. What Thomas proposed has gone down in history under the name of the Missouri Compromise. Viewed from the standpoint of a slaveholder, on the one hand, or from that of an abolitionist, on the other, the thing was completely idiotic.[2] It established no principle, it settled no controversy, it was not based on any logical geographical, social, or other scientific consideration. It decreed that the southern boundary of Missouri should thereafter be the northern boundary of slavery, but at the same time it admitted Missouri as a slave State. It asserted the power of Congress to deal with slavery and at the same time renounced formally any intention of dealing with it.

Perhaps Clay found a sardonic pleasure in the very irrationality of the Thomas compromise. To his mind the whole controversy was irrational, so to seek an irrational solution may have appealed to him as having a sort of crazy logic. Such sour humor was not altogether foreign to his nature.

It is unnecessary to range so far into the field of speculation, however, to discover a reason why, when the Thomas suggestion came up, Clay flung all his great influence into the fight to get it adopted. He was blamed at the time, and has been blamed ever since, for his supposed fatuity in assuming that an arrangement as preposterous as the Missouri Compromise could settle the slavery question permanently; but there is not the slightest evidence that he thought it would do so. He wasn't trying to settle the slavery question. He depended upon time and economic pressure to do that; and he had excellent reasons for be-

[2] Its wording was this: "*And be it further enacted*, That in all that territory ceded by France to the United States, under the name of Louisiana, which lies north of thirty-six degrees thirty minutes north latitude, excepting only such part there-of as is included within the limits of the State contemplated by this act, slavery and involuntary servitude, otherwise than in the punishment of crimes whereof the party shall have been duly convicted, shall be and is hereby forever prohibited."

lieving that they would do it. He did think that the Missouri Compromise would prevent the slavery question from splitting the country in 1820, and he was right.

Clio is an exasperating jade. She has a trick of inscribing in imperishable characters all sorts of trivia about her favorites and then, when she comes to a really critical point, calmly leaving the record blank as regards the essentials. This is a case in point. How Henry Clay managed to drive the Missouri Compromise through Congress we do not know. All contemporary records agree that he played a very important part in doing it, and most of them assign him the leading part, but his exact procedure is left to the imagination. There is doubtless a reason. Mr. Clay was a great man, but he certainly was no plaster saint; on the contrary, he was an extremely practical politician, and the methods of a practical politician in a fight so sternly contested and so bitter that a single vote may turn the scales are usually methods that would cause some lifting of the eyebrows even among the less austere. It may be just as well that the younger generation doesn't know too much about how Henry Clay won his fight; we may safely dismiss outright bribery, first because Clay did have limits beyond which he would not go, and, second because there was no great financial interest involved and therefore no one to put up the money. But the political dealing and dickering that went on in the first half of February, 1820, might make a story that would startle even modern Washington. When it came to the final vote something decidedly curious happened to eighteen members. Three were absent, and fifteen, on whom the anti-slavery element had counted, voted for the compromise. One of the absentees later offered an explanation of his part in it that is interesting both for its ingenuity and as an illuminating commentary on the tension that pervaded the House. The session had lasted all day and this member had not left his desk even for meals. Eventually a representative named Mercer, otherwise little known to fame, rose to address the House and the member in question, ingenuously confessing that he knew his colleague would say nothing worth hearing, decided that now was the time to get a bite, for he was certain that Mercer would maunder for an hour or two. When he returned to his seat he received the dismaying news that the vote had been taken. Mercer, it seems, was not as nerveless as dull fellows are usually supposed to be; after talking for a few minutes he had suddenly fainted, and the Speaker seized this unscheduled closure of debate as the moment to put the question.

This, in itself, is evidence that Clay was railroading the measure through with no overscrupulous observation of the niceties of debate, but an incident even more convincing occurred the next day. John Randolph of Roanoke, the chronic troublemaker, who had come perilously close to wrecking the schedule on several previous occasions, rose to move a reconsideration of the previous day's action. Clay was appalled, for the vote had stood ninety to eighty-seven the previous day. With Randolph apparently changing his vote and the non-admirer of Representative Mercer with, perhaps, the other absentees, back in the House, the situation was critical, for Clay, unfortunately, had the bill still in his desk. Had he already signed it and sent it to the Senate, no reconsideration would have been possible. He therefore ruled Randolph's motion out of order until after the receipt of petitions, normally the first item of business after the reading of the journal. Randolph appealed to the House, but the House sustained the Speaker and the clerk proceeded to call the roll of the States for the presentation of petitions. When Virginia was called, Randolph rose and renewed his motion. Clay ruled him out of order again. At length, when the petitions had all been received, the Virginian returned to the attack, only to be blandly informed that the Speaker had already signed the bill and returned it to the Senate, therefore no reconsideration was possible.

Clay had signed the bill while the clerk was calling the roll, and had instantly dispatched a messenger with it to the Senate. It was a scandalous trick, but the situation was desperate, and Clay was not the man to lose a hard-won victory for lack of a little practical politics at the right moment.[3] It is, then, no wild

[3] Adams inserted the incident in his *Memoirs*, vol. v, p. 4, and McMaster checked it up in the *Annals of Congress*. See McMaster, vol. iv, p. 592.

flight of imagination to fancy that he had employed more than a little practical politics in rounding up those ninety votes in the first place. He would never have played that trick on Randolph had he been satisfied that his votes would stick. He alone knew how he got them. He knew they wouldn't stick. The inference is plain to anyone with even a superficial knowledge of political methods.

The famous Missouri Compromise thus was passed with only three votes majority to begin with and by the assistance of a bit of political chicanery to end with. Yet, at the moment, Henry Clay was quite satisfied as, from his point of view, he had a right to be. He was not trying to settle the slavery question, but only to release the energies of Congress so that they might be devoted to other purposes. He thought that slavery was a question that could never be settled by Congress, but that in the course of time would be settled elsewhere; as, indeed, it was, although not by the means Clay hoped for and expected, to wit, the economic collapse of the institution itself.

He undoubtedly believed that the entire incident might soon be forgotten, for it was his hope that Congress would proceed with a program of legislation far more memorable than the flurry over the admission of Missouri, or even setting a definite northern boundary to the "peculiar institution." Already a gigantic, if nebulous, dream was taking shape in Clay's mind. The spirit of the new America, the titanic America whose mere size was now beginning to be the inspiration, rather than the terror, of her citizens, was taking hold of him; but he, ever the leader, even in his dreams strode ahead of most men. Not the Mississippi, not the Indian country, not even the Pacific, limited his imagination; the hegemony, if not the empery, of half the globe was the lodestar that drew him as, the Missouri Compromise safely enacted, he turned with relief to matters that he regarded as far more important.

But later generations have stubbornly refused to subordinate the achievement to the dream. Today few except students of history think of Henry Clay when they hear the words "American System," while practically every American who has survived the rigors of the seventh grade in school thinks of Clay when the Missouri Compromise is mentioned. For more than a hundred years he has been alternately, sometimes simultaneously, praised and blamed for his part in that fight, while other achievements of the Sixteenth Congress are known only to specialists.

This book is certainly no addition to the long list of volumes that have been written on the effect of the Missouri Compromise on American history; but a study of the statecraft of Henry Clay would be inept indeed if it paid no attention to this achievement as an example of that statecraft in operation. At the time it was almost completely misunderstood by friend and foe alike; yet among both friends and foes there were men who came nearer understanding it than did Henry Clay himself. At the distance of more than a century it is easy to see how both the exultation and lamentation that filled the air were grotesquely misapplied. Almost without exception, those who lamented should have rejoiced, and those who rejoiced should have wailed. Clay did neither. He merely preened himself a little on having successfully overcome a rather nasty obstacle, and looked about for a really important job. Yet he, above all others, had occasion both to exult and to lament, for he had set on the enduring record of history a vivid demonstration both of his power and of his frailty.

To dispose first of the matter of least importance, it is evident now that the politics, as distinguished from the statesmanship, of the Missouri Compromise was superb. This does not refer to the document itself. Historians have frequently pointed out, with a touch of disdain, that the Missouri Compromise was not devised by Henry Clay at all; the statement is true enough, but the excuse for the disdain is not immediately apparent. Clay can well afford to yield to Senator Thomas whatever credit may accrue from the writing of that curious amendment; the loss will not be great.

The excellence of the politics is proved by the feat of getting any compromise of any nature adopted. When feeling was running so high that a man like Mercer would actually faint in the House, the politician who could round up and deliver ninety votes out of a hundred and seventy-seven obviously knew his business; and this is true regardless of the issue. More than that, the immediate effects upon the political fortunes of the Speaker were excellent. It created hatred for him in certain quarters, both North and South, but only in places where dislike of Clay already existed. A middle-of-the-road man can never hope to hold the support of extremists in any case; but in this case the extremists on both sides were given overwhelming proof that Clay was highly effective and therefore formidable. If a politician can in no wise hope to secure a man's support, then it is frequently good politics to secure that man's fervent hatred, especially when the man is an extremist the frenzy of whose attack frequently creates sympathy for his victim.

But in a far wider area the compromise created respect for and confidence in the Kentuckian. Moderate men everywhere were shocked by the virulence of the passions released by the long deadlock, and Clay's success in smoothing things over aroused widespread relief, which was reflected in a feeling that here was something more than merely a clever politician, here was a statesman. The White House looked appreciably closer to Clay when that bill went through.

But statecraft covers a much wider field than mere politics, and in the wider field there is a good deal that is not to be approved without question.

For awhile it was the fashion in the North to pretend to believe that the Missouri Compromise merely perpetuated slavery and made war not only inevitable, but more frightful in its effects when it did come. Schurz demolished that notion half a century ago.[4] He pointed out that if the issue had been pressed to a conclusion at that time there could have been but one outcome, to wit, the triumph of slavery. There were three reasons for this: in the first place, there was as yet no unanimity of sentiment in the North against slavery, and even among those who sincerely opposed it, very few considered it worth a war; in the second place, secession was accepted as theoretically possible, even by as stout a patriot as John Quincy Adams and any effort by the

[4] Schurz, vol. i, p. 195 ff.

Federal government to coerce a State would have been resented, and probably resisted, in the North; in the third place, the South's relative strength, in man power, in money power and in war material was much greater in 1820 than it ever was again. In other words, in 1820 the North did not want to fight over slavery, would have been as likely to fight for the right of secession as against it and if it had fought the South at all probably would have been defeated. Even after losing ground steadily for forty years from this date the South put up a tremendous battle. There can hardly be a doubt that in 1820 the South would have won even against a united North, while against a doubtful and divided North there can be no reasonable doubt.

The Missouri Compromise, in short, was the first of three great victories that Henry Clay won for the North and Negro freedom. He was not aware of it. He was not consciously fighting for either North or Negro. But that was the effect.

It has been assumed by the critics of Clay that this argued a deplorable moral obtuseness on his part. But this assumption is based on the typical arrogance of the righteous, rather than on the facts. That the enslavement of the Negroes was an evil is incontestable; but that it was the greatest evil that afflicted the country is open to serious doubt.

In the minds of Clay, Webster and Calhoun alike the great threat that overshadowed all others was the threat of disunion, and as they were all able men the possibility that they may have been right deserves more than passing attention. It was only too clear to them that events outside the field of politics were subjecting the fabric of the union to great and increasing strains. They were none too clear as to what should be done about it, but they were very clear indeed as to the necessity of doing something. The tremendous expansion of population, of wealth, and of area that filled the country with pride also filled its wiser leaders with anxiety. The Constitution had not been designed to fit any such country, and to make it fit without tearing it apart would have been difficult work had there been no question of slavery to complicate it further.

We know what actually happened. In the end, the skill of

ANDREW JACKSON

". . . collected the most magnificent array
of enemies in American history."

MARTIN VAN BUREN

"... a dapper little red-head from up-state New York, always
polite, always smiling, always imperturbable and always deadly,
commonly called the Red Fox of Kinderhook."

statesmen was not sufficient; the country split and the Constitution was torn apart violently. The orgy of bloodshed released
all the evils that customarily follow wars. Brute force, having
replaced reason in the settlement of one problem, spread far
afield. Men who have walked arm in arm with Death for months
and years, usually end by setting too much value upon mere living and too little value on the quality of life.

The years that followed the Civil War are admittedly among
the blackest in our national history, not in the defeated South,
only, but also in the victorious North. One historian, Bowers,
has ignored the years when men were dying in battle by the hundred thousand to give this time the name of the Tragic Era. Unquestionably, it is the period when politics, business and society
were debauched to an extent almost, if not quite, without parallel
in our history. It was then that greed entrenched itself so strongly
in our political system that it came close to throttling democracy
altogether. It was then that the criminal spoliation of the continent was established, not as robbery, but as progress. It was
then that the concentration of wealth and the distribution of
want were cleared of disgrace and held up to admiration as the
fulfillment of civilization, instead of its failure.

Such reversals of values are always part of the price of war.
Clay and Calhoun had observed it at close range—although on
a small scale—after the War of 1812, and Webster was close
enough to the center of events to gain a pretty clear realization
of the truth.

But apart from the prevention of war, it was the center of the
policy of each of these men to achieve a regular, orderly development of the great domain that belonged to the country. This was
long before the term "planned economy" had ever been heard
in America, but the idea is present in every speech of the period.
Calhoun arguing for use of both the legislative and taxing power
of the Federal government for "the ultimate attainment of national strength and the perfection of our political institutions"
is certainly pleading for a planned economy. It was Calhoun,
incredible as it seems in view of later events, who retorted to
the argument that it was unconstitutional to use tax money to

promote the general welfare, "I am no advocate for refined arguments on the Constitution. The instrument was not intended as a thesis for the logician to exercise his ingenuity on. It ought to be construed with plain good sense." As late as 1825, speaking with reference to the gigantic program of public works at Federal expense which he had proposed when Secretary of War, he said, "I gave my zealous efforts to all such measures."

Thus Calhoun, later the very incarnation of the opposition to all Federal interference with the affairs of the individual States. Is it necessary to quote Clay and Webster? Any public utterance of theirs, practically any speech, chosen at random, will sustain the point.

The statecraft of these men was far from negative, in that it was applied solely to the prevention of war, or static, in that it was applied solely to preservation of the Union as it existed then. It was positive, it was energetic, it was flexible. It envisaged not merely the possibility but the existence of change, and the accompanying necessity of revision or reconstruction of our political institutions. They were not blind to the existence of dangers which the experience of a century has revealed. It did not escape them that the increasing size, wealth and complexity of the country carried the potentiality of a new slave system, larger in extent and more ruthless in character than the one existing in the South. Perhaps they did not foresee breadlines and famine-smitten children in the richest country on the globe, but they certainly foresaw the possibility that the agricultural interest might be reduced to virtual serfdom by a bad economic policy, and that commerce and industry might come under thralldom to finance by a bad fiscal policy. They foresaw the possibility that the continent might be sacked and pillaged— although they probably never guessed that it could be done within a hundred years—in the absence of wise legislation regulating its development. They foresaw the possibility that political liberty might become a shadow and a mockery if economic opportunity were shut off.

If combating these evils seemed to them of more importance than securing the immediate liberation of two and a half million

Negro slaves, is that proof that they were morally obtuse? The charge seems somewhat radical. Certainly it was never made by the man who actually freed the slaves. Abraham Lincoln admitted freely that if he could preserve the Union—and he meant if he could preserve it as the home of liberty under law, not as the happy hunting ground of the looters who came in with Grant —by keeping every Negro in the country in slavery, he would do it. In bending every energy to achieve that end Clay, Calhoun and Webster were obviously no more obtuse, morally, than Lincoln.

Yet if the achievement of Clay in the Missouri Compromise was historically effective and morally justifiable, nevertheless the circumstances of its achievement reveal his weakness, as well as his strength.

Clay paid too much attention to the ninety votes he won on that memorable day and not enough to the eighty-seven that he lost. He observed, but he did not estimate accurately the significance of this revolt against his leadership; and it was an error that he was to repeat at several critical points in his career.

The truth was that the boys had heard from the country, and Clay never got it through his head that the country ever spoke with decision. Every politician knows that when party leaders, financial leaders and business leaders are agreed on a program, nine times out of ten that program can be put through; but Clay made the mistake of believing that it can be done ten times out of ten. He was aware of the existence of popular movements, of course, but he clung to the theory that they are always—not usually, which would have been within the fact, but always— manufactured by agitators of one sort or another, so that if a man were able to get on his side all the agitators, or most of them including the most skillful, he would inevitably have the people.

This is close enough to the truth to constitute a pretty safe working rule, but it isn't absolutely true. At intervals, usually widely separated, the American public really makes up its mind; and when that happens, all the agitation in the world is simply waste of breath.

[151]

In 1800 Clay himself had seen it happen, but the lesson was lost on him. Thomas Jefferson was a good politician, perhaps the best this country has ever produced; but Clay was wrong if he assumed, as he seems to have assumed, that Jefferson's political wizardry was solely accountable for the success of his party, not only in 1800, but in 1804, 1808, 1812, 1816, and 1820 as well. Political manipulation may put a party in power once, but it cannot keep it there for twenty years. In 1800 the people had really made up their minds that they wanted no more to do with Federalism, and thereafter the Jeffersonians simply couldn't lose. In fact, once he was in power Jefferson was compelled by circumstances to repudiate every promise he had made and to do the exact opposite, but it didn't matter in the least. The more platform promises he broke, the more his majorities increased. The "best people" were against him, almost to a man; practically every newspaper of any reputation was against him; bankers and business leaders fell into apoplexy at the very mention of his name; while as for the attitude of the clergy, or at least of the sleek and well-fed among them, it is not much distorted by the famous lamentation of President Timothy Dwight, of Yale, in 1801: "We have a country governed by blockheads and knaves; the ties of marriage with all its felicities are severed and destroyed; our wives and daughters are thrown into the stews; our children are cast into the world from the breast and forgotten; filial piety is extinguished, and our surnames, the only mark of distinction among families, are abolished. Can the imagination paint anything more dreadful of this side of hell?" Yet nineteen years later Connecticut seemed to be getting along happily and contentedly in hell, for it had gone Jeffersonian, like the rest of the country.

Now, in 1820, the northern part of the country was leisurely, but definitely, making up its mind again. It had not yet gone to the length of determining to do away with slavery; but it had arrived at a pretty definite decision that the thing was wrong and ought not to be encouraged in any way. The eighty-seven members who voted against the Missouri Compromise knew it, but Clay did not. He still cherished the delusion that this was an issue that could be thrust aside, if it had to be handled at all, right in Washington. He still believed that if gentlemen could only get together, discuss the situation reasonably, and decide on what was the right and proper course, the country would acquiesce.

The immediate event seemed to justify his belief, for the country did acquiesce in the compromise, but that was only because it did seem to put a limit to the spread of slavery. The average man in the North was not so much interested in having Missouri come in a free State as he was in having some limit laid down somewhere. The line of thirty-six thirty might be objectionable in some ways, but it would do, and it was decidedly better than splitting the country. But Mr. Clay made the mistake of his life when he assumed that the decision was reached on the floor of the House of Representatives when ninety Congressmen voted for the bill and only eighty-seven voted against it. That was the preliminary formality. The decision was made by ten thousand firesides, North and South, when ordinary men who never held a political office and never wanted one, read the news, or heard it from some passing traveler, thought it over awhile and finally determined that on the whole it was not worth while to raise a fuss over it.

The political philosophy of Henry Clay was defective in that it failed to make allowance for the fact that while democracy functions rarely, sometimes it does, and when it does the ablest and strongest politicians in the world are whirled along by its current as straws are swept on a spring freshet.

CHAPTER X

INTERLUDE IN PARTIBUS INFIDELIUM

Inquiring into the nature of Mr. Clay's romantic notions concerning Greece, South America, Hungary, et alii

WHEN we read that Mr. Calhoun suffered his very soul to be ground to powder between the upper millstone of his logical principles and the lower one of unalterable circumstances, those of us who are not heroes, philosophical or of any other kind, are left fumbling. It is hard for us to make any psychological contact with such a man, hard to realize that such men exist, all but impossible to realize what they may be like. Mr. Calhoun differs from ordinary people, not in degree, only, but in kind.

When we read that Mr. Webster, on his deathbed and knowing that the end was only a few hours away, said, "Wife, children, doctor, I trust that on this occasion I have said nothing unworthy of Daniel Webster," we are left speechless. Vanity is familiar enough; but such vanity, and such vanity carried right to death's door, is quite out of the realm of experience of most of us. It seems hardly human. It drives home the conviction that, not in mental power, only, but in other things as well Mr. Webster was far away from us, and we distrust our estimates of what he was like.

But when we read that Mr. Clay repeatedly made a fool of himself in trying to deal with foreigners, we note the information with a sort of glad recognition, for haven't we all done so? It is not only a human trait, it is an intensely American trait. The main difference is that while we small men have done it only in a small way, Clay, being a big man, did it in a big way. But we can guess at what drove him to it, and we can imagine how he felt.

The enduring charm of the man is largely due, without a doubt, to his resemblance, except in degree, to very ordinary people. It is what Bradford had in mind when he spoke of the "humanness" of Henry Clay. Even in his extravagances, Clay ran true to type; they were precisely the sort of extravagances that you or I might imagine ourselves committing, were we presented with the opportunity and the ability to commit them. Therefore, in whatever he said and did, Clay, while frequently astonishing, is rarely, if ever, incomprehensible. Perhaps the greatest mystery about him is the fact that he, so easily understood by the common man, proved himself so frequently utterly unable to understand the common man.

His first excursion into foreign affairs took place in 1818. His political enemies, of course, had a highly discreditable explanation. They said he had no other motive than the hope of embarrassing the President who had refused to make him Secretary of State. The event that brought Clay into the field was the condition of Spain's South American colonies, particularly the group known as the United Provinces of La Plata, which had actually won their independence in 1813 and under the guidance of Puyredon showed signs of ability to establish and maintain a reasonably stable and orderly government. But they had been thrown into a turmoil again by the scheme to use the territory to form a kingdom for the egregious Felice Pasquale Bacciochi, the sum total of whose achievements in life was his success in marrying Elisa Bonaparte, sister of Napoleon. Napoleon had made them Prince and Princess of Lucca and at one time he toyed with the idea of making them King and Queen of La Plata. All that came of the scheme was to discredit Puyredon, who was suspected of favoring it; and as there was no other leader in whom anyone had much confidence, a long period of bloodshed followed. At the same time, Bolivar and Morillo were fighting a hideous war of extermination in the northern part of the continent, a war in which each side massacred non-combatants in an earnest and thoroughgoing fashion. That South America was in an appalling condition nobody could deny; but what, if anything, the United States ought to do about it was by no means as obvious.

Monroe was very much in the position of another President, a hundred years later—Wilson, who said his only way of getting at an approximation of the truth about Mexico was "by balancing lies." A dozen factions had each its propaganda agent in Washington; and in the clamor they raised it would have taken more than human wisdom to detect and identify the truth. The President therefore evolved the idea of sending what later generations learned to call a "fact-finding commission" to Buenos Aires to examine conditions there and make an independent report by which he might be guided. But when he applied to Congress for an appropriation to cover the expenses of such a commission, Henry Clay fell upon the proposal furiously. At this distance the project of Monroe seems reasonable enough; but Clay would hear to nothing except full recognition of the La Plata government and the appointment of a fully accredited diplomatic representative at Buenos Aires.

Naturally, skeptics questioned his sincerity. This was in 1818, when Clay was still supposed to be smarting under the disappointment of losing the Secretaryship of State. These skeptics refused to be convinced that Henry Clay was so violent a protagonist of human liberty that even a short delay in paying due deference to its ostensible defenders would compel him against his will to assail the administration in Washington; nor did they believe that Clay was totally unacquainted with facts which altered materially the view he chose to present of the South American revolutionists. Monroe, in particular, was aggrieved. In the first place, he entertained the friendliest sentiments toward the South Americans, and was willing enough to recognize any government that seemed to have a fair chance of surviving and maintaining diplomatic relations. But the reports that came to him were conflicting at almost every point, and as regards atrocities, not only was each side accusing the other of perpetrating every imaginable barbarity, but was presenting embarrassingly convincing proof. The President's desire to proceed with cau-

tion)therefore is understandable and Clay could have understood
it had he set his mind to it. Without doubt, the acerbity of his
attack was due, in part, to the fact that Monroe was his target.

But, as Schurz points out, if it is impossible to acquit him of
all malice on this occasion, it is equally impossible to pretend
that all his enthusiasm for South America was cooked up simply
to make head against the administration. To rebut this charge
it is necessary only to cite Clay's record back in the administration of James Madison, when he had warmly supported the revolt against Spain. Indeed, in 1816 he was seriously discussing
the possibility of armed intervention on the southern continent.
Clay was fascinated by South America before James Monroe
entered the White House.

After the lapse of a century, however, his motives in this
affair are less significant than his methods, or, rather his attitude. Certain passages in his great speech of March 24, 1818,
reveal much about the speaker, if not about the situation. For
instance: "There can not be a doubt that Spanish America, once
independent, whatever may be the form of the governments
established in its several parts, these governments will be animated by an American feeling, and guided by an American policy. They will obey the laws of the New World, of which they
will compose a part, in contradistinction to that of Europe."
Then, a little later, "I contend that self government is the natural government of man." Shortly after that, "We are the natural
head of the American family."

It would be hard to frame a more perfect expression of the
typical North American viewpoint toward our Latin American
neighbors. That viewpoint has always been strangely com-
pounded of generous enthusiasm and magnificent condescen-
sion, with all trace of a factual basis carefully eliminated. Sometimes it has profited the South Americans, frequently it has
puzzled them, but more frequently still it has maddened them.
Yet centuries of explanation and expostulation on their part
have not availed to change it.

At the moment when Clay spoke, the South American conception of political liberty and political rights was even further

removed from ours than it is today. The contest that was raging was, in fact, a contest to determine whether the masses of South Americans should be ruled by Spaniards or by the stronger and abler of their own countrymen. Clay devoted a blistering passage to the attempts made by the royal army, under Morillo, to terrorize the common people into loyalty to Spain; but he conveniently forgot the equally hideous methods applied by the revolutionists, under Bolivar, to terrorize them into disloyalty.

The history of the very government to which he wished a minister accredited, the United Provinces of the Rio de la Plata, afforded ample evidence that it was in no wise "animated by an American feeling and guided by an American policy." Generations before either Adolph Hitler or Benito Mussolini first saw the light of day, Latin America had adopted as its ruling political doctrine the "principle of leadership." Such peace and order as the United Provinces had enjoyed—their boundaries wavered with the success of battling armies, but they included much of what is now the Argentine Republic, part of Bolivia, and sometimes part of Chile—it owed to the dominance of one man, Puyredon. When the affair of the Prince of Lucca shattered confidence in him, the system collapsed, and as Clay was speaking the unfortunate country was seeing something very much like the contest among the generals of Alexander the Great. Was this American feeling and American policy?

It is easy, however, to be too scornful of this American trait. Grant that it runs frequently into deplorable sentimentality; nevertheless the fact remains that it stems from an authentic generosity. The American does possess—or did possess at this time and for many years thereafter—the capacity for enthusiasm divorced from profit or the hope of profit. At least twice within comparatively recent years American public opinion has supported heartily deliberate sacrifice of a potential profit in pursuance of an ideal. The first of these occasions was the American withdrawal from Cuba after the war with Spain, in 1898. This may have been a shrewd move. Further occupation might have been both economically and politically unprofitable; but that was not why the mass of the American people approved it. They approved getting out simply because they thought it was the right thing to do. The affair had cost us some hundreds of millions, and some thousands of lives, but we started in to free Cuba and we had to keep our word. That was what the plain people saw in it, and that was all they saw. The second occasion was our refusal to claim territory or reparations, other than the actual expenses of the Army of Occupation, from Germany after the World War. There is no manner of doubt that the American people approved of this refusal. The cost in that case had run to thirty billions and nearly half a million lives; but we had not gone into that war hoping to gain either colonies or cash, and when our representatives at Paris refused to claim either, the country approved. Apparently we were denied at that conference even the thing we did hope to gain, to wit, the permanent safety of democratic government; but that has nothing to do with the fact that representatives of the United States at a peace conference refused to attempt to secure any financial advantage for their country, and their country thought well of them for refusing.

Therefore when Clay rose to speak for the South American revolutionists, he gave voice to an American sentiment that may have been illogical and badly informed, but that was far from being empty and insincere. It was the common possession of the men of his time. He quoted from Washington, who was certainly not given to extravagant utterance, "Born in a land of liberty, my anxious recollections, my sympathetic feelings, and my best wishes, are irresistibly excited, whensoever, in any country, I see an oppressed nation unfurl the banners of freedom." One may easily discover absurdity in Mr. Clay's attitude toward the United Provinces of the Rio de la Plata; but there was nothing absurd in his attitude, which was the attitude of the majority of his countrymen, toward human freedom.

Moreover, if he harried the administration out of pure joy in making it uncomfortable, there were, nevertheless, sound public reasons for keeping it stirred. Monroe was an earlier Coolidge, a man without ideas of his own, and cherishing deep suspicion of men who did have them. Even his Secretary of State, Monroe sometimes regarded questioningly, for Adams was capable of developing unexpected enthusiasms, which annoyed Monroe extremely. Occasionally, to be sure, they were convenient, as when the Secretary of State cheerfully agreed to clean up after General Andrew Jackson; but Monroe's considered opinion was that the sound man was the man who had attained the wisdom to let well enough alone. There have been periods in our national history when a policy of masterly inactivity has worked admirably. It may be argued, not without plausibility, that in the years between 1817 and 1825 the inertia of Monroe may have saved the country from a great deal of trouble that would have been precipitated had the stern truculence of Adams, the philosophical rigidity of Calhoun, or the brilliance of Clay or Webster been determining the policy of the White House.

But the most that can be said for this view is that there were arguments in support of it. Certainly it isn't obviously true, for there were also arguments, and very powerful ones, on the other side. Europe, in 1818, was in a state curiously similar to its condition a hundred and twenty years later. After a war, or series of wars, unprecedented in destructiveness, the continent had endured a period of appalling confusion, during which the forces of reaction, little by little, had secured the upper hand again. At last autocracy, under one form or another, had been pretty generally restored except in Spain. That unhappy country, fantastically misgoverned both by Joseph Bonaparte and by Ferdinand VII, had been converted into a shambles, and the great powers were acutely aware that its flames might spread at any time to set off a new conflagration. England, France, Austria, Russia and Prussia all understood the necessity of doing something about Spain, and intervention was the final outcome.

But the kings regarded the Spanish American colonies as part of the problem of Spain and every scheme for general pacification included some sort of disposition of the colonies so as "to restore order" which meant, in fact, turning them over to some powerful ruler. In this, the United States had an inevitable and legitimate interest. We had learned by experience that Spain was not a dangerous neighbor. Her own territory she held precariously, if at all; so she was extremely unlikely to invite additional trouble by invading us. But England, Russia, Austria or France would have presented a very different problem.

If this reasoning seems rather farfetched today, it is because we forget, or choose not to remember, the status of the United States in the period following the Napoleonic Wars. America has been highly respectable for so long that it is difficult to realize that it ever was a leper nation. Nevertheless, in 1820 it was regarded by Europe very much as the rest of Europe and the United States regarded Russia in 1920. It was the one country in the world that had introduced and successfully maintained a system of government at variance with and obnoxious to all the previously existing systems. The United States was the country of the Reds. Not only did it stand out as a government antagonistic to monarchy and every other form of autocracy, but it furnished both a text and a refuge to the radicals of all other countries. Nor had it ever lacked enthusiastic propaganda agents. Tom Paine was dead, but it was a rare American, traveling in Europe, who saw fit to suppress his political beliefs and our embassies and consulates abroad were almost invariably nests of what autocratic governments must needs regard as subversive radical agitation.

Fortunately, from the standpoint of the autocrats, America was fairly remote from the centers of European population, so stamping out radicalism in the United States was no such imperative necessity as was its elimination from, say, France. A costly and difficult expedition against this country therefore seemed hardly worth while, especially since British experience in the War of 1812 had proved that such an expedition would be very costly and very difficult. At the same time, the eradication of democracy in the United States would have been welcomed in Europe exactly as the eradication of Communism in Russia would be welcomed today. It was only too clear that Spain, in her distracted and paralytic condition, could never contribute importantly to this result; but if some "safe and sane" power, for example, Austria, could be established on the shores of the Caribbean, that would be at least a step toward the establishment of a sanitary cordon against the American Reds. Conceivably, in the course of time, such an establishment might be used as a base for operations against the stronghold of radicalism; but in any event, a strong European power close at hand would serve as a useful check upon the spread of democratic ideology.) ⨯

From the safe distance of a century it all seems rather fantastic, but there was nothing fantastic about it to the men charged with the conduct of American affairs. They were under no illusions as to their own popularity in the chancelleries of Europe. Like the modern Russians, they knew that their destruction was, if not actively plotted, at least greatly desired by rulers to whom their mere existence was a standing threat; which included the rulers of all the great countries in the world. They saw, in fact, nothing particularly unreasonable in this attitude of the kings, for they actually were hostile to autocracy and not a bit backward about proclaiming the fact. At no time in their national history have the citizens of the United States been conspicuous for the mildness of their bearing and the sweet reasonableness of their argumentation. It is true enough that at this time they hoped to avoid actual collision with any European power, but that they were inimical to the European system was too obvious to require statement and that Europe returned the enmity was a fundamental assumption of their political thinking.

All this had been thoroughly understood for years, and James Monroe saw no reason why he should do anything about it. Nor did he see why Clay should be raising such a clatter in the House of Representatives—or, rather, he thought he did see, all too well. Clay simply wanted to make things difficult for him, Monroe. Adams observed that it was becoming an obsession with the President: "The subject which seems to absorb all the faculties of his mind is the violent, systematic opposition that Clay is raising against his administration," the Secretary of State wrote in his diary. Adams, of course, did not acquit Clay of cherishing ulterior motives. "If Mr. Clay," he observed, "had taken the ground that the Executive had gone as far as he could go with propriety towards the acknowledgment of the South

Americans, that he was well disposed to go further, if such were the feeling of the nation and of Congress, and had made his motion with that view, to ascertain the real sentiment of Congress, it might have been in perfect harmony with the Executive. But between that and the angry, acrimonious course pursued by Mr. Clay there was a wide difference."

So there was indeed. The Speaker, whose motives were rarely unmixed, was playing a little politics, and pretty dirty politics, at that. However, regardless of his motives, the incessant clamor he raised was doing more than merely making things uncomfortable for a President he disliked; it was also slowly driving the United States toward a pronouncement that was to modify the whole course of the history of the Western Hemisphere for a hundred years, and that is, indeed, still modifying it.

Nobody, not even Henry Clay, could inject real energy into James Monroe, but that was not essential. He had plenty of energy at hand in the State Department, if he could only be persuaded to release it. Little by little Clay drove him in that direction, and eventually developments in Europe brought him to the point where he perceived that he would have to take some sort of steps, or he would open the way for Clay to redouble the noise.

The Congress of Vienna, adjourned to Verona, had served formal notice on Spain that her affairs must be reduced to some sort of order and when that produced no effect a French army of intervention crossed the Pyrenees. It was instantly apparent that the time had come. Everyone realized that as soon as the peninsula itself had been straightened out, the allies would take up the question of the colonies. England was wary of the whole business. She had too many other irons in the fire to desire to get involved in any American schemes; moreover, she had come to a fairly satisfactory *modus vivendi* with the United States and her ardor for the extirpation of democracy was rapidly cooling. So the Prime Minister, Canning, passed along a friendly tip to Rush, the American ambassador, and Rush notified Washington that London could endure it quite cheerfully if Washington took a strong stand.

[163]

This was enough for Adams, if not for Monroe. There is no doubt that if the hand of the President wrote the message that went to Congress on December 2, 1823, the voice of the Secretary of State had dictated a good deal of what that message contained.⟩

The first of the three significant passages read, "The occasion has been judged proper for asserting, as a principle in which the rights and interests of the United States are involved, that the American continents, by the free and independent condition which they have assumed and maintained, are henceforth not to be considered as subjects for future colonization of any European powers."

This passage was diplomatically divorced from any suggestion of a threat by the "occasion" referred to. It was not any of the Spanish American troubles, but the debate on the rights of the United States on the northwest coast; so it seemed to be aimed, if toward any one European power, at England. But the use of the plural, "continents," made its real application plain.

The second of the significant passages was more directly to the point: "We owe it, therefore, to candor, and to the amicable relations existing between the United States and those powers, to declare that we should consider any attempt on their part to extend their system to any portion of this hemisphere as dangerous to our peace and safety. With the existing colonies or dependencies of any European power we have not interfered, and shall not interfere. . . . But with the governments who have declared their independence and maintained it, and whose independence we have, on great consideration and on just principles, acknowledged, we could not view any interposition for the purpose of oppressing them, or controlling in any other manner their destiny, by any European power, in any other light than as the manifestation of an unfriendly disposition toward the United States."

The third passage introduced an ambiguity that has not yet been entirely cleared up. It read, "Our policy in regard to Europe, which was adopted at an early stage of the wars which have so long agitated that quarter of the globe, nevertheless remains the same, which is not to interfere with the internal affairs of any of its powers. . . . But, in regard to these continents, circumstances are eminently and conspicuously different. It is impossible that the allied powers should extend their political system to any portion of either continent without endangering our peace and happiness; nor can anyone believe that our Southern brethren, if left to themselves, would adopt it of their own accord. It is equally impossible, therefore, that we should behold such interposition, in any form, with indifference."

These passages together constitute what has come down in history as the Monroe Doctrine. To this day its full implications have never been determined with finality, but its instant significance, in 1823, was clear beyond a doubt. It meant that if any attempt were made to set up a sanitary cordon, the American Reds would fight.

Furthermore, to Canning it meant that he escaped the danger of becoming involved in a series of international tangles for which he had no taste; so the British received the message with cheers. That, in turn, meant to the other allies that if they persisted in their attempt to draw a ring of steel around the western democracy, they might as well count without the British fleet; and that, in the vernacular of a later day, put the lid on it.

There were skeptics in this country who denounced Monroe for risking the ruin of the country by making threats which he could not possibly back up; but these were not experienced and well-informed military men. The high command in every European country knew that the resources of the United States were formidable, considering the geographical situation. The census of 1820 showed that there were just under four million white men in the population, which meant that the country ought to be able, at a pinch, to find a million men of military age. It was therefore out of the question even for the Holy Alliance to transport across the Atlantic a force numerically superior to the potential American army. Furthermore the British knew, and officers of other nations doubtless knew it as well, that such British successes as were won in the War of 1812 were due, almost without exception, to the poor equipment and worse

[165]

command of the Americans, rather than to the poor quality of the troops. On the contrary, in the one action of that war in which the Americans were skillfully disposed and ably commanded, at New Orleans, 2,500 of them had defeated and well-nigh destroyed an army of 5,500 British veterans. In Europe, perhaps, the Americans would not have been very formidable; but any nineteenth-century army, operating three thousand miles from home, would have had a fearful campaign against them. Take away, then, the co-operation of the British fleet, and the thing became hopeless. If the United States intended to fight, conquest of South America simply was not practical, from the military standpoint.

The enunciation of the Monroe Doctrine, and its reception by the British, unquestionably flattened any schemes the Holy Alliance may have been formulating to extirpate political radicalism in its western stronghold.

What else it did is still hotly debated by historians. The third section may be read, and frequently has been read, as tantamount to a guarantee of a republican form of government for every nation on this side of the globe. The bland assumption that "our Southern brethren" think on this subject as we do is typical of a style of thinking that has brought us much trouble in the last century; but even American statesmen, with all their romanticism, have drawn the line at trying to make that guarantee effective. Sporadic efforts to do so have been so uniformly woeful in their results that we have acquiesced in the existence in South America of more dictatorships than Europe ever dreamed of having.

But as regards the personal fortunes of Henry Clay, the Monroe Doctrine had two interesting effects. Temporarily, it threatened to extinguish him, politically; and permanently it inspired him, philosophically.

As is frequently the case in politics, the statesman who did the lamb's share of the work, walked off with the lion's share of the credit. The driving forces behind the Monroe Doctrine were Henry Clay and John Quincy Adams. Clay's gadfly tactics in the House had stung the inert Monroe until he was willing to do anything, even to take action; and when the time came Adams was ready with the knowledge and skill to put the thing in form. But when it was announced, the country burst into a delirium of enthusiasm that for a moment made James Monroe seem the greatest man in the world. The thing happened that always happens when the American people are moved to regard a President with unusual favor—it was proposed to give him a third term. The argument was, "Don't swap horses while crossing the stream." It was pointed out that within a few months there would be five candidates for the Presidency in the field. The election was likely to be thrown into the House of Representatives and if any other than Monroe were chosen Europe might construe it as repudiation of his Doctrine.[1] It is amazing to think how close the weakest President thus far to hold the office came to being the only one after Washington to be elected unanimously, and again close to being the one to break the two-terms tradition.

This was a suggestion appalling both to Mr. Adams and Mr. Clay, as well as to Mr. Calhoun and Mr. Webster, not to mention the Secretary of War, Mr. Crawford, and the uproarious westerner, General Jackson, all of whom were being assiduously groomed for the race by their various backers. In the first flush of enthusiasm Clay had presented to the House a resounding resolution, loudly committing Congress to support of the Monroe Doctrine; he now explained somewhat lamely that it seemed that the Holy Alliance, after all, was not preparing to attack us immediately, therefore it was probably wiser to take no risk of seeming to be truculent, so he proposed that his own resolution lie on the table. In a short time, however, the third term movement subsided and was heard of no more.

But if this aspect of it soon ceased to engage his attention, the Monroe Doctrine unquestionably fired Clay's imagination with regard to an idea that he had cherished for years, and that he never abandoned entirely. This was his conception of the United States not merely as a nation, even a nation continental in extent,

[1] See McMaster, vol. v, p. 51.

but as more than a nation—as "the natural head of the American family."

It was a conception of dimensions so gigantic that it eluded the grasp not of his contemporaries, only, but of succeeding generations. What Clay called the "American System" has been degraded into mere advocacy of the protective tariff. It was vaster, far, than that. Clay foresaw a time when the democracy of the United States would attain the hegemony of the Western Hemisphere. In that he was a true prophet, for it came to pass. But he foresaw this attainment, not by the development of our military and financial power but through the moral power of a demonstration that the rule of the people may guarantee the national safety, promote the general welfare, and secure the blessings of civilization. In this, unfortunately, he did not prophesy so well. But is it to his discredit that he failed to predict calamity? He did not believe that his country's statesmen, in the end, would fail lamentably, that the Union would be rent by civil war for four years, and that afterward one third of it would be held in economic bondage for three-quarters of a century and another third be given over to economic pillage for an equal length of time.

He thought too well of us to foretell the future accurately; but it is a hard judgment that would condemn him utterly for that fault. It was after his death that his protective tariff system became the instrument of an oppression more strongly intrenched by far than the rule that Ferdinand VII imposed on Spain. As he planned it and advocated it, it was to be the intelligent use of the legislative power to correct a serious imbalance in the national economy. So at that time—before slavery had become an overshadowing moral issue—did Calhoun see it, and other leaders among the Jeffersonians. True, there was death in the pot. Even then there were men who pointed out to the enthusiasts that this same instrument might be employed to rifle the wealth of one section and one class for the enrichment of another. But these men, young, then, and confident, felt that it was a chance that had to be taken; and so impressed were they with a con-

viction of the essential honesty of America that they felt it was
a remote chance.

If there is one thing about Clay which the biographer can
assert with absolute certainty, it is that he was not avaricious.
He sought a balanced economy—manufactures sufficiently strong
to supply the needs of the agricultural population and to relieve
us of the necessity of importing essentials in case of war—because he believed that the straight road to the greatest happiness
of the greatest number, and that he considered the way toward
the greater goal.

Henry Clay had a noble dream of empery—impossible, no
doubt, fantastic, perhaps, but not mean, not touched with greed,
nor stained with cruelty, and arrogant only in that it attributed
to his fellow-men a loftier spirit than they possessed. He believed
that the Hemisphere could be, and should be conquered, not by
the might of American arms, but by the irresistible might of
American happiness. He foresaw a country peaceful because too
strong to be attacked with any hope of success, wealthy by the
cultivation of its own enormous resources, not by raids upon
others and pillage of their store, impregnable from within because no man would have just cause to complain of oppression by
its government. It would be a happy country inevitably and as
such it would as inevitably be a beacon among the nations.
The countries of South America would submit to its guidance
not out of fear, but out of admiration, and would follow it because it led where every honest man would wish to go.

There is biting irony in the fact that out of this mighty vision
all that remains is the protective tariff, which long ago produced
such another imbalance in our national economy that the whole
structure fell into ruins, driving us today to adopt every sort of
desperate expedient to prop up the shaking fabric. "The evil
that men do lives after them; the good is oft interred with their
bones." Henry Clay's American System is a shockingly apt illustration of the text.

As practical statecraft the original American System was full
of flaws, the first, and most obvious, being the fact that the
American people have proved to be by no means as competent,

politically, as Clay assumed they would be. However, to be fair one must note that Clay never advanced it as practical statecraft, but only as an ideal toward which American statecraft should work by degrees, hoping to attain it, not at once, but in the indefinite future.

Yet when one has made due allowance for the nebulosity of an ideal, and when one has forgiven Clay for the amiable error of thinking too well of his countrymen, there remains an element in this project which is, indeed, characteristically American, but not lovely. It is the arrogant assumption that we are the people and that wisdom shall die with us.

Perhaps this is, after all, less an American than a human trait. At all events, it is the active and virulent element in what is currently termed nationalism, using the word in the derogatory sense. The American System was necessarily based on an assumption of the universality of our values. Doubtless this assumption is an element of national strength, but it is also the basis of national bumptiousness. Over wide areas and over long periods the Latin Americans have persistently rejected democracy, and even today we have not quite managed to get over being horrified by the rejection. When they were just emerging from subjugation by Spain it seems to have occurred to hardly any American that they would hesitate to adopt the system that had worked admirably for us. Monroe did not refer specifically to democracy in his message, but when he said of the European political system, "nor can anyone believe that our Southern brethren, if left to themselves, would adopt it of their own accord" there is little reason to doubt that he supposed democracy to be the only alternative. The experience of the century that has elapsed since he wrote his message has proved him wrong.

It is a truism of politics that the government of any nation—taking it at its average for a considerable period, not at one of its unusually high or low points—is never the best government the people of that nation can devise, but the worst government they will tolerate. Clay had worked in politics long enough to understand this; but he failed to take into account the fact that the point of tolerance is found at different levels in different populations. Ardent nationalists of all nations commonly fail to take it into account; or, when the fact is forced upon their notice, invest it with moral significance. Americans, after more than a hundred years' experience, can hardly be oblivious of the fact that the people of most of the South American countries will tolerate military dictatorship; and because it is, to us, an abhorrent form of government, we tend to assume a certain moral superiority whose relevance is hard to establish. Political liberty probably has an ethical aspect in strengthening individual character; but so has discipline, and he would be a mighty philosopher indeed who devised scales in which one could be weighed against the other.

Such subtleties have rarely troubled the political thinking of Americans, however, which may go far to account for our remarkable unpopularity in South America. Certainly they never troubled Henry Clay. His creed, unexpressed but undoubted, was that a political system that was good enough for the United States certainly was good enough for the United Provinces of the Rio de la Plata, or for New Grenada, or for any of the other countries slowly and bloodily taking shape in the southern continent. In that he was at one with his countrymen. It was the buoyant assurance of a new and successful country, not yet old enough to be tolerant, not yet conscious enough of its own mistakes to be humble. It was the assurance of the provincial American, unfamiliar with any other country and not at all convinced that any other country held anything worth learning.

In certain respects this was admirable. It led to an impulsive generosity, if nothing more. Clay was sincerely willing to furnish assistance to the South American revolutionists, and that without any thought of gain. This was recognized in Latin America, which explains the fact that the capitals of the southern continent are studded with statues of Henry Clay, its cities have streets named after him, and its schoolboys are taught that he was one of the noblest and most disinterested of American statesmen. As regards them and their affairs, it is true; for if he used South America as a spike with which to prod James

Monroe for his own satisfaction, it was at no cost to South America.

The attention here given to Clay's connection with the Rio de la Plata undoubtedly would have seemed disproportionate to him. But it is not disproportionate in a study of his statecraft; the reasons are two; first, this was the one occasion on which his activity played an important part in forcing a significant and memorable event in American foreign policy, to wit, the enunciation of the Monroe Doctrine; and, second, because this incident exhibits to perfection the good qualities and the defects of Clay's manner of dealing with foreign countries. His activities in behalf of Greece, his later negotiations with Bolivar and Miranda, his Pan-American Congress scheme, all exhibit the same pattern of thought. Understand Clay in the Rio de la Plata affair, and you understand Clay throughout.

Criticism of the vices of a man prominent in history is easy, but a correct appraisal of his virtues is extremely difficult. It is especially true in this case because Clay's vices were negative and his virtues positive. His vices were ignorance of the history, both the political and the social, but especially the social history of the nations that excited his interest, and lack of the imagination that would have enabled him to understand that history had it been set before him. Incidentally, because these vices were shared by vast numbers of his countrymen, Clay's foreign policy was easily understood by them, and therefore usually popular. It is not difficult at all to comprehend how they handicapped him and prevented him from formulating any really great foreign policy.

What are not easy to assay are his virtues. These included tremendous faith in the form of government adopted by his own country, a sincere love of liberty, and a generous enthusiasm for making the blessings of liberty available to all men, an enthusiasm that was not damped by the threat of cost and pain. These are positive, not negative, virtues. They are kinetic, vital, moving and for that very reason difficult to weigh. Clay's ignorance of the Latin-American temperament tended to have one effect on our relations with the countries of South America, and his generous enthusiasm tended to have a diametrically opposite effect; but when it comes to measuring the relative importance of the two, the calculations promptly become so abstruse that the attempt becomes absurd.

About all that can be said is this: Clay, for reasons that are perfectly apparent, never worked out a really satisfactory formula for dealing with "our Southern brethren"; yet Clay, for reasons which are by no means so plain to our eyes, left upon those brethren an impression, startlingly deep and clear, of a great statesman and a high-minded, generous friend. He left us the liability of a bungling foreign policy, and the asset of a great reputation for good will.

CHAPTER XI

ON ADMINISTRATION

*Observations as to how Mr. Clay conducted himself as Secretary of State,
with some notice of bargains and corruption, and of Mr. Calhoun's entry
into silence for eight years as Vice-President*

THE approach of the year 1824 was watched by the leaders in American public life with extraordinary interest. Everyone realized that it meant the end of an epoch. The great Virginia Dynasty, which had held the Presidency for thirty-two of the thirty-six years of its history, must end with James Monroe. A soldier of the Revolution at eighteen, a United States Senator at thirty-two, Governor of Virginia at forty-one, he was the youngest and the last of the Revolutionary heroes. The mighty line, beginning with George Washington, continuing with Thomas Jefferson and then with James Madison, must stop with James Monroe, simply because there were no more of his colleagues left. Nearly fifty years had elapsed since the Declaration of Independence, and the time had come when the Chief Magistracy must necessarily pass out of the hands of the companions of Washington.

Where, then, would it go? There were at least five men each of whom by reason of his talents was popularly regarded as worthy of being mentioned in connection with the great office. It was generally agreed that the time had come for Virginia to step aside, even the Virginians themselves not making any very serious effort to deny it. But as to which State, or which section, should succeed Virginia, there was no agreement at all. Each of the main divisions of the country desired the honor, and each had an eminent man to put forward as embodying its claims. New England stood ready with a son of the only non-Virginian

President. The old South had John C. Calhoun and the new South had William H. Crawford, the brilliant Georgian. All three had served in the Cabinet and served ably. But there was a new voice now in national affairs, that of the West. The North had had the Presidency once, the South had had it four times; when was the West to be recognized? Here was the Speaker of the House, the dazzling Clay, negotiator of the Treaty of Ghent, pilot, if not architect, of the Missouri Compromise, orator and statesman of the very first rank. Thus said the Westerners in Washington; and away from Washington there were others who pointed to Andrew Jackson, hero of New Orleans, captor of Florida, deliverer of the West from Spanish and Indian domination, idol of the common people.

The jockeying for position that took place in the two years preceding the election makes one of the most interesting and amusing chapters in our political history; but it was all straight politics, having little to do with anything properly to be classified as statecraft, so it must be skimmed over lightly here. A good many historians are convinced that, but for the interposition of fate, Crawford would certainly have carried off the prize. The Secretary of the Treasury had a brilliant record, good in the Cabinet and even better in Congress; he was honest, he made a fine appearance on the platform, and he was tremendously popular among the members of Congress who made up the caucus that usually designated the candidate. If precedent held, Adams, who was Secretary of State, would be named; but as time passed it became increasingly clear that precedent could not be trusted to hold against Crawford. If the nomination were made by the usual method of the Congressional caucus, Crawford would almost certainly win. In these circumstances, Mr. Adams, Mr. Clay and Mr. Calhoun were visited by inspiration. It was suddenly revealed to them that the caucus was really an abominable method of nominating a President. It was undemocratic. It excluded the people from any participation in choosing their President. It was shocking, outrageous, and ought to be abandoned at once.

The Crawford men were not impressed by this high-minded

interest in the plain, ordinary voters. They thought, or at least they said, that the supporters of the other candidates were fighting the caucus simply because that was the only way to stop Crawford. Clay happened to be in a good position on this point, for he had denounced "King Caucus" eight years before, when Crawford was nowhere in sight. But in any case, the plea was a good one, regardless of the *bona fides* of its makers. The caucus was undemocratic and did exclude the people from participation in Presidential elections; therefore the fight against it received widespread popular support. State after State instructed its delegation not to participate if a caucus were called, and State after State proceeded to do its own nominating, either in the legislature or in conventions specially called for the purpose.

But the Crawford men were undaunted. They were under the command of an extraordinary leader, one of the ablest political generals in American history, a dapper, little red-head from up-State New York, always polite, always smiling, always imperturbable and always deadly, commonly called the Red Fox of Kinderhook, but named Martin Van Buren. This bland cynic was quite unmoved by the overwhelming evidence that the people were strongly against the caucus. Many times, in New York State, he had successfully carried through projects that the people detested, and he had little doubt of his ability to overcome the obstacle afforded by their opposition to the caucus. In February, therefore, it was called; and although only sixty-six members showed up out of two hundred and sixty-one, Van Buren insisted on going ahead[1] and Crawford was duly named as the candidate for President. It was promptly dubbed the "Treasury Caucus" by the opposition newspapers, but it was a caucus, of sorts, and it put Crawford in the field as the only man nominated by the traditional method which made him, in the eyes of many, the regular candidate.

But although the Red Fox dared to disregard blithely the will of the people, he couldn't contend against the hand of God. In the summer of 1824 his candidate was stricken with paralysis, and that was too much, even for Van Buren. He made a gallant

[1] McMaster, vol. v, p. 64.

effort. The truth about Crawford's condition was suppressed as far as was humanly possible. Selected callers were permitted to visit him in rooms whose windows were carefully shaded to prevent his condition's being too plainly apparent. All sorts of mechanical devices were brought in to aid him to make a show of having recovered, but in spite of everything before the voting was under way the country knew he was a paralyzed man. Even so, by the time the returns were all in—Presidential elections in those days were held at the convenience of the several States, not all on one day, and in the autumn of 1824 they continued for several weeks—Crawford had more electoral votes than Henry Clay. The technique of the political manager had not then been developed to anything like its present perfection, and few Americans comprehended it at all; therefore few realized that Crawford's forty-one electoral votes really were an astounding tribute to the political craftsmanship of Martin Van Buren. Clay, who was intimately acquainted with the inner workings of politics, should have understood; but there is little, if any, evidence that he did.

Long before the actual voting began Mr. Calhoun had taken stock of the situation and come to the accurate conclusion that he had no chance for the first prize, so he prudently decided to make sure of the second. Ideas as to the Vice-Presidency were pretty nebulous. There was a notion abroad that the wild Westerner might take it and in the South, especially, there was much militant chanting of

> John Quincy Adams,
> Who can write,
> And Andrew Jackson,
> Who can fight,

but when Mr. Calhoun delicately intimated, through trusted friends, that he was in a receptive mood, partisans of the other candidates were only too glad to put him in second place on their tickets. Therefore the electoral college gave him one hundred and eighty-two votes for Vice-President, a safe majority.

But for the first place General Jackson had ninety-nine, Mr.

[177]

Adams had eighty-four, Mr. Crawford had forty-one and Mr. Clay had thirty-seven. As it took one hundred and thirty-one to constitute a majority, this was no election, and it was necessary to apply the procedure provided in the Twelfth Amendment of the Constitution.[2] Since only the three highest names could be considered, Clay was out; and since Crawford was half-dead, Crawford was out, and the thing came down to a choice between Andrew Jackson and John Quincy Adams.

With the election thrown into the House of Representatives, the Speaker had it in his hands, and everyone knew it. It was the supreme test both of the statecraft and of the political prescience of Henry Clay, and he botched it; he swung his strength to Adams and then accepted the portfolio of State at his hands.

The volumes that have been written attacking and defending the course of Clay at this point in his career would fill a library of respectable proportions:[3] nor is the battling to be dismissed as mere sound and fury, for if one wishes to assess the ethical quality of Henry Clay accurately the question of his governing motive in this crisis is of the very first importance. But if the object is not the formulation of any moral judgment whatever, but merely an estimate of the efficacy of his statecraft, the question of motive is far less important, and the impossibility of determining it with certainty is far less hampering.

As a matter of fact, from the standpoint of ethics it is easy to make out a case either for Clay or against him. The assertion of the Jacksonians that in voting for Adams he deliberately defeated the will of the people is supported by impressive evidence. Jackson had ninety-nine electoral votes against Adams' eighty-four. He had 153,544 popular votes against Adams' 108,740. He

[2] The relevant passage reads as follows: "If no person have [a] majority, then from the persons having the highest number, not exceeding three, on the list of those voted for as President, the House of Representatives shall choose immediately by ballot the President. But in choosing the President, the votes shall be taken by States, the representation from each State having one vote; a quorum for this purpose shall consist of a member or members from two-thirds of the States, and a majority of all the States shall be necessary to a choice."

[3] An admirable summary of both sides of the controversy is to be found in two recent books, Marquis James' *Andrew Jackson; Portrait of a President*, for the prosecution, and Van Deusen's *Life of Henry Clay*, for the defense.

carried eleven States against Adams' seven. More than that, the legislature of Kentucky, carried by Clay, passed a resolution calling on the Kentucky delegation in Congress to vote for Jackson after Clay was eliminated, and there is little doubt that he was the second choice of Ohio, also carried by Clay. In the House, these two would have given him thirteen States, constituting a majority. But in the House, Clay not only delivered his own three States to Adams, but he pulled away the delegations of three States whose electors had given a majority of their votes to Jackson and delivered these also,[4] thus making up the necessary thirteen. At the last moment he swung the senile General Van Rensselaer over to his side, thereby capturing the vote of New York, but as the New York electors had been chosen by the legislature, not by popular vote, this was defeating the will of Martin Van Buren, rather than that of the people of New York. All told, there is little reason to doubt that if Clay and Crawford had never entered the race, the General would have beaten Adams decisively, so when Clay made Adams President, he was not carrying out the will of the people.

On the other hand, there is no convincing evidence that Clay was anything but a sincere believer in representative government. He was a member of Congress, bound by oath to support the Constitution, which he regarded as the organic law of a representative government; therefore he regarded himself as bound by oath to use his best judgment in preserving, protecting, and defending that government, regardless of what anyone, even his own constituents, might think.

Now Henry Clay had no great affection for John Quincy Adams. On the contrary, ever since their days together in Ghent he had regarded the Puritan as about the most poisonous individual the country could show; which, indeed, he was. But as between Adams and Andrew Jackson it is easy to understand how Clay might persuade himself that there was no doubt where his duty to his country lay. His personal animosity toward Jackson was at this time not yet highly developed; perhaps he even

[4] They were Illinois, Maryland and Louisiana.

believed that he preferred Jackson, personally, and was sacrificing his feelings in supporting Adams.

Whether or not he demanded, and Adams promised, his appointment as Secretary of State as the price of his support is really not important; but unless politicians have changed their ways marvelously within the last century the story is all but incredible. Business simply is not done that way, on the higher levels. Both men were experienced politicians. Both men knew that if Clay made Adams President, Adams could not decently do less than offer Clay the first post in the Cabinet. In such a situation why should Clay make an embarrassing request? Why should Adams promise to do what circumstances would render inevitable? When the Jacksonians began to shout "Bargain and corruption," the indignant denials of Adams and Clay were doubtless technically true; which does not alter the fact that when Clay swung to Adams he was well aware that the refusal of the State Department would be his.

The reasons that underlay his course were probably much more subtle than anyone, including Henry Clay himself, realized. Those on the surface, those that he advanced in explanation of of his course, were both obvious and highly respectable. Mr. Adams was, to begin with, a man whose personal integrity was as unimpeachable as that of his opponent, so nothing could be urged against him on that score. Then he was a man of long experience in national affairs, in Congress, in the diplomatic service and in the Cabinet, while Jackson had only brief service in Congress to his credit, all his other public service being either military or in the State of Tennessee. More than that, there is every reason to believe that Mr. Clay thought Adams had more brains than Jackson. This was a grievous error, but, in the circumstances, a natural one; Mr. Clay was not the first man, nor the last one, to mistake inequalities in education for inequalities in intellectual power. Finally, his distrust of the elevation of a military chieftain to the Presidency doubtless was sincere enough. Why not? The history of republics proves beyond peradventure that it is a dangerous expedient.

But underlying all this argumentation, there was another

reason that Mr. Clay perhaps never acknowledged even to himself. It was simply the fact that Mr. Adams was one of the boys, while General Jackson wasn't. To introduce this rank outsider into the Presidency simply because a lot of people in the backwoods had voted for him would be to transfer control of affairs from Washington to God knew where. To Mr. Clay, as, indeed, to most of his colleagues, this was revolutionary in the worst sense. From the beginning the American republic had been run by gentlemen. They conferred with the people, yes, and within reasonable limits they allowed themselves to be swayed by the people's wishes. But they were the leaders, they determined policies; above all, they chose Presidents, allowing the people at most the right to choose between two or more gentlemen all of their own type. Then for Clay to employ his influence to bring Jackson into office over a gentleman of the old school, a man familiar to Washington, a man who, whatever his objectional idiosyncrasies, undeniably was a member of the ruling class, would have been a sort of abdication. At the very best, it would have been an admission that this revolt of the people marked a permanent change in their attitude, which Clay did not believe for a moment. After the usual manner of conservatives, he laid it all to the pernicious activity of agitators.

Martin Van Buren was better informed. In the phrase of a later day he "went down the line" for Crawford because he was committed to the Georgian and he was too good a politician to break his word openly and blatantly. But by the time the campaign was finished, he was keenly aware that a change had come over the spirit of the country. He knew all about the agitators. He knew that countless malcontents had rallied to Jackson for no better reason than that they were Outs, willing to rally to anybody who gave any promise of being able to beat the Ins. He knew all about Felix Grundy and John Henry Eaton, the swashbuckling major whom Henry Clay regarded as the personal devil at the bottom of the trouble. He knew all about a man vastly more important than Eaton, the almost imperceptible Major William B. Lewis, to whom nobody paid any attention but who has, after Van Buren himself, perhaps the best claim to be considered the inventor of modern American politics.

But in spite of his acquaintance with the agitators, Van Buren realized that there was much more in this movement than their persuasive powers. The old republic, dominated by country gentlemen of the Washington type, was gone. For one thing, the census of 1820 had shown New York with a population of 152,-000, Baltimore with 62,000, Philadelphia with nearly 60,000, and Boston with 43,000. The republic of Washington had had no such great cities. More than that, the streams of people pouring into the West broke with the old tradition as they moved, and the streams of immigrants pouring into the East had never had it. As the conquest of the wilderness proceeded, the growing confidence of the people in themselves made them increasingly resentful of any suggestion of tutelage. As newspapers multiplied, and the ordinary man became better informed on public affairs, he formulated more and stronger opinions. Mr. Van Buren never argued against a fact. For good or for ill, whether one liked it or not, control had definitely gone from the Washington group; so Mr. Van Buren, observing the fact, trimmed his sails accordingly.

The greater man of the two was in this instance the more foolish. Instead of trimming his sails, Clay crowded on canvas, and drove straight into the hurricane. It is not at all inconceivable, indeed, it is probable that he felt, in making Adams President, that he was doing his duty; but it was no part of his duty to become Secretary of State in Adams' Cabinet. Perhaps he did not bargain for the office, but he accepted it, and that was enough.

The proof, if needed, may be found in the career of Mr. Webster. It is pretty generally admitted that he actually did bargain for the post of Minister to England; even his friendly biographer, Lodge, doesn't deny it. Nor is there any doubt that Webster was the decisive influence in pulling Maryland away from Jackson and turning it over to Adams. Yet Webster was never subjected to any such drumfire as burst upon Clay, and the reason is plain—he never got his pay. The storm that followed the Clay appointment may not have been Adams' only reason for with-holding Webster's nomination, but it was a sufficient one.

Clay knew exactly what he was doing when he accepted the Cabinet post. The cry of "Bargain and corruption!" was already resounding, and Clay had managed to get himself into a ridiculous position by denouncing and offering to fight the author of an anonymous newspaper article making the charge. When the authorship was promptly claimed by George Kremer, a Pennsylvania member regarded as a harmless eccentric notable chiefly for the leopard-skin coat he wore in the House, the laughter was more damaging to Clay's pride than the charge. He understood what his enemies would say, for they were already saying it; what he did not understand was to whom he must explain his course. He still believed that if he could convince a few party leaders in Washington that his course was correct, no more would be required. He still refused to believe that henceforth any political leader must plead, not to a caucus, but to the country.

Incredulity as to the ability of the American people, on some occasions and on some issues, to make up their own minds regardless of what they are told by their leaders was Clay's undoing.

It is striking how little the Triumvirate accomplished during the Adams administration, when two of its members occupied high offices and the third was administration leader in the House. True, Mr. Calhoun's office was that of Vice-President which, in the American system, amounts to virtual political exile. The Vice-President, as a rule, exerts small influence upon the course of legislation and still less upon Cabinet decisions. "They also serve who only stand and wait," no doubt, but it is not often apparent to observers how they serve. It was not long after the beginning of the administration that both Mr. Adams and Mr. Clay developed certain suspicions as to how Mr. Calhoun was serving. They thought the South Carolinian was employing his abundant leisure to strengthen and extend his political fences. Schurz declares flatly that it was about this time that Calhoun turned into a sectional leader[5] and began to identify his cause with that of slavery.

As for Mr. Webster, at first his eloquence was employed to good effect in the House to defend the administration. But as time passed and Rufus King, first of Adams' ministers to England, was succeeded, not by Daniel Webster, but by Albert Gallatin, Webster's enthusiasm cooled noticeably. Toward the end he was much more interested in the logrolling that resulted in the Tariff of 1828, the notorious "Tariff of Abominations," than in the success of the administration.

Clay, in these years, actually accomplished something, but not much by comparison with what he had hoped, or what might reasonably have been expected, considering his ability and experience. The reason is not far to seek. The "bargain and corruption" idea hung around his neck like the Ancient Mariner's albatross. Never for a moment did he escape it, and he made the capital error of explaining. Not once, but repeatedly, he went over the story, calling on witnesses, citing documents, piling up evidence, even going so far as to shoot at John Randolph of Roanoke[6] by way of establishing his innocence. But he wasted his breath; he could deny the betrayal, but he couldn't deny the thirty pieces of silver, and the more he explained the worse the thing looked.

It was directly responsible for the defeat of his effort to bring his great dream, the American System, a step closer to fulfillment. During a moment when the program of reciprocal murder was being prosecuted somewhat less frantically than usual in South America, some of the leaders in that tortured continent conceived the idea of a great Congress of American nations to

[5] Schurz, vol. i, p. 265.
[6] That master of invective had picked two of the most unpleasant characters out of Fielding's *Tom Jones*, one a canting hypocrite, the other a thorough-going rascal, and had used them to characterize the alliance between Adams and Clay as "the coalition of Blifil and Black George—the combination, unheard of till then, of the Puritan with the black-leg." Clay put a bullet through Randolph's coat, but Randolph fired in the air and the practical results were nil, except, perhaps, to make a great many people read *Tom Jones* who had never looked into the book before.

be held at Panama and invited the United States to participate. To Clay it seemed a heaven-sent opportunity, and he welcomed it with an enthusiasm that carried even the cautious Adams along. Here was the hegemony of the Western world offered to us voluntarily, and Clay was all for accepting it fully. Adams, however, was not ready to go that far. He toned down Clay's proposals sharply and sent to Congress a project that seems, upon reading it now, as harmless as can be imagined. He proposed the dispatch of two plenipotentiaries to Panama to consult with the Central and South American nations upon such matters as reciprocal trade treaties, the definition of blockade and neutral rights, the suppression of piracy and the slave trade and other matters that obviously needed clarification and concerted agreement. He thought, too, that it might be well to explain to the southern nations that the Monroe Doctrine did not assert any right on our part to interfere with their internal affairs and at the same time to do something for freedom of religion by requesting guarantees of the right of free worship for United States citizens domiciled in South America. It was, in short, no more revolutionary than an expression of approval of the Ten Commandments.

But from the uproar in Congress a foreign observer might have inferred that Adams and Clay had proposed the demolition of the republic. It was in this debate that Randolph precipitated the duel with his "Blifil and Black George" taunt. The attack was completely disingenuous. Nobody had any real objection to the Panama Congress and public opinion seemed to be strongly in its favor. But it was a glorious opportunity for the Jacksonians —unobtrusively assisted by the Crawford and Calhoun men—to make war medicine and they improved it to the fullest possible extent. In the end, Congress had to accept the President's project because there was no reasonable ground for rejecting it; but the ranting and the roaring were kept up so long that the Panama Congress had adjourned before our tardily appointed representatives could arrive.

This was Clay's one opportunity to do a conspicuous and memorable thing as Secretary of State, and it was lost. For the rest, his record is that of a conscientious, hard-working and sensible official. He negotiated excellent trade agreements with half a dozen nations, and although he got nowhere with Great Britain in this matter, he did secure payment for the slaves her forces had carried off in the War of 1812. He opened the way for successful solution of several other difficulties with the British, although the final settlements were made years afterward, and, in general, made an excellent Secretary of State.

This, though, was to be expected, because there was no doubt of Clay's ability. Where he confounded his enemies and rather astonished his friends was in maintaining amicable relations with John Quincy Adams from start to finish. Neither of these men was in any degree a yielding personality; yet somehow Clay managed to keep constantly in mind the fact that not he but Adams was President, and when Adams ruled against him he submitted with good grace and made sincere and vigorous efforts to execute his orders. Not immediately, but eventually Adams realized that Clay was thoroughly loyal—the virtue for which most may be forgiven by any man in public office. The Department of State was well managed and its head could be relied on to give advice that was always sincere, if not always judicious. The Puritan was nothing if not honest. He paid his debts, to whomsoever they were due. If the devil himself had served J. Q. Adams well, J. Q. Adams would have made prompt and public acknowledgment of the fact. He never liked Clay, but he did come to esteem him; so at the end of the administration it was probably with real pleasure that he challenged any man who questioned his motives in appointing Clay.

"Let him," he thundered, referring to such a questioner, "look around among the statesmen and legislators of the nation and of that day. Let him then select and name the man whom, by his pre-eminent talents, by his splendid services, by his ardent patriotism, by his all-embracing public spirit, by his fervid eloquence in behalf of the rights and liberties of mankind, by his long experience in the affairs of the Union, foreign and domestic, a President of the United States, intent only upon the honor and welfare of his country, ought to have preferred to Henry Clay."

All this, though, while a splendid tribute to his subordinate officer, was but begging the question. The error was not Adams'. Under the circumstances he should have offered the post to Clay. But Clay should never have accepted it.

Long before Adams' term had ended, the Secretary of State realized his error. Political considerations were not all that forced the realization upon him. He was not happy in the job. In part this was due to domestic tragedy. Shortly after his appointment he had started gaily for Kentucky to bring Lucretia and the family to Washington; but one beloved daughter was taken ill and died on the way, and another was mortally stricken within two months. His house therefore was a house of mourning. He worked hard and long, much harder and longer than he had worked as a member of Congress, and confinement to a desk told on his own health. What with illness, sorrow and worry, he came close to lapsing into melancholia, and more than once begged the President to be relieved of his office; but Adams, keenly sensible by that time of his worth, always persuaded him to stick it out.

Undoubtedly another contributory cause of his discomfort was a sense of frustration in that he was missing great opportunities in Congress. Webster was a good man in the House, at least in the beginning, but Clay knew he was every whit as good and later, when Webster's enthusiasm began to cool, Clay knew he could have done a great deal better. To see the administration forces led into battle apathetically, not to say reluctantly, when the enemy was becoming momentarily more violently aggressive, must have been maddening to a really great parliamentary leader unable, by reason of his office, to lead.

So they were for Clay four rather miserable years, for Webster rather dull years, for Calhoun rather dubious years that led up to the great crash of 1828.

CHAPTER XII

ON THE REIGN OF TERROR

The melancholy tale of how the Triumvirate jauntily undertook the destruction of the indestructible General Jackson and how it worked the ruin of Mr. Calhoun

THE campaign of 1828 has come down in history as by long odds the filthiest in American history. Even the campaign of 1936, although it rivaled the earlier one in bitterness, did at least keep its worst scurrilities in the mouths of the more verminous camp followers of politics. No newspaper with any pretensions to respectability fouled its pages by printing the slanders that were whispered; but in 1828 they were shamelessly embalmed in the permanence of type.

Randolph may have been merely a picturesque liar, but here was, indeed, a coalition of the Puritan and the blackleg, and also —what is equally anomalous—a coalition, in the other camp, of Don Quixote and Black George. It is quite true that, despite vigorous and long-continued efforts, no proof has ever been discovered that either of the two candidates, President Adams or General Jackson, had anything to do with the mud-batteries; but it is also true that neither ever used, or threatened to use, a horsewhip to silence those on his own side. Perhaps, considering the manners and customs of the times, neither could have gagged the slanderers; but neither made any violent effort to do so, hence, let their apologists say what they will, both stand somewhat befouled in the light of history.

The depths to which the scavengers dredged are almost incredible today. Even a generation that knows the whisperers do not hesitate to accuse the President of the United States of being a petty thief is shocked to read that in 1828 the President—and he the rigidly upright Adams—was accused, not in a backstairs whisper, but publicly, of being a procurer for the Emperor of Russia. This was done by one who purported to be a supporter of the quixotic Jackson, and Jackson failed to stop it. On the other side, not only was Jackson himself accused of every crime from murder down, and not only was his wife spattered with slime, but even his mother was accused of being a loose woman. As it happens, that woman lies in a grave unknown to this day, somewhere around Charleston, South Carolina; she died of ship fever, contracted while ministering to American prisoners of war held in the British hulks in Charleston Harbor during the Revolution. Think of attacking the character of Florence Nightingale, or Edith Cavell, as an argument for a candidate in a modern political campaign! Think of making such an attack in support of a Puritan of the Puritans; and think that the Puritan failed to stop it!

Parton asserts[1] that this was the one attack that broke the General down. Mrs. Jackson found him in tears, with the newspaper in his hand.

In any event, such a campaign was bound to presage an orgy of vengeance, whoever won. It is inconceivable that even Adams would have been mildly tolerant of political opponents who accused him of being a pander; and Adams didn't win. Jackson swept the country, except for New England and scattering votes from States as far down as the Potomac. He was always a good hater, but right after the election his wife died and he was convinced that the slanders of the Adams newspapers had precipitated the heart attack that killed her. He had been devoted to her, so he came to Washington filled with such hatred as made all his passions of the past seem mere trifling irritations, by comparison. He did not rave, as in the old days. He was beyond that. His associates noticed that for months the General did not even swear, and for a man whose profanity had astounded and enthralled an army on active service, that had a sinister significance. The only outward manifestation of his feelings was his flat refusal to call on his predecessor. The *National Journal*, of

[1] Vol. iii, p. 141.

Washington, reputed to be the personal organ of President Adams, had been particularly infamous in its attacks on Mrs. Jackson, and Jackson would not shake the hand of the man he held responsible for these attacks, no, not had he been twenty Presidents. It has since been established that Adams had nothing to do with this phase of the *National Journal's* campaign, but Jackson didn't know it, nor was there any way he could know it, for the President had neither stopped the assaults, nor publicly denounced them.

Next to Adams the man Jackson held chiefly responsible for the scurrility of the campaign was Henry Clay. Again he was in error, but again he had no way of knowing it. The truth probably is that Clay regarded the whole business of appealing to the voters with more than a touch of disdain; he could do it, since it was necessary, but his preference was to work with leaders only and to leave the appeal to the masses to be directed by underlings. What they did he regarded as something entirely aloof from his own activities. If they chose, in the politicians' expressive if inelegant phrase, to "fight with stink-pots and contagious diseases," he would disapprove, but hold his nose and endure it, for he could not believe that the appeal to the rabble was the appeal that counted. He played a large part in directing the campaign on the higher levels and doubtless he thought honestly that that was the real campaign.

The result of the balloting therefore was a shock to him on more than personal grounds. His bewilderment was not pretense. He knew that the Adams administration had been honest and patriotic. He thought that it had been successful. He was aware that most of the attacks made on it in Congress were essentially fraudulent, trumped up by men whose anxiety was not over the ostensible issue but over the next election. He could perceive no reason for its repudiation, except that the voters had been deceived by self-seeking demagogues; and if the voters could be so deceived, then the end of the republic was in plain sight.

The trouble with this reasoning was that it ignored the point on which the people had not been deceived. This was the point that the Adams administration had been put in power not by the clearly expressed will of the people, but by the will of a group of politicians in Washington, and chiefly by the will of Henry Clay. Thus the virtues of that administration became irrelevant. True, Mr. Clay had only exercised his constitutional powers. True, he may have believed that he was giving the country the best President available. But the country believed that he had defied its will; and that it did not propose to tolerate. The era of the rule of the "best people" was definitely over; henceforth the people who were less than "the best" were taking a hand in the game hitherto played by gentlemen in Washington.

In extenuation of Clay's blindness, it may be pointed out that this was only the second time in history that the phenomenon had occurred; and on the other occasion, when the second-best people had intervened in behalf of Jefferson, even then they had done no more than transfer power from one group of gentlemen to another group composed of men of a very similar type. John Adams and Thomas Jefferson belonged to the same small world; when age was upon them, and the battles were all over, they discovered it and showed it to the world in the series of wise and charming letters that passed between them. This revolt of 1828, however, swept power away not from one group but from the entire class that had hitherto been the ruling class. Never before had it happened in this country, and it was impossible for it to happen in any other.

But against Clay's sagacity must be registered the fact that other and smoother men understood what was happening and took precautionary measures. Conspicuous among them was Calhoun. The astute Vice-President perceived two things, neither of which could have given him any comfort. He marked the new and aggressive spirit that filled the country. He knew that it was not demonstrated in politics alone, nor principally, but was bursting forth in a dozen directions. It was shown in the vigor with which the West was being subdued. It was shown in the mushroom growth of the cities. It was shown in the amazing industrial development that was altering the national economy with startling speed. A new and different America, a sort of

America that George Washington had never dreamed, was already in existence.

The second fact that presented itself to the mind of Mr. Calhoun was the fact that his own section, the South, was less affected by the new spirit than any other. In certain ways this may have given him satisfaction, for he was growing steadily more conservative, but it did not escape him that continuance of the process meant eventual isolation; and this he regarded with increasing anxiety.

General Jackson was plainly the people's man and before the Adams administration was half over Calhoun had not the slightest doubt that the Tennesseean would win the next election. General Jackson was also the leader of the West as Calhoun was of the South, and as Adams was of New England. Neither Calhoun nor the South had much to hope from New England; their interests lay too far apart. More than that, Adams' rigidity, austerity and fanatical devotion to principle were duplicated in Calhoun, as well as some measure of the New Englander's bitterness. They were too much alike to form a strong and permanent alliance. Therefore fairly early in the administration Calhoun began quietly shifting over to Jackson. Adams and Clay, of course, saw nothing in this but politics, and it was a good move, politically; but it was also a good move for the southern leader as a statesman, and not merely as a politician. The isolation that Calhoun feared was in fact encircling the South, and it was more sensible for her to seek to make terms with the West than with New England, for she had more in common with the West.

The mid-term elections bore out his predictions. The Jacksonians swept Congress and the bull-like voice of Thomas Hart Benton kept up a continuous roar against the administration. Calhoun moved faster. Then the disgraceful logrolling of the Tariff of Abominations came to give him all the justification he needed. Not until the twentieth century was the country to see another tariff comparable to that one, either in the scandalous way in which it was put together, or in its ruinous effects on essential interests. Most regions suffered in some degree from this almost fabulously bad law, but the South suffered worse than any other; and although plenty of Jacksonians—now beginning to call themselves Jacksonian Democrats, or merely Democrats—including Benton, of Missouri, were far from blameless in connection with it, the thing furnished a perfect excuse for any Southerner to abandon the administration altogether. Mr. Calhoun accordingly abandoned it, and gracefully accepted the nomination for Vice-President on the Democratic ticket, being swept into office on the Jackson landslide.

Equally astute, although by no means as well justified by reasons of statecraft, was Mr. Van Buren. Quite early Mr. Van Buren perceived that Jackson would inevitably win, and the Red Fox could imagine no better, if, indeed, any other, reason for transferring his allegiance to that leader. Mr. Van Buren, be it repeated for emphasis, never argued with a fact. That the country was for Jackson was a fact. Therefore Mr. Van Buren was for him, too.

Nobody ever accused Martin Van Buren of being a profound thinker, and that he gave much consideration to the deeper significance of the changes that were coming over the country is improbable. But far better than Clay, better than Calhoun, better than any other man of that generation, he understood the new political methods that were applicable to the new situation. The reason was simple. The changes had affected New York earlier and more rapidly than any other State, and Van Buren had been playing politics in New York State all his life. He had observed at close range the operations of such masters of political chicanery as Aaron Burr and George Clinton, and he was not unacquainted with some of the shifty expedients adopted by a vastly greater man, but a cunning politician, Alexander Hamilton. He therefore did not merely shift his allegiance to Jackson. He took over the Jackson campaign and managed it with superb adroitness. It is improbable that he handled any of the dirt, personally. He was too shrewd for that. But it is at least equally improbable that he was profoundly revolted by the use of any method whatever that promised to bring in the votes.

Clay, of course, could not have shifted his allegiance if he had wished to do so. He was a member of the administration and to make any attempt to curry favor with Jackson would have been to play the Judas. But he had not the slightest desire to do anything of the sort. He had no conception of the power that was behind Jackson and no comprehension of the source of that power. He honestly believed that the people had been tricked into supporting the military chieftain, and confidently looked forward to their discovery of the trickery. The fact that it was he, Clay, who had tricked the people was beyond his power to grasp.

Therefore he had to stand and take it. Even after the election he did not understand fully what had happened. Knowing the honesty of his own course, he was incapable of seeing how it looked to others. The cry of "Bargain and corruption!" he had regarded contemptuously as political trickery; he could not realize that others actually believed it. But Jackson did. Moreover, the General's erroneous belief that Clay had been personally responsible for some of the filth thrown at him, and at his wife, during the campaign led him to the conclusion that the Secretary of State was capable of any depth of rascality. Jackson had determined to make Martin Van Buren Secretary of State, but Van Buren was Governor of New York and could not immediately vacate that office to come to Washington. Therefore on the morning of Inauguration Day the President-elect called in Colonel James A. Hamilton, gave him a written order to take charge of the State Department pending the arrival of Mr. Van Buren and ordered him not to attend the inaugural ceremonies but to proceed to Clay's office and, as soon as he heard the cannon shot announcing the inauguration instantly take over. What General Jackson feared Clay might do, Colonel Hamilton would never reveal; but it is evident that the newcomer to the White House had the lowest opinion of the personal, as well as the political character of the Kentuckian.

So Clay went into retirement for two and a half years, beaten, but still unaware of what had struck him.

Calhoun, as Vice-President, was debarred by the rules of the game from taking a very active part.

Of the Triumvirate, only Webster was left on active duty, so to speak. The others were active enough, in all conscience, but they were practicing politics, not statecraft, and while the story of their activities in these years is diverting and in many ways illuminating, it is aside from the purpose of this inquiry.

It was during this temporary absence of both his great colleagues that Daniel Webster rose to be the dominant figure in parliamentary history that he has remained ever since.

There seems to be a stage in the development of every democracy when it falls for a time completely under the thrall of the Silver Tongue. Of course, mankind is never entirely immune to the enchantment of the orator's personality, but fashions in eloquence change, and neither the eighteenth century nor the twentieth yielded or yields to sonority as promptly as the nineteenth did. The United States is now by an appreciable margin the oldest democracy, for democratic rule in Great Britain dates from the Reform Bill of 1832, and that of France is the age of the Third Republic. Our last great Silver Tongue was William J. Bryan, and even he was more celebrated for his ideas than for his oratory after 1896. France, a younger democracy, had Briand until a few years ago, and Great Britain still has Churchill and Lloyd George, although neither seems to possess the old magic. Woodrow Wilson's eloquence was of a different type—harder, sharper and more complex than that of the nineteenth century. On the other side, Patrick Henry's was harsher and simpler. The most effective contemporary American speaker, the second Roosevelt, is a radio speaker, which is to say, he practices a completely different art, one element of which is studious avoidance of what passed for eloquence a century ago.

But when Andrew Jackson came to power, oratory was in its Golden Age. Curiously enough, Jackson did not speak very well. He had neither the voice, the figure nor the stage presence of an orator. True, he had been known to speak with such effectiveness as to freeze a column of mutinous troops into stone, but the text of his address on such an occasion was, to put it delicately, unsuitable for publication. The old soldier climbed to really great eloquence only in the profane language.

But the country swarmed with great, or at least much-admired, orators. The fire of John Randolph's genius was flickering out, but Benton, Cass, Everett, Grundy, Hayne were all at the height of their powers and the country resounded to rolling periods. Yet in a country swarming with orators none, by general agreement, compared with the mighty trio, Webster, Clay and Calhoun; and *primus inter pares* was Webster.

His art is worth more than merely passing attention, both for itself and for its significance as an American phenomenon. It was by no means as effective a political weapon as Clay's. Never once did Webster drive a crowd into such transports of delight as Clay did on half a dozen occasions; yet Clay's speeches were rarely, if ever, used as declamations by schoolboys of later generations, whereas Webster's have been heard in every schoolhouse in the land. Clay's speeches, read today, seem pedestrian, if not intolerably dull, while the purple and gold of Webster's rhetoric are as gorgeous as ever. But Clay had an electric personality that was better, on the platform, than sonority; his angular figure, his ugly face, his inordinate length of leg and arm might seem, at first glance, to render ridiculous any comparison between him and the imposing Webster, massive, handsome, the personification of dignity. But Clay had, like Lincoln, the elusive quality that made men forget his outward aspect—nay, like him the better for his lack of beauty—and when he was on the platform he was utterly plausible, completely persuasive.

If Webster could not appeal to the emotions as successfully as Clay, neither could he appeal to the intelligence as successfully as Calhoun. The South Carolinian's logic, indeed, was perfect; Calhoun has never been answered yet, as far as his main argument is concerned. As a very young man he permitted his jingoism to carry him into untenable positions, and in later life he was capable of falling, in a heated moment, into such absurdities as the famous declaration that slavery was "a positive good." But his prepared addresses to the Senate were usually

WEBSTER REPLYING TO HAYNE

"The political effect was prodigious."

"Sun of Intellectual light & liberty,
stand ye still, in masterly inactivity,
that the italian of Carolina may continue
to hold negroes & plant Cotton till the
day of Judgment!"

CALHOUN AS JOSHUA, COMMANDING THE SUN TO STAND STILL

"His conscience was clear . . ."

invulnerable, as far as their logical reasoning is concerned, while those of Webster were rarely so.

Webster, however, had two qualities which neither of his great rivals possessed, and these two enabled him to hold his own, and more than hold his own, against them. One was a really superb ear. Few Americans have appreciated as keenly as he did the sound of the English language; few have known half as well how to take advantage of its rhythms, its stresses, its tonic accent. A speech of Webster's was a musical experience; and intelligent men, when they analyzed it after hearing it and found that it really meant something, tended to ascribe to it, in their astonishment, a much greater profundity than it really possessed.

The second quality that gave Webster tremendous power over the minds of Americans was his singular ability to bestow upon emotionalism the aspect of philosophy. The classical example of this came in January, 1830, when Webster reached the apogee of his fame with the unthinking. This was the occasion of his immortal "reply" to Hayne, the South Carolinian who was occupying what everyone regarded as Calhoun's seat in the Senate, while Calhoun was occupying the Vice-President's chair.

The curious and interesting thing is that Webster's reply to Hayne was not at all a reply to Hayne, but so intensely American was it that it served Webster's purpose better than any possible reply could have done. Hayne had made a long and closely reasoned argument against the Tariff of Abominations. He proved beyond a reasonable doubt that the thing could have no other result than to reduce the South to economic serfdom. He prophesied exactly what happened in the century that followed his speech—prophesied it with an accuracy that is little short of uncanny. He exposed mercilessly the fallacy of the whole protectionist argument. He foresaw and foretold the exploitation of the South and the West precisely as it occurred. It was to this argument that Webster made his famous reply; and the substance of that reply is summed up in its closing words: "liberty and union, now and forever, one and inseparable."

As far as its bearing on Hayne's argument was concerned, he

might just as well have recited the multiplication table; but its political effect was prodigious. Emotionally, New England and, to a lesser extent, the rest of the North, wished to believe in the Tariff of Abominations, because it afforded an opportunity for the East and North to exploit the West and South; therefore when Webster linked up the tariff with human freedom, the exploiters found themselves suddenly elevated from the status of robbers to that of crusaders. Naturally, they regarded it as a great speech. So, indeed, it was—a downright miraculous speech. Any speech that can convert grand larceny into a virtue unquestionably deserves to rank with the great oratorical efforts of all time.

But it was not only, nor mainly, in the debate with Hayne that Webster did the work that proved more lasting by far than anything accomplished either by Henry Clay or by John C. Calhoun. In countless other speeches, in legislation he introduced, most of all in quiet work in committee rooms and lobbies, Webster labored assiduously and, in the end, successfully to forward the theory of Alexander Hamilton that this country really belongs to "the rich and well-born." The New Englander, however, was somewhat less fastidious than the Jamaican; he, apparently, would have been quite content to eliminate the "well-born." Perhaps because his origin, while not exactly exalted, was somewhat less obscure than that of Hamilton, he never betrayed any noticeable respect for aristocracy. But his respect for plutocracy was profound.

Because Webster was the first conspicuous representative of the moneyed interest in the Senate, democrats of the violent type have been inclined to accuse him of hypocrisy. This is, however, a somewhat intolerant assumption. There have always been, and there are today, plenty of men who believe in all sincerity that possession of money, while it may not confer virtue, is prima facie evidence of virtue. The widespread acceptance of the democratic dogma has cowed most of them into silence, but it has convinced few, if any, and occasionally there is still to be found one bold enough to speak his mind. Few rational men would accuse the late E. W. Howe, of Kansas, of hypocrisy, yet he boldly proclaimed his belief that possession of money indicates, in the absence of evidence to the contrary, industry, frugality and intelligence in the possessor. Ed Howe may have been hopelessly romantic, but he was no hypocrite.

It is hard to see why Daniel Webster may not have been a man of the same general type. Grant that he was more intelligent than Howe, and you must still take into consideration that he had seen far less than later generations have seen of the way in which wealth is more frequently won by piracy, or by luck, or by a combination of the two than by industry and frugality. More than that, in the early days of the Industrial Revolution it was true that industry, frugality and intelligence would more often than not win a man at least a competence, if not wealth. It was still the day of the small entrepreneur, when any man with a good mind and good health could set up in business for himself with a fair chance of success.

At the same time, even at the moment when Webster made his reply to Hayne, the assumption that money is prima facie evidence of character was a pretty shallow assumption. The fact that Webster made it is incontrovertible evidence that he never was a man of the first order. But as between the essentially shallow man and the conscious hypocrite there is a wide difference; and there is no convincing evidence that Webster belongs on the less reputable side of that division.

But as the first Senatorial chargé d'affaires of Big Business Webster established a political function that has outlasted almost everything his illustrious colleagues accomplished. Succeeding generations time and again have seen Congress without leaders worthy of the name, without real parliamentarians, but never without a representative of the business interests in the Senate. It does not follow, however, that the advent of Webster marked the beginning of a period of moral decay. It was simply that not until the rise of industrialism did business, and especially manufacturing, become sufficiently well integrated and differentiated to require a representative in the Senate. In Alexander Hamilton's time "the rich and well-born" consisted largely of planters, with merchants coming more and more into the foreground and with finance slowly gathering power. The sharpness of the present divisions between agriculture, commerce, manufacturing, and finance had not been established. Hamilton could argue plausibly that he was representing the true interest of Thomas Jefferson as much as that of Robert Morris, or John Hancock.

Webster's lasting contribution to American politics was his demonstration to successful manufacturers and bankers of how valuable an able friend in the Senate could be to them. The lesson was learned thoroughly, and the acquisition of Senators has ever since been regarded as one of the primary objectives of collective business. Of course "acquisition" is by no means a synonym for "purchase." The opinion to the contrary of muckrakers notwithstanding, the outright purchase of legislative votes has always been disapproved and opposed by astute American business men. Nor is it a question either of price, or of tenderness of conscience; it is, rather, a matter of common sense. A bribed legislator is rarely worth the money. What Big Business, and every other special interest, needs is a legislator who is not consciously dishonest, one who believes that in serving his special interest he is serving the country. Such men are easy to find and frequently easy to elect; they are usually efficient and sometimes extremely able, nor is there any danger that a disastrous scandal may at any time destroy their work.

The first and greatest of this type was Daniel Webster. Some may be scandalized by the implication that he was not consciously dishonest. They will cite the fact that he consistently borrowed right and left, and was careless about repaying. They will cite the fact that he took $32,000 from the Bank of the United States, while it was under fire in the Senate. Above all, they will cite that famous letter to Nicholas Biddle, president of the Bank, while the fight over removal of the government deposits was raging: "I believe my retainer has not been renewed or *refreshed* as usual. If it be wished that my relation to the Bank should be continued it may be well to send me the usual retainers." That these were the acts of a thoroughly honest man cannot be seriously maintained.

But that they prove that Webster was consciously collecting bribes is by no means so certain. Against it, but frequently omitted from the calculation is the factor of the man's colossal vanity. Never in his life did he underestimate the value of his services to any client; he may have believed sincerely that he was being ridiculously underpaid for the value he was giving, and he may have been right, at that. The fact that he had already sold his services to the people when he drew his salary as a United States Senator, and had, therefore, no right to resell them, affected him not at all; and had the point been raised, he would have considered it mere casuistry. As for the people, he believed that in protecting the rich he was protecting them; for he harbored all the fear of the people that, a hundred years later, could throw a rich man's club into a frenzy of excitement over the mildest sort of social legislation, not from fear of the legislation itself, but from fear that it might prove to be the camel's nose thrust into the tent of privilege. If his labors in behalf of the general welfare were highly beneficial to certain individuals, why should not those individuals share the benefits with him who had brought them about? When he wrote that letter to Nick Biddle it may be that Mr. Webster was disturbed by gnawing doubts of Nick's honesty, seeing that he had not promptly furnished the retainer which the tribune of the people had richly earned.

Yet in spite of his curious conception of the position of a representative of the people, Webster seems to have had a keener conception of what was behind Andrew Jackson than either of his great colleagues. He never made the mistake of assuming that the violent old man in the White House was a mere political accident, and that the people would repudiate him as soon as gentlemen of intelligence and education pointed out the error of his ways. Webster sensed an elemental force in Jackson. Perhaps he never clearly understood its nature, but he perceived its existence and understood something of its strength; therefore he neatly avoided anything that would bring him directly in its path. He opposed Jackson, but in a carefully impersonal way. He denounced the President's policies, but never the man. So he never drew upon his own head the blasting wrath that fell upon Clay and Calhoun. Incidentally, Webster thereby demonstrated the error of the opinion, long current, that Jackson was unable to discriminate between political and personal opposition.

However, Webster could make so little headway against Old Hickory that not even the delightful position of being incontestably the greatest man in Congress could compensate for his futility; so, before the end of 1831, he was writing Clay urging him to return to the Senate[2] and to become head of the anti-Jackson party. This was not magnanimity on Webster's part, but a triumph of common sense over personal vanity. He would have preferred to head the party himself, but with that strange sense of the movement of the tide he realized that he was not the type to bring down such a popular idol as Jackson. Clay was the one hope.

In the meantime, political disaster had overtaken the Vice-President of the United States. Ever since 1819 John C. Calhoun had been living over a powder house, and now a spark was dropped into it, not by accident.

The truth of the Cabinet discussion after the Florida campaign was suddenly revealed to the President.

It was the work of Major William B. Lewis. Until 1830 Andrew Jackson was under the false impression that it was Crawford who had tried to have him cashiered and that Calhoun and Adams had labored together to save him. So content was he with Calhoun that he had stuffed his Cabinet with the Vice-President's men, notably Branch, Secretary of the Navy, Ingham, of the Treasury, and Berrien, Attorney-General. But Calhoun proved a source of weakness, rather than of strength, to the administration. He and his party were obviously drifting more and more toward nullification and Jackson was growing uneasy. Then the storm broke over the absurd Peggy Eaton affair, and Floride Calhoun was one of the first to send Peg to Coventry. Jackson got the idea that the whole business was engineered by

[2] Schurz, vol. i, p. 347.

Clay³ assisted by the collusion of Calhoun. He was therefore in the right mood to believe pretty much anything to the discredit of the Vice-President. This was the moment the wily Major Lewis chose to start a conversation in the President's hearing regarding Calhoun's course in 1819. Jackson had just returned from the famous Jefferson's Birthday dinner at which the Calhoun men had endeavored to entangle him with nullification by making him listen to a long series of toasts, poisonously nullificationist in tone; but he had smashed the scheme with his own toast, "Our Federal union—it must be preserved." In his thunderous mood the careful negligent remarks of Lewis⁴ caught his attention and he demanded a full explanation. This involved a great deal of letter writing, interviewing and complicated politics, but by May, 1830, the President had the essential facts, and Calhoun's name went on the list of the proscribed.

This is usually cited as an example of the way in which Jackson's personal antipathies were permitted to sway his political

³ As a matter of fact, there is no evidence that Clay had the slightest connection with the Eaton affair, except to enjoy it hugely. Eaton, Secretary of War, had married Margaret O'Neal, daughter of a tavern keeper in Washington. Scandalmongers said she had been his mistress before the marriage and the ladies of the Cabinet refused to receive her, to the vast indignation of Jackson, who remembered the cruel slanders of his own wife, in 1828. There is not much reliable evidence to convict Peggy O'Neal of adultery, but there is plenty to convict her of something far worse, to wit, the offense of being above her position. She was lowborn, yet had the audacity to be vivacious, witty and extraordinarily attractive to men. Therefore her case was hopeless from the beginning, even with the violent support of the President. Clay did not start the scandal, but he did laugh at the discomfiture of the administration, which Jackson never forgave.

⁴ Nobody but Parton seems ever to have taken Lewis seriously, and Parton took him much too seriously, at his own valuation, in fact. Marquis James, in *Andrew Jackson: Portrait of a President*, handles Lewis with great severity, rating him far below the rather egregious Donelson, the President's secretary. Yet Lewis had built a superb political machine before either Amos Kendall or Martin Van Buren came into the Jackson camp; Lewis was completely loyal to his chief to the end; and Lewis apparently never profited, or tried to profit personally from his services. The methods of political organization Lewis devised were taken over by Van Buren and remain standard American political practice to this day. James thinks, on grounds not very clear, that Lewis swelled up in his own conceit and finally became a nuisance to Jackson; but it may be argued just as plausibly that Van Buren and Donelson found him annoying and contrived to get rid of him. In any event, the man was an important contributor to American political practice, and therefore a potent figure in our national history.

policies, but there is a good deal of evidence that the truth is rather in the other direction—that Jackson seized upon personal antipathies as excuses for political acts that he had determined upon regardless of the personal element. He had been suspicious of Calhoun for some time and had reasons for desiring a break with the Vice-President before Lewis' studied carelessness led him to the truth about the Cabinet meeting of 1819; but this affair gave him his first chance to pose as the outraged victim of deception.

The Peggy Eaton business, too, may fall into the same category. There is no reason to doubt that Jackson was genuinely indignant over the treatment accorded her; but there were several excellent reasons for kicking out the Cabinet, the first, and most important, being the fact that it was full of Calhoun's agents. This was not, however, a good reason to give the country. The Peggy Eaton affair may have been absurd, on its face, but at least it put the President in the position of a valiant defender of a woman attacked by gossip, and while this position may evoke snickers from the sophisticated, among the common people—at least in 1830—it was a strong one. A little later, in the Bank fight, Jackson produced, as unimpeachable documentary records show, appalling outbursts of rage that were wholly synthetic. More than once, after fairly blasting a delegation off its feet and sending it pelting out of the door, he sat down and coolly filled his pipe, chuckling over the excellence of his own performance as the raging madman.[5] Be that as it may, the fact is evident that Andrew Jackson's personal indignations often served his political schemes admirably.

However, the President's motives are less important than the event. Calhoun was under the ban, and this eliminated Calhoun definitely as a possible successor of Jackson in 1832. It did more. It eliminated him as a contender for the Presidency in any capacity for at least eight years, possibly longer. It was already fairly evident that Jackson would endeavor to succeed himself in 1832 and the opposition was already rallying around Henry Clay as his opponent. If Clay succeeded, he would reasonably ex-

[5] For example, see James, *op. cit.*, p. 366.

pect to remain in the White House eight years. If he failed, he would still be in the logical position to oppose Jackson's choice in 1840. It was plain that Mr. Calhoun might as well give up all thought of the Presidency for a long time to come, probably forever.

Here was one of the turning points of American history, if the individual really affects the course of history. This is the development that drove Calhoun definitely into sectionalism, thereby giving sectionalism its greatest leader. He had started his political career as a thoroughgoing nationalist. Emotionally, he preferred nationalism to the end of his days, and as a logician he realized that any man who aspires to national leadership must preserve the nationalist point of view. But from the moment of his break with Andrew Jackson the field of national leadership was closed to him. If he did not realize it immediately, it was soon borne in upon him. Only sectional leadership could be his henceforth, and remorseless logic dictated that a sectional leader should develop a sectional viewpoint.

Calhoun's development probably would have pursued approximately the same course without the intervention of the tricky Major Lewis. A break was on the cards, and Jackson would doubtless have found some other pretext to make it, even if this one had not served. But the ingenious Lewis does furnish us with a convenient date to mark the transformation of John C. Calhoun from one of the Union's strong defenders into one of its disruptive influences.

Henry Clay, summoned back to Washington to do battle with the wild man, entered upon his campaign with a serene and foolish confidence.

Even in Kentucky there were ominous portents. Everyone understood that he was returning to the Senate to fight Andrew Jackson, and although the State was intensely proud of its distinguished representative, there was murmuring against sending him back for that purpose. Instead of being instantly and unanimously returned by a delighted legislature, he found himself sternly opposed; indeed, in the Senate he lost by one vote to Richard M. Johnson and on the combined vote of House and Senate skinned through by only nine ballots in a total of one hundred and thirty-eight.[6]

Still he refused to hear the roll of thunder. Still he chose to believe that this man Jackson was President by virtue of political trickery, and not by virtue of the profound belief of the common people that he, above any other man in public life, was really their friend. Therefore Mr. Clay assumed that, since the man had won by political trickery, by counter-trickery he might be overthrown. It was a sound enough conclusion had he been right in his premise; but with a false premise, the sounder the reasoning, the further it takes the luckless logician from the truth.

The campaign of 1832, which really centered in the fight about the Bank of the United States, is of no real importance in this story and might be dismissed with a line save for its demonstration of the collapse of the statesmanship of Henry Clay. This was the occasion on which he most conspicuously abandoned statecraft and sank to the level of tricky politics; hence it is essential to a true picture of the man.

Fate seems to have a way of picking some men to be great and denying them the capacity to be anything less than their best selves; and of laying upon others the destiny of being small, visiting severe punishment upon them when they attempt to rise above their true level. Henry Clay and Martin Van Buren are cases in point. Whenever he attacked problems of statecraft, Clay was remarkably successful. Even the grandiose scheme of the American System was defeated by factional opposition in Congress, not by any error on the part of its proponent; and at critical moments when the fate of the nation was wavering in the balance, Clay never failed. But on every occasion when he abandoned statecraft and descended to slick politics, he took a terrible beating. He was marked out for greatness by destiny, and only his efforts to be small were ruinous.

Van Buren, on the other hand, seems to have been marked

[6] Epes Sargent, *Life of Henry Clay*, p. 133.

from the cradle for smallness. As long as he apparently never gave a thought to anything higher than tricky, and usually dirty, politics, he marched from triumph to triumph, arriving at last at the summit of political ambition, the Presidency of the United States. But immediately after his installation, he was confronted with an appalling crisis, the great panic of 1837, and in the face of that disaster he rose above his ward heeler's instincts and took the course of an honest man and a statesman. The firmness, the courage and the intelligence with which Van Buren faced his hour of trial astonished his friends, confounded his enemies, and ruined Van Buren. Hurled into outer darkness by a Fate which will permit no tomtit to play the role of an eagle, he reverted to his old pettifogging and by trickery and double-dealing so far retrieved his political fortunes that he became once more a serious contender for the Presidency; but at the critical moment, on the question of slavery, he refused to equivocate and spoke up resolutely for human freedom. Once more he touched greatness—and suffered the fate of Uzzah when he laid impious hands on the Ark of the Covenant. He was destined to be small, and only his efforts to be great were ruinous.

Clay, in the campaign of 1832 devised a scheme that looked invulnerable, and that would have been invulnerable had the situation been what he thought it was. The public resentment of the Tariff of Abominations was so intense that some sort of tariff bill obviously had to be framed. The charter of the Bank of the United States was to expire by limitation in 1836, and there was a good deal of opposition to the Bank, but not among people whom Clay deemed important. Clay's scheme was to get that charter renewed immediately, so that important people would have no more to expect of Jackson; and at the same time to present to him a tariff bill so villainous that he would have to veto it, thus leaving the Tariff of Abominations, on the whole satisfactory to important people, in effect. Thus Jackson would be weakened from two directions and Clay, with the solid support of important people, would win in a walk.

From the standpoint of statecraft, it was an appalling scheme. It dragged the fiscal agency of the government, and with it the whole currency system, into the politics of a Presidential campaign; and it cynically sacrificed the economic interests of the South and West by denying them any real tariff reform. But from the standpoint of politics it looked smart. Clay assumed that Jackson would have to sign the bill rechartering the Bank, on pain of wrecking the whole financial system, and even if he signed the tariff bill, the hollowness of that pseudo reform would be made plain enough in the campaign.

But Clay omitted from his calculations the most important factor, to wit, the amazing political astuteness of Andrew Jackson. He omitted it for a simple, but sufficient reason—he did not believe in its existence. Jackson relied on the people, and in Clay's opinion this was not astuteness, but folly. Therefore, even when Jackson, instead of vetoing the tariff and signing the Bank bill, neatly reversed the process, signing the tariff and vetoing the Bank bill, Clay did not understand what had happened. On the contrary, he was happily assured that the old General was even crazier than he had believed. So certain was he that now he had Jackson exactly where he wanted him, that his enthusiasm swept along all his colleagues, including even Nicholas Biddle. The banker termed the message "a manifesto of anarchy" and, incredible as it seems, actually had printed and circulated at the Bank's expense thirty thousand copies.

"When the laws undertake," declared the message, "to add to . . . natural and just advantages artificial distinctions . . . to make the rich richer, and the potent more powerful, the humble members of society, the farmers, mechanics and laborers, who have neither the time nor the means of securing like favors to themselves, have a right to complain of the injustice of their government. Its evils exist only in its abuses. If it would confine itself to equal protection, and, as heaven does its rains, shower its favors alike on the high and the low, the rich and the poor, it would be an unqualified blessing. In the act before me, there seems to be a wide and unnecessary departure from these just principles."

This was the doctrine the Bank, in its folly, spent its money to circulate.

Clay's triumph was short-lived. Instead of having Jackson where he wanted him, it soon became apparent that Jackson had *him*. As for the tariff, all the South and West could see was that the Tariff of Abominations had been repealed. As for the Bank, the important people who were its friends had everything except the votes; they were to be found among the unimportant people who hated Nicholas Biddle and all his works. When the dust settled, Jackson had 219 electoral votes and Clay had 49. It was catastrophic. Even Adams, in 1828, had not taken such a drubbing, for he had carried eight States for a total of 83 electoral votes against the General's 178. Betraying the farmers and wrecking the Bank had been worse than useless; instead of elevating Clay to the Presidency they left him one of the worst-beaten candidates who ever ran.

But he never knew what hit him. To the end of his life he did not realize that the people, while weak on issues, possess an extraordinary perspicacity with regard to men. Perhaps a man who cannot get that through his head is thereby disqualified to sit in the President's chair.

CHAPTER XIII

ON REPARATIONS

*Setting forth how Mr. Clay, appalled at having conjured up the devil,
exorcised him with great labor*

PERHAPS somewhere in the fastnesses of New England, or at the back of the remoter prairies there may yet be elementary schools where pupils are stuffed with the misinformation that the Civil War was fought on the one issue of Negro slavery; but surely such schools must be few. Elsewhere that notion has long since gone with the wind; indeed, in recent years some of the more radical historians have been advancing, at least by implication, the theory that the part played in it by slavery was negligible; that is a little extreme, although if it were limited to the processes by which the war was precipitated, excluding the development of the conflict after hostilities began, a pretty good case could be made out in support of the theory that slavery played an unimportant part. Certainly Lincoln was almost painfully anxious to repudiate the idea that he was attacking slavery; and Jefferson Davis was no less anxious to convince the world that it was not primarily the "peculiar institution" that he was defending. Both were human, therefore both may have been lying; but it seems improbable.

In any event, whatever may have been true in 1861, slavery was not the primary issue in 1833, when civil war was escaped by a margin so narrow that men were inclined to regard the man who patched up the differences as little less than a magician. The doctrine happened to be advanced on this occasion by slave-owners, but that there was no necessary connection between nullification and slave-owning is sufficiently proved by the fact the South Carolinians borrowed it from the New Englanders, who had advanced it with great vigor only nineteen years earlier. Hartford had ceased to be a slave market long before 1814 nor was the Essex Junto composed of fire-eating cavaliers.

The Ordinance of Nullification, passed by the legislature of South Carolina November 24, 1832, to take effect on the first day of February of the following year, was no defense of slavery. It was a protest against a tariff little, if any, less infamous than the Tariff of Abominations. In an important sense it was Henry Clay's tariff. He did not write all the schedules, to be sure, but he had laid down the law to his colleagues in what John Quincy Adams thought a "peremptory and dogmatic" manner, and when someone complained that a tariff of the sort he proposed would infuriate the South, he retorted, according to Adams, that "to preserve, maintain, and strengthen the American System he would defy the South, the President and the devil." Well, the incantation worked. With thunder and lightning and a terrific smell of brimstone, Mephistopheles appeared—the leering, red devil of civil war, and Faustus Clay was appalled.

Henry Clay had been playing a game, the game of Presidential politics, but the men opposite him were in deadly earnest. If ever there were two figures in public life whom no rational man would have called frivolous, they were Andrew Jackson and John C. Calhoun. They understood Clay's maneuvers perfectly, and they were not amused. Jackson had seen with the clear eye of a strategist the trap Clay had laid for him in posing the dilemma of the Bank and the Tariff; and although he had escaped neatly, he resented the trap. Calhoun had perceived equally clearly that Clay was cynically ready to sacrifice the whole agricultural population to the exigencies of his game; and he was determined to force the thing to an issue then and there. He resigned the Vice-Presidency and Hayne promptly resigned his seat in the Senate to make room for him in that arena of battle. Clay realized, to his horror, that both of them actually meant business.

The drama of this combat, accentuated by the grim determination of the principals, tends to obscure the personal stresses under which the men labored. It is generally assumed that Jackson, at least, found a stern joy in it, and that Calhoun was filled with a sort of cold, Calvinistic fury. James[1] has demonstrated fairly conclusively that behind his belligerent front the President was tortured with anxiety; and there is no reason whatever to doubt Calhoun's repeated asseverations that he was driven into his course against his every emotional instinct and in defiance of his personal interest. Benton[2] and others might have been sincere in their expressed belief that Calhoun was playing the great White House game in supporting nullification; but at this distance it is easy to see that if he played the game at all, it was not when he went into the nullification scheme, but when he consented to its withdrawal.

The terrible sincerity of Calhoun was, indeed, the dynamite in the situation. Calhoun was an upright man; he believed with all his soul that any man, conscious of the purity of his intentions and of the righteousness of his cause, ought to go ahead regardless of consequences. He was now fifty-one years old, yet life had not taught him—it never did teach him—that the man who is absolutely certain he is right, is inevitably wrong; for in politics, at least, there is no certainty of being right. Calhoun was not the man to play with paradox. He was a serious man, and the profound frivolity of human existence was utterly beyond his comprehension; he was a strong man, and the prevailing weakness of humanity earned only his contempt; he was a righteous man, and so never carried the uneasy conscience that endows publicans and sinners with a humility out of which arises, sometimes, a wisdom transcending that of the virtuous.

Two years earlier[3] he had exposed the whole difficulty in words whose truth has only grown clearer with the passage of time. "The great dissimilarity and, as I must add, contrariety of interests in our country . . . are so great that they cannot be subjected to the unchecked will of a majority of the whole without defeating the great end of government, without which it is a curse—justice."

With this there is little disagreement today. The consistent

[1] Marquis James. *Andrew Jackson: Portrait of a President.* Chapter **xiv**, *passim.*
[2] See, for example, his *Thirty Years' View,* Chapter lxxxiv.
[3] In the *Address to the People of South Carolina,* dated at Fort Hill, July 26, 1831.

THE SENATE IN 1849   "The great debate was heard by a brilliant audience."

1. Henry Clay	5. William H. Seward	9. John C. Calhoun	13. Stephen A. Douglas
2. Daniel Webster	6. Millard Fillmore	10. James A. Pearce	14. Pierre Soule
3. Thomas H. Benton	7. William L. Dayton	11. Robert F. Stockton	15. Truman Smith
4. Lewis Cass	8. William M. Gwin	12. Henry S. Foote	16. Salmon P. Chase

17. William R. King	21. Willie P. Mangum	25. Jeremiah Clemens
18. John Bell	22. Samuel Houston	26. Arthur P. Butler
19. James M. Mason	23. John P. Hale	27. John Davis
20. James Cooper	24. Asbury Dickens	28. Dodge (Wis.)

FRATERNAL LOVE

The substance of Mr Clay's letter to his friends :—" My dear whig friends ! You seem to believe that I am too old and feeble, again to be a candidate for the Presidency. You know I never cared to be President, but I have always felt anxious to see the right kind of a man in that high position. Especially do I feel anxious on the present occasion, as there is a strong probability that Mr Webster will receive the nomination. Now, you know, my dear whig friends, that Mr Webster has never acknowledged me as his leader and political idol ; he always would be independent Now, put a quietus upon his hopes. Go in for Fillmore. He is a good easy soul, who does just as I wish him. He has been tried ; he is docile in harness. Mr W. is not ; but will have his own way. Talks much to the public about *availability*. Tell them that, as Mr Fillmore has been tried as President, you know he will answer ; and as Mr. Webster has never been tried, of course he won't answer. I've owed Dan a grudge for twenty years, and now is the time to settle it."

Yours, ever,

H. CLAY.

A POLITICAL CARTOONIST READS BETWEEN THE LINES

exploitation of the South and of the West which Calhoun foresaw has reduced the South to the point at which a President of the United States describes it as the Nation's Economic Problem Number One and the West to the point at which, a few years ago, milk farmers were on the verge of starting a civil war of their own and mortgage-ridden farmers of all sorts were nullifying the decrees, not of a distant Congress, but of their own courts.

What Calhoun was constitutionally incapable of grasping was the fact that reason itself is not infallible in governing an unreasonable world. The South was falling under the oppressor's heel. The South had just cause for resistance. Nullification seemed to be, at the moment, the only way she could prevent exploitation. All this Calhoun proved with irrefutable logic. But he never cast up the account on the other side, because his logic taught him that it is the duty of a righteous man to resist wrong. It was probably beyond his comprehension that this is one reason why a completely righteous man, if there were one, should never be a governor. It certainly is not always the duty of a governor to resist wrong. Lincoln understood the point: "If I could save the Union without freeing any slave, I would do it; and if I could do it by freeing all the slaves, I would do it; and if I could save it by freeing some and leaving others alone, I would also do that," he declared when war had already been raging a year. To say that the responsible head of a nation should not always resist all evil is illogical, but right.

Calhoun was too clear-sighted not to be able to see the logical result of secession. A dozen years earlier he had told John Quincy Adams[4] that if the Union ever split on the slavery question it meant, in his opinion, a reversion of the South "pretty much" to British colonial status. Well, the worst that Calhoun feared has duly come to pass. The Union has been split. The South has been beaten in the field, sacked and pillaged by the conqueror, and for seventy years subjected to ruthless economic exploitation. Yet with it all the Southerner who would express regret today that the section is not a British colony would be re-

[4] See his Diary for February 24, 1820.

garded by his fellow-Southerners as highly eccentric, if not downright insane.

His antagonist, Jackson, was gifted with no such power of prophecy and troubled by no philosophical subtleties whatever. Jackson was simply in a terrible position from which he saw no means of emergence save by plunging straight ahead. He was himself a Southerner and a slaveowner. He believed himself to be a native of Calhoun's own State.[5] The tariff law against which South Carolina was protesting had been devised for his undoing, and he knew it. Emotionally, therefore, he must have been drawn toward Calhoun's side of the controversy.

More than that, when it came to nullification *qua* nullification, there was nothing in it to perturb Jackson. He had looked on with apathy, if not with complacence, as Georgia nullified the judgment of the Supreme Court of the United States in the matter of the Creek Indian lands. Perhaps he did not actually say, "John Marshall has made his decision; now let him enforce it," as his critics asserted; but he thought it, and he acted as if he had said it. Georgia had arrested two white men in the territory held by the Creeks; the Supreme Court ruled that the State had no jurisdiction there, and ordered the men released; Georgia flatly refused to comply, and the President did nothing except warn the Indians that if a collision occurred between them and the whites "the arm of the government is not strong enough" to protect them.

But while nullification of a decision of the Supreme Court moved him little, nullification of the government's power to col-

[5] John Spencer Bassett and Marquis James have both rejected the evidence of Jackson's birth on the North Carolina side of the boundary for the curious reason that this evidence was too well put together. It was presented by a lawyer, with a lawyer's skill in marshaling facts; and it hangs on the memory of a little girl, who was taken along by her mother, one of the neighbors called in at the time of the birth. Bassett rejects testimony from such a source, overlooking the fact that, psychologically, it is the best possible testimony. Among all the witnesses present, the little girl is the only one to whom the event is likely to have been memorable; why should anyone else remember clearly the circumstances connected with the birth of one more child in a poverty-stricken family? Only to the child could it have been tremendously exciting and therefore unforgettable; and the child testified that it took place in the house that stood on the North Carolina side of the line.

lect its revenues moved him powerfully. Jackson was a lawyer, and had been himself a judge, but he was little afflicted with legalism. He cherished none of the legalist's mystic belief in the courts as the arcanum in which rests the sovereignty of the nation. In his eyes the courts were merely implements through which the government acted; and disrespect for one of those implements was not particularly shocking. The active principle of government, to his way of thinking, was not in the judiciary, but in the legislative and executive. He did not believe for a moment that refusal to obey a mandate of the Supreme Court, made in interpreting a contract, was comparable in seriousness to refusal to obey a law passed by Congress and signed by the President. Jackson knew through years of experience that it is perfectly possible to maintain government without courts, but that it is out of the question to maintain courts without government; he believed, therefore, that the complete destruction of the Supreme Court would not necessarily mean the end of the republic, but he realized that destruction of the government's power to enforce its own laws would be the end.

Therefore his thunderous proclamation, issued on December 10, 1832, was sincere in every word. "Fellow-citizens of my native State, let me admonish you . . . I have no discretionary power on the subject . . . disunion by armed force is treason . . . your first magistrate cannot, if he would, avoid the performance of his duty." In the face of this blast Calhoun came to Washington, a journey that Parton likened to Luther's to the Diet of Worms, to take his seat in the Senate. This simple act is enough to give the lie to those who questioned the South Carolinian's physical courage. Jackson had announced that the moment his trusted agent in Charleston, Joel Poinsett, reported an act of violence against the authority of the United States he would seize the chief nullifiers and "hang them as high as Haman."

People afflicted with legalism have belittled this, asserting that there really was no danger to Calhoun. "An empty threat this most certainly was, if it was ever made," asserts Von Holst, scornfully. "Jackson was not now the general commanding in in the wilds of Florida, but President of the United States; and

[215]

Calhoun was not an Arbuthnot or Ambrister, but a senator of the United States."[6] But the fact remains that, Senator or no Senator, Calhoun was a man with a neck that would break; and the fact remains that the President of the United States had at his command men who would have put a rope around that neck without the slightest hesitation; the fact remains, also, that this particular President was one who had seen Georgia slap the Supreme Court in the face and had not been shocked; and the fact remains that his most conspicuous characteristic was his readiness to assume the responsibility for doing whatever he thought was right. If he had given the order, it would have been executed, law or no law, courts or no courts. The evidence that he was incapable of giving it is anything but clear. There is excellent reason for believing that Calhoun actually took his life in his hands when he returned to Washington; and the fact of his return was a fine display of physical courage.

Henry Clay was rendered speechless by these events. Too late he saw the fascinating game turned into deadly earnest. Webster, who had worked with him in framing the iniquitous tariff, was in a fine position. Sonorously and majestically he rallied to the support of the President he had opposed, gaining loud applause for his magnanimity in praising the man who, for once, was doing exactly what Webster wanted done. John Quincy Adams rallied, too, gaining less praise, but deserving more. Adams cared not a straw for the tariff, and it was inexpressibly bitter for him to say a good word for Andrew Jackson; but when the President of the United States was fighting for the Union, there was only one course for an Adams to take, and he took it.

But Henry Clay was in a quandary. He had before him the alternatives of playing the politician safely, or of rising to the stature of a statesman, and incurring risks.

As a politician, his position was excellent. The American System, the thing he had closest at heart, the thing that he regarded as his great contribution to statecraft and to the welfare of the nation, the thing by which he hoped to be remembered, was at stake. By ironical circumstance, his bitterest political foe and a

[6] H. Von Holst, *John C. Calhoun.* p. 104.

man he had come to regard and who had long regarded him as a personal enemy was defending Clay's work, not because he wished to, but because he had to. That defense involved the gravest of risks, and might very easily work the irretrievable ruin of Andrew Jackson.

So to contrive that one's enemy must needs fight one's battle and court destruction in doing so—did politician ever dream anything more perfect? No real risk need be incurred by Clay. It would have been safe for him to follow the course of Webster and Adams, but not even that was necessary. Mr. Van Buren found it convenient to attend to pressing business in New York at this juncture; Clay could have found equally pressing business in Kentucky. After some sharp prodding from the White House, Van Buren put through the New York legislature a resolution of indorsement of the President so watery and weak that Clay might have put through a stronger one in Kentucky without at all committing himself to the Jacksonians. But he was under no compulsion to do anything whatever. As a politician he had only to sit tight and let things ride.

But from the viewpoint of a statesman things were far less pleasant. Clay knew perhaps better than anyone else how weak a position was concealed behind Jackson's bold front. The proclamation had electrified the country for the moment, but if war actually began would that enthusiasm hold? Clay doubted it. Van Buren, frightened half to death, was quite sure it would not, at least in New York. Jackson himself was drearily aware that the roots of nullification struck deep—how deep, he dared not ask himself.

From the military standpoint, the South was strong. Jackson talked of throwing thirty-five thousand men into South Carolina instantly, with fifty thousand behind them, but where were those men to come from? North Carolina, on one side of the trouble center, and Georgia, on the other, were both supporting the President "in principle," as the diplomatists say; but when it came to the point of actually invading their neighbor, there would be powerful opposition in both States. Virginia was already talking of blocking the passage of United States troops across her territory. Indeed, it was far from certain that either New York or Pennsylvania would fight. The military odds against South Carolina were sufficiently heavy to give the nullifiers extreme discomfort; but the psychology of the situation was in her favor. It would be a very nasty war, in any event, and if any considerable portion of the North refused to fight the disruption of the Union would have been certain.

It was the American System against the Union, and it is to the glory of Henry Clay that he hesitated not at all. With the resolution of Abraham in the land of Moriah, he laid the knife to the throat of his brain child and there was no intervening angel to prevent the consummation of the sacrifice.

Since it had to be done, he insisted on doing it himself. Into the House of Representatives, quaking as the lightning blazed and the thunder rolled, rushed Gulian C. Verplanck, of New York, with a bill to reduce the tariff approximately to the level of the tariff of 1816. This would have been surrender unconditional and for that neither Clay nor the country was prepared. However, the introduction of the Verplanck bill gave South Carolina an excuse to back down from her extreme position. The State, taking notice that Congress had tariff legislation under consideration, graciously postponed the date of its contemplated suicide by suspending the Ordinance of Nullification until Congress should act.

"A prompt passage of the bill might have been expected," commented Benton, sourly; "on the contrary, it lingered in the House, under interminable debates on systems and theories, in which ominous signs of conjunction were seen between the two extremes which had been lately pitted against each other, for and against the protective system. The immediate friends of the administration seemed to be the only ones hearty in the support of the bill; but they were no match, in numbers, for those who acted in concert against it—spinning out the time in sterile and vagrant debate."[7] Old Bullion was disinclined to see good in anything done by either Clay or Calhoun; and to his ardent Jack-

[7] Thomas H. Benton, *Thirty Years' View*, vol. i, p. 309.

sonian eye, when they acted together whatever they did was
sure to be doubly poisonous.

The debate in the House that held up the Verplanck bill until
February 25, 1833, just a week before Congress expired by constitutional limitation, was in truth "sterile and vagrant" and was
intended to be just that. The debate was for the purpose of killing
time, nothing else, while the leaders worked desperately behind
the scenes trying to frame a bill that would satisfy the South
without setting off as disastrous an explosion in the North. By
February 25, they had succeeded. The compromise bill carried
some immediate reductions and provided for a gradual lowering
of the whole tariff barrier over a period of nine and a half years.
The South won a promise of economic freedom. The North won
a postponement of the immediate destruction of the protective
system. Calhoun surrendered the possibility of an independent
South; Clay surrendered the American System. For both, it was
a Peace of Munich, "peace in our time," but it was peace.

Once the compromise bill was agreed on, it was rammed
through both houses in a highhanded fashion that left Benton
sputtering with wrath. The Verplanck bill was amended by
striking out all save the enacting clause and the compromise substituted for it. Then Clay and Calhoun cracked the whip in unison
and members obediently jumped through the hoop—and very
glad most of them were of the chance.

Webster, indeed, was acidulous. He had not been consulted,
and Benton makes a great ado over this slight to the third member of the Triumvirate. But why should he have been consulted?
He was publicly committed to support of the ironhanded policy
outlined in the Nullification Proclamation, and it would have
been difficult and embarrassing for him to come down. Leaving
him out of the negotiations, under the circumstances, seems to
have been considerate, rather than contemptuous, on the part
of the other two.

Later, when war had heated passions to incandescence, it became the fashion in the North to denounce Henry Clay for the
compromise. As late as 1883, Lodge, in his life of Webster,
makes the first assertion that but for this compromise "we

should probably have been spared four years of civil war."[8] The only possible basis for such an assumption is that the odds against South Carolina in 1833 were so great that she must have been bluffing; but, as a matter of fact, for the next twenty-eight years the South steadily lost strength, relatively to the rest of the nation, yet in 1861, when the matter was put to the test, the odds against her were barely great enough. South Carolina was not bluffing in 1833; and instead of making war inevitable, the chances are that the compromise of 1833 had only the effect of making the conflict successful, instead of disastrous, for the North.

It would be rash to assert that Clay's motives in this business were as pure as distilled water. Undoubtedly, he tried to salvage all that he could from the wreck. Undoubtedly, he made all the political capital he could out of it. Nevertheless, it is indubitably true that for his country's good he deliberately sacrificed his most cherished political possession, his American System and— what is equally remarkable for a politician—he helped pull his deadliest enemy out of a deep and dangerous hole. This is patriotism. This is statecraft. For the second time Henry Clay had risen above the ruck of politicians, out of the low-lying fogs of partisanship, and stood in clear air, touched with a gleam of greatness.

[8] Henry Cabot Lodge, *Daniel Webster*, p. 223.

CHAPTER XIV

ON FOXHUNTING

Explaining how General Jackson, not content with beating Mr. Clay again, subjected him to the humiliation of beating him with Van Buren

IN THE year 1832 Calhoun and Webster were both fifty years old and Clay was fifty-five. Each member of the Triumvirate was in what may reasonably be expected to be a statesman's best decade, that decade in which he is old enough to be experienced, ripened, purged of the greenness of youth, and yet not old enough for senility to begin to sap his powers. It may have been the case with these men; indeed, there is no lack of evidence to indicate that between 1832 and 1842 they were at the top— never more brilliant, never more skillful, never more powerful.

But in statecraft of lasting importance this period is strikingly unfruitful. The obvious explanation is that the three were in opposition and debarred from active participation in government; for although Calhoun never formally joined the Whig party, remaining technically a Democrat to the end, he was as frankly an opponent of the administration as Alfred E. Smith, also technically a Democrat, was a hundred years later. The parallel between Calhoun and Smith is, indeed, striking. Not only were both party rebels against a swing to the Left, but both were honest, both were able, both were haunted by dreams of the Presidency, both saw men whom they had patronized succeed where they had failed, and both sacrificed their political power little by little, to their loyalty to the slave-owning class. However, Calhoun died seeing nothing ahead for his country but ruin; it is still possible to hope that his great successor may evade that dismal fate.

The Triumvirate were in opposition during these years, it is true, but that does not fully account for their relative sterility. Calhoun, indeed, was no longer a national statesman, but frankly the leader of a sectional party; but Clay and Webster were still regarded as Americans, first, and Westerner and Northerner afterwards. Simply being in opposition to the administration does not necessarily render a statesman impotent; plenty of men have found it a good strategic position. Hamilton, out of power, delivered the country from the menace of Burr in 1800—certainly one of his most important public services. John Quincy Adams, after he left the Presidency, attained a stature in the estimation of history that he had never reached before. Abraham Lincoln's greatest campaign was not any of his successful ones, but the one he lost to Douglas. Andrew Johnson did more for his country as an opposition Senator than he had as an ill-starred President. For twenty years William J. Bryan, beaten consistently whenever he ran for office, nevertheless steadily forced his ideas, one after another, into the policy of the majority party, and the most disastrous of them all, prohibition, he forced into the policy of both parties.

It was not solely because they were out of power that Webster and Clay accomplished so little of note in these years. It was rather because they were out of touch with the realities of the situation. Perhaps Webster maintained his sense of proportion better than Clay, or perhaps it was here that his tremendous sense of his own dignity became profitable, but at any rate, he fell into rather fewer absurdities than the Kentuckian. As usual, however, Clay was the positive force, the active element, in the combination, and Webster, for the most part, was content to follow his lead, revolting only when Clay went entirely beyond reason.

Clay has incurred much criticism for the arrogance with which he dictated the course of the opposition at this time. Doubtless he was too dictatorial in dealing with his followers, but the ill effects of his arrogance were borne by himself, rather than by the country. Perhaps it prevented him from being President, but it did not prevent him from accomplishing anything worth while as a practitioner of the art of government. That failure was due to another cause.

Basically, this cause was his ingrained contempt for democratic processes. He believed in the aristocratic theory that had been common to the founders of the republic. Even Jefferson, founder of democracy, did not believe in direct rule of the people. He did not think that the people, or men of the people, are wise rulers; he differed from Washington and Hamilton only in believing that the people are capable of profiting by their own mistakes, and with time and experience do develop the capacity to choose wise rulers. Hamilton was not so optimistic; he thought it essential to have the government in strong hands, not, as his critics tried to make out, for the benefit of the strong hands, but for the benefit of the people themselves.

Clay, although he resented being called a Federalist, was of the same opinion. He did not believe that the Jacksonian regime represented the deliberate, reasoned choice of the people because he was honestly unable to imagine any reason for such a choice. Nevertheless, Jackson was President and his followers held all the offices. If it was not the firm will of the people that they should be there, how did they arrive? The only possible answer was, by trickery. It was an answer that was the easier for Clay to accept because it moved in line with his emotional, as well as his logical processes. These people constantly frustrated and annoyed him; how easy it was to become persuaded that they were essentially tricksters and scoundrels!

This reason contained, however, one fallacy so glaring that even passion and self-interest could not ignore it. Bitterly as he hated the man, Henry Clay could not persuade himself that Andrew Jackson was a subtle schemer who could perpetrate an elaborate hoax. A tyrant, yes, he could believe that; an incompetent blunderer, a destroyer of every kind of excellence, a bloody-minded menace to civilization, a deep-dyed villain—he could fit his enemy into any or all of these categories. But subtle—the suggestion was so preposterous that even Henry Clay had to reject it. Yet if the Jackson regime had been established and maintained by shrewd, well-planned deception of the people,

[223]

there must be a deceiver somewhere; and he would be the key-stone of the arch, whose destruction would probably bring down the whole fabric in ruin.

Clay had no difficulty at all in finding an actor to play this role. Martin Van Buren was obviously cast for it by nature. "Tally-ho!" cried Clay and launched into a furious pursuit of the Red Fox of Kinderhook—one of the most bootless enterprises in which an American statesman of the first rank ever engaged. It was twice futile—in the first place, he never captured the Red Fox, and, in the second place, had he done so the result might easily have been more helpful than harmful to Jackson. The idea that Van Buren was in any important matter responsible for the strength of Jacksonism could have been entertained only by a man in search of a personal devil and determined to find one somewhere.

But the hunt was prodigiously noisy and, as one looks back on it now, amusing. It got really well under way after what Van Buren himself called "the Eaton malaria" had furnished a convenient excuse for cleaning the Calhoun men out of the Cabinet. As Congress was not in session, Van Buren was given a recess appointment as minister to England, replacing Edward Livingston, called back to become Secretary of State. The appointment, of course, had to go before the Senate for confirmation at the next session, but this was assumed to be a matter of form and Van Buren proceeded to his post.

Normally, it would have been a formality. There was no reason why Van Buren should not be minister to England, or certainly none of which the public was aware; and there were good reasons for believing the appointment an excellent one. Whatever Van Buren's failings, his bitterest enemies had to admit that he was shrewd and that he had good manners. All too well he had demonstrated both qualities in the Eaton affair. Van Buren was a widower, therefore unhampered by any intransigent feminine influence at home when the dazzling Peggy became the center of the political and social storm. He therefore made it his business to be exceptionally polite to her, being well aware that whenever he called upon Peggy, or danced with Peggy, or gave a dinner for Peggy, the incident was known to Peggy's grim old champion in the White House. It has been asserted, with some plausibility, that when the dapper little Secretary of State knocked at Peggy's door, in the days of her ostracism, he made himself President of the United States.

Be that as it may, the envoy of this country at the Court of St. James's is not hampered by possession of good manners and is lost if he lacks shrewdness. In the short time he was allowed to remain there, Van Buren made an excellent impression; and there is every reason to believe that he would have made an efficient and successful representative of this country among the British.

But the Triumvirate would not have it. Obsessed with the delusion that Van Buren had risen to power by deluding the people, instead of by shrewdly aligning himself with the people, they assumed that they could delude the people, too. They determined, therefore, to reject the nomination, not on the true ground that the nominee was a political enemy, but on the grounds (a) that he had mismanaged the negotiations regarding a West Indian trade treaty with Great Britain, (b) that he was responsible for the break between Jackson and Calhoun, (c) that he had broken up the Cabinet to further his own political ambition, and (d) that he had introduced the "spoils system" into American politics.[1] If all of these charges had been true, only the first could have had any bearing on the nominee's fitness for the post of minister to England; but it happened that none of them was true. The treaty was negotiated successfully; Lewis, not Van Buren, gave Calhoun away to Jackson; the Cabinet reorganization was for Jackson's benefit, not Van Buren's;[2] and it happened that the State Department, under Van Buren, had experienced fewer removals for political reasons than almost any other.

For fifty-one days the solemn farce was played. A round dozen

[1] Benton, in his *Thirty Years' View* (Chapter lix.) lists these as the ostensible reasons for the opposition.

[2] Benton thought Van Buren had cut his own throat, politically, by going to England, and was very sour over the disruption of the Cabinet. *Thirty Years' View*, vol. i, p. 218.

orations were fired at the target—just twice as many, Benton notes, as the speeches that were made against Warren Hastings. It is a curious and ironical fact that the Triumvirate were so pleased with their work that everyone insisted on taking a hand in it. Clay and Webster could, and did, speak from the floor; but Calhoun was in the Vice-President's chair. He was volubly represented by his men on the floor, but that was deemed insufficient. The Triumvirate had more than the necessary number of votes from the beginning, but on two occasions enough of their men deliberately left the Senate chamber at a roll call to assure a tie vote in order that the Vice-President might have the opportunity to cast the deciding vote against Van Buren.

At last the thing was done. The nomination as minister to England of Martin Van Buren was rejected by the Senate of the United States.

In Washington Benton said grimly, to Moore, of Alabama, "You have broken a minister and elected a Vice-President!"

In London, Lord Aukland, meeting the American minister at Prince Talleyrand's the night the news came in, said, "It is an advantage to a public man to be the subject of an outrage."

These were the voices of prophecy; but the voice of the Triumvirate sounded in Calhoun's fatuous comment on the rejection: "It will kill him, sir, kill him dead. He will never kick, sir, never kick."

So Martin Van Buren, who could hardly have played American politics very successfully at a distance of three thousand miles, was brought home, where he could easily thrust a deft finger into every pie.

The irony of the whole episode is that the great campaign to deceive the American public did deceive it although not in the direction it was intended to take. The Triumvirate really were trying to kill the Red Fox, but nobody believed it for a moment. The public, that had never taken Mr. Van Buren too seriously, could not believe that the three great parliamentarians took him seriously enough to stage such a campaign against him; the prevailing opinion was that poor Mat was served up as a burnt offering on the altar of his friendship for the President. The charges publicly brought against him were dismissed as the tosh they were; but the real charge, that was never brought against him, to wit, the Triumvirate's delusion that he was the real power behind the Jackson administration, was not even suspected. The conclusion of the people was that here was a man who had taken a beating because he was loyal to his friend; and Van Buren became a popular hero overnight.

It must be admitted that in some of his manifestations the Red Fox was superb. Seething with wrath and mortification when he was dismissed, within a very short time he began to perceive his real situation; so when he arrived in this country again and faced his exultant foes he was as serene, as bland, as imperturbable, as ever. Never a whimper came from Mr. Van Buren, no recriminations, no threats of vengeance, not even a protest that wasn't perfectly good-humored. The country took note, and its admiration for the man went up another notch; not only was Matty an innocent victim in the cause of his friend, but he was a sportsman, too. He could take a beating that he had done nothing to deserve and take it without a single yelp. What a man!

Still the hunting of the Red Fox went on. Wedded to the delusion that there was a trick in it somewhere, the great Three could not gain the consent of their minds to the theory that Andrew Jackson was his own man; and year after year they wasted their time in vain searches for the mirrors with which it was done. The attack on the Bank of the United States, for instance, they could by no means ascribe to the simple indignation of a farmer against a financial corporation that had him by the throat. The truth is that all Jackson's principal advisers, Van Buren included, were horribly afraid of the Bank, and were sincerely appalled by the President's headlong assault upon it. The Triumvirate, contemptuous of Jackson's reasoning powers, were convinced that some Machiavellian intelligence behind the scenes was putting him up to it; they wasted incalculable time and energy trying to bring it home to Van Buren, but they failed because nobody had put him up to it.

In Jackson's opinion, preventing renewal of the charter had

scotch'd the snake, not killed it. In September, 1833, he gave it the final blow. After great difficulty with his Cabinet—he had to transfer one Secretary of the Treasury, McLane, to another post and dismiss outright another, Duane, before he found in Roger B. Taney a man with the courage and resolution to smash the Bank—he ordered no more government money deposited in the Bank of the United States after October 1; and as checks would continue to be drawn against the $9,000,000 already there, this meant withdrawal of the deposits.

It is remarkable how this, one of the most perfectly characteristic acts of Jackson's whole career, was persistently referred to some concealed actor behind the scenes. Even in 1882 William Graham Sumner was repeating it,[3] although Parton had exploded the theory in 1860.[4] Here was a man who, throughout a long and stormy career, had been celebrated for the promptness and fury with which he carried every war swiftly into the enemy's territory. He was also a man whose reckless courage, physical and moral, was a byword. Here was a man under attack by a formidable enemy, by the most formidable enemy in the country, one so formidable that it had terrorized nearly all his counselors. If that man suddenly attacked the foe in a headlong, furious assault, utterly regardless of consequences, was the explanation to be looked for in the mind of some member of the terrified entourage he dragged along with him?

No, if there ever was a government policy that could have originated in the mind of Andrew Jackson and no other, that must have originated with him because no other imaginably could have devised it, that policy was the removal of the deposits.

Nevertheless, Clay, Webster and Calhoun ignored all that they knew about the man, all that they had heard about him, all that they had seen him do and went a-hunting the Red Fox again. In truth, the Red Fox, appalled by the storm, had taken to earth. Van Buren was comfortably ensconced in New York,

[3] William Graham Sumner, *Andrew Jackson*, p. 349. True, Sumner probably was as completely incapable of understanding Jackson as any man who ever lived, but he did have the reputation of being able to understand the English language, and if he had read Parton he had seen the facts.

[4] James Parton, *Life of Andrew Jackson*, vol. iii, pp. 500ff.

and behind the earthworks he remained until the shooting was over. He was so completely out of it this time that the Triumvirate could pin nothing upon him; yet so determined were they to have a Master Mind to explain why Jackson acted precisely as Jackson always had acted that they were reduced to bringing out the so-called "Kitchen Cabinet," Kendall, Lewis, Blair and Hill, politicians who were extremely useful to Jackson on many occasions, but who never imposed a major policy on him in their lives, as the real foes of the Bank.

This led Clay and Calhoun—but not Webster—into a grotesque error. Fishing around for some documentary evidence that might enable them to identify the ghost behind Andrew Jackson, they put through a Senate resolution calling on the President to present to the Senate a paper he had read to the Cabinet, explaining his reasons for removing the deposits. This was obviously not a genuine request for information, since the substance of the paper had already been given to the newspapers by Jackson himself. It was simply to establish the right of the Senate to call for Presidential documents. Naturally, Jackson curtly refused to transmit the paper.

Then Clay and Calhoun were guilty of the incredible folly of supposing that they could damage the President by causing the Senate to rail at him. The shattering failure of similar procedure in the Van Buren case had apparently taught them nothing. At this point, if we are to trust Benton,[5] Webster decided that he had had about enough of it, and although he gave the other two his vote when it was required, he let them supply all the oratory. It led up to the passage of a resolution, reading, "Resolved, That the President, in the late executive proceedings in relation to the revenue, has assumed upon himself authority and power not conferred by the Constitution and the laws, but in derogation of both."

This silly project laid them open to a terrific counter-attack from the President. It was terrible, not because of its violent language, since it was, for Jackson, notably restrained, but because of the careless way in which the resolution had been

[5] *Thirty Years' View*, vol. i, p. 423.

framed. The President, in a protest transmitted to the Senate, pointed out that he had been adjudged guilty of impeachable offenses, to wit, assuming power not conferred by the Constitution and laws, but in derogation of both. But, although the Constitution provided a method of impeaching a President, this had not been used; the President had simply been found guilty without a trial. More than that, the vote had been twenty-six to twenty, whereas the Constitution provides that a President cannot be found guilty of an impeachable offense by the votes of less than two-thirds of the members present.

It was deadly, and one of the worst features of it was that Clay and Calhoun had walked into it with their eyes open. They were both lawyers and there was no excuse for their not having seen the weakness of their legal position. They helped matters not at all by a blustering refusal to receive the President's protest or permit it to be spread on the Senate Journal. The truth is they were so busy hunting the supposititious fox that they were never able to realize where the big game lay until they fell over it, and were mauled.

The futility of these years is all the drearier when one considers what Clay and Webster, at least, might have accomplished by taking a different course. Calhoun, one feels, was out of it. If he had been capable of taking a different course, he would not have been Calhoun. The logic of events pointed sternly in one direction, and he was incorrigibly logical. Nullification had sealed his fate. The continuance of the Union meant the gradual economic enslavement of the South. He regarded disunion with a distress that was not in the least feigned, but he would have regarded acceptance of the inevitable and dedication of his talents to making it as bearable as possible, not with distress, but with contempt. He might have avoided some relatively minor blunders, such as the resolution of censure, but he could never have worked with and for Jackson.

Clay could, and to a lesser extent so could Webster. Clay, in particular, has been blamed for permitting his ambition to be President to blind him to all else; but was it ambition that blinded him? Ambition never blinded Martin Van Buren. On the contrary, it gave him an eagle eye when it came to seeing who was the inevitable winner. In 1824, Van Buren had been not merely a Crawford man, but Crawford's manager, and he put up an amazingly good fight, considering the fact that his candidate was known to be half dead. In fact, he eliminated Clay, when the election went into the House of Representatives, for his paralyzed man had more electoral votes than the Kentuckian. Therefore, if Van Buren could not be called more strongly anti-Jackson than Clay, he had certainly done more damage to Jackson than Clay had done.

Yet when the dust settled, and he had estimated the situation, none came into the Jackson camp more easily and gracefully than the Red Fox.

Clay could not have done that either easily or gracefully. But his error was not in failing to make terms promptly. His error was in failing to realize that the reign of King Caucus was over. As an honest man, he might have felt compelled to make Adams President; but no rule of honesty compelled him to give substance to the "bargain and corruption" cry by accepting a glittering reward at Adams' hands.

Again, after 1828, he might, spurred by ambition, have contributed immensely to American statecraft. The determination of the people actively to participate in the control of their own destinies has never been entirely broken since the first election of Andrew Jackson; but it has been thwarted, evaded and avoided. If he had understood clearly what was afoot, Henry Clay certainly could have served his country and probably could have served his own ambition marvelously well. In the one instance of the fight over the Bank of the United States, his genius as a mediator might have softened the collision between democracy and capitalism to an extent that would have contributed immeasurably to the well-being of both rich and poor. In a thousand ways the ingenious and affable Mr. Clay might have reduced the crudities of triumphant democracy, on the one hand, and eased the shock of the change to the quondam rulers of the nation on the other, to the great profit of all concerned, including Henry Clay.

No, it was not ambition that blinded him. It was the old, familiar blindness of those who are satisfied with the existing order, which leads them to attribute any stirring against it to the mischievous activity of "agitators." It was that fatal lack of imagination that Louix XVI exhibited when De Liancourt burst into his room with news that the Bastille had fallen and the head of the Governor was being paraded on a pike. When Jackson crashed into Washington Henry Clay took note of a revolt; and there was no mental voice to correct him sternly with, "No, Sire, it is a revolution."

Yet even Clay, after being thrown downstairs on the question of the Bank charter, thrown down again on the matter of Van Buren's appointment, thrown down again in the election, and thrown down again in the matter of the removal of the deposits, began to suspect that his presence was not urgently desired on the upper levels. Long before the election of 1836 he read the handwriting on the wall. Van Buren it would be, beyond the shadow of a doubt.

It was the bitterest of pills, but it had to be swallowed. Being beaten by Jackson, after all, was being unhorsed by Lancelot; but being beaten by Van Buren would be an overthrow by Lancelot's squire—Clay would probably have said by his kitchen scullion. Yet to turn the nomination over to another was in some sense to resign the party leadership. Clay was irritated by the indecorous enthusiasm of some of his friends for a new candidate. Calhoun was a flat impossibility—not even a Whig. Webster? Oh, a good enough man, no doubt, but a sectional candidate. William Henry Harrison? Perhaps the best of the lot, but hopeless at that. No one could win, and it was merely a question of selecting a victim to be thrown to the wolves. Before the world Clay acknowledged that Jackson had beaten him again, and beaten him with Van Buren before the race had started.

Calhoun valiantly undertook to create a diversion by running Hugh L. White, of Tennessee, to divide the Democrats, but the Whig Achilles continued to sulk in his tent. Such dour support as he gave went to Harrison. The result was pretty much what he had expected. Massachusetts voted stoutly for

Webster. South Carolina, erratic as ever, threw her vote away on a man not in the race, Mangum, of North Carolina. Georgia and Tennessee voted for White. Van Buren and Harrison divided the rest in the proportion of one hundred and seventy Van Buren electoral votes to seventy-three for Harrison. It was no revolt. It was a revolution and the Triumvirate could not put it down.

CHAPTER XV

ON THE GOLDEN FLEECE

*An account of the search for the Presidency by Clay and Webster, with
notice of the increasing hardness of "the cast-iron man"*

BIOGRAPHERS owe much to and suffer much from that quirk of
human nature which makes historical characters most interesting at moments when they are doing nothing of importance. The compilation of the Code Napoleon was certainly
more important than the courtship of Josephine de Beauharnais;
Washington arguing with Congress for supplies is more significant than Washington dancing again and again with Mrs.
Nathanael Greene, not that either wanted to do so, but because
he knew no polite way of getting rid of her and she did not dare
dismiss the commander-in-chief; Jackson in the Bank affair
meant more than Jackson in the Eaton affair; but in each case
the more insignificant affair is the more interesting. Biography
as an art profits by this circumstance; but biography as a science
is frequently betrayed by it.

Biographies of Henry Clay grow so interesting, as they deal
with the thirteen years following the inauguration of President
Van Buren, that the reader is unlikely to observe that they record
next to nothing of real and lasting significance in the development of American statecraft. It was not that Clay was idle;
on the contrary, he was never busier; but his business was running for the Presidency which is, although an interesting, even
enthralling, occupation, to be classified as politics, not as
statecraft. Even the political party that Clay organized and
commanded during this period proved evanescent, surviving its
organizer by a few years only. The period has given rise to an
incalculable amount of political philosophizing and moralizing,

but in a commentary on the statecraft of the Triumvirate, there is remarkably little to say about the Kentuckian in these years.

The activities of Calhoun, on the other hand, were duller, but far more significant. In 1833 the South Carolinian won a Pyrrhic victory. The threat of nullification brought down the American System, but it did not bring down the Union; and as the years passed Calhoun saw ever more clearly that the continuance of the Union, as it was then constituted, meant the inevitable enslavement of the South. At the same time, he was convinced that destruction of the Union was a horrible alternative; at best it would mean the reduction of the South "pretty much" to British colonial status; at worst it would mean the Mexicanization of the South. For Calhoun there was no way out; ruin faced his beloved country, no matter which alternative it chose.

In many respects John C. Calhoun is the most interesting figure that the public life of this period presents. He is easily the most obscure and contradictory figure. He baffles the biographer and historian because, looking in one direction, he could see so far, while, looking in the other, he could not see what lay right under his nose. His estimate of the ultimate effect of protectionism, with its tremendous stimulation of concentrated industrialism, was so uncannily accurate that ordinary economists a hundred years later were only beginning to catch up with him. He saw plainly that protectionism, lacking economic checks and balances not yet provided, was bound to result in the erection of a nation half slave and half free. That prediction has been fulfilled with such precision that writers in the second quarter of the twentieth century have inclined to the theory that Calhoun was inspired, not, perhaps, divinely, but certainly far beyond any other political philosopher of his generation.[1] Not the South, only, but the agricultural West, as well, has lived in economic bondage to the industrial Northeast for decades that are now running into generations. The evidence is not far to seek. The primary wealth of any nation consists of the products of its

[1] See, for example, Donald Davidson, *The Attack on Leviathan*, and Herbert Agar, *The Pursuit of Happiness*, both published in 1938 and both of which bear testimony to the remarkable rightness of John C. Calhoun.

farms (including ranges), its forests, and its mines. This primary wealth is produced very largely in the South and West, the sections that have profited least by protectionism; but of the accountable income of the country in 1935, estimated at fifty-five billion dollars, nearly twenty-three and a half billions, or forty-two per cent, went to the States that have benefited most by protection, to wit, New England, plus New York, New Jersey, Pennsylvania and Ohio, which comprise seven per cent of the whole area of the country. When forty-two per cent of the income goes to seven per cent of the country, the rest of the nation is obviously in economic bondage to that favored section. To be sure, the favored seven per cent of the area has much more than seven per cent of the population, in fact, over thirty-one per cent, but this only adds to the disparity; this favored area has carried off the people, as well as the income, from the rest of the nation.

This condition did not become conspicuous until Calhoun had been dead for many years; nevertheless, he foresaw it with great clarity. It is not without reason, then, that modern writers look upon him with a certain awe and, noting his perspicacity in this respect, are inclined to credit him with a clarity of vision in other respects which he did not, in fact, possess.

The peculiar characteristic of Calhoun's vision was, that while it was extraordinarily keen when it was turned upon the future, it became myopic the moment it was turned upon the past, and purblind when it was turned upon the present. He saw in vivid and astonishingly accurate detail what was to happen; he saw in blurred and distorted fashion what had happened; and a great deal of what was happening directly before him he could not, or would not, see at all. In his youth he had declared, "I am no advocate for refined arguments on the Constitution. . . . It ought to be construed with plain good sense." Yet by 1832, when the nullification movement was coming to a head, he was asserting, "Not a provision can be found in the Constitution authorizing the general government to exercise any control whatever over a State by force, by veto, by judicial process, or in any other form,—a most important omission, designed, and not accidental." This was construing the Constitution as having set up no government whatever, although the government had been functioning forty-five years, constraining States, too, as New England in the case of the Embargo and Nonintercourse Acts. It took a nearsighted statesman to see that as construing it "with plain good sense."

But his distorted view of the past was of small significance by comparison with Calhoun's great failure, his inability to obtain even a dim comprehension of the significance of the present. Some of its politics he understood. The effects of its legislation he understood only too well. But its life was to him a sealed book.

When Martin Van Buren was inaugurated, the Baltimore and Ohio Railroad had already been pushed west to Harpers Ferry and the practicality of rail transportation over long distances was thereby established. On that inauguration day it was already five years since his friends had begun to suspect the sanity of one of the country's most distinguished portrait painters, a man named Morse, who had abandoned a brilliant career to devote his time to perfecting "the magnetic telegraph." It was not apparent to Mr. Calhoun, although it was plain to some of his more alert colleagues, that these two innovations were destined to alter the country tremendously and above all to speed the already apparent obsolescence of the economic and social system that Mr. Calhoun represented.

A good many people—Benton was one example—never doubted that the South Carolinian's stern refusal to be swayed by the facts was due to personal ambition. He could not have accepted any criticism of the southern system without endangering his political career. That may be part of the answer—doubtless it is a small part, for Calhoun was certainly ambitious, especially in his youth. But no such facile explanation covers the whole ground. Calhoun was not blind to the significance of the enormous economic and social upheaval going on around him solely because it was politically convenient to be blind.

The tragedy of Calhoun is no shabby melodrama of ambition overreaching itself, no smug morality play, showing the engineer hoist by his own petard. It is on a kinglier scale, it is high tragedy, for it deals with an honest man immeshed in the threads of a destiny he can in no wise either understand or evade. Salvation lay within arm's reach of Calhoun; he had only to thrust out his hand to grasp it; but since this was precisely the thing he could not do, the means of escape might have been as far removed as Betelgeuse without increasing the impossibility of his reaching them.

What Calhoun needed was the advice Cromwell gave to the Scotch Presbyterians: he should have prayed God to show him that it was possible for him to be mistaken. It would have taken nothing less than divine power to open his eyes to this possibility, for he was a man of principle and men of principle are frequently equipped with a moral arrogance that, in a statesman, is likely to be very expensive, if not ruinous, to the country. Calhoun's career went far to establish the theory of the cynical Englishman: "A principle is a rule of inaction which states a valid general reason for not doing, in a particular case, what to unprincipled instinct would seem to be right."

To unprincipled instinct, in these years, it seemed to be right for the South to do something toward setting her own house in order to meet the changing conditions of a new world. Regardless of questions of abstract morals the slave system was economically ruinous, and most intelligent Southerners were beginning to realize it. The ablest of them saw more than that—they saw that the development of swift means of transportation and communication, drawing the country more compactly together, would emphasize, rather than minimize the obsolescence of the slave system.

If Calhoun had been of this number, he might have been ejected from public life; on the other hand, it is conceivable that he might have been just the man to effect the transition from the slave system to a system of politically free labor with a minimum of jarring and jolting. A scheme of gradual emancipation, worked out by Calhoun, would have been a good one, because his amazingly keen perception of the distant future would have been invaluable in such work. He would have foreseen and provided against the most formidable of the difficulties; and if his plan had

[238]

worked he would have deserved, and might have won, a greater fame than Jefferson's.

But one of his principles was that a nation that submits to coercion is no longer free. As an abstraction, it may be sound; but as every nation has submitted, and must always submit, to coercion in some form, and as no nation has ever been completely free, it is an abstraction that has little application to statecraft in this world. Moreover, Calhoun was committed to belief in the existence of a personal devil; a man capable of saying that malarial fever among his friends and relatives in Charleston "may be considered as a curse for their intemperance and debaucheries" was not the man to spend much time seeking to identify great, impersonal forces which might account for the objectionable acts of his enemies. Technological advances, with the economic changes they enforced, were coercing the North to oppose slavery, independently of the crusade of the moralists; but this truth Calhoun never envisaged.

His conscience was clear—perhaps too clear. Even Andrew Jackson, certainly as unyielding by nature as Calhoun, had certain joints in his armor through which modesty might strike. There were men in the world who were better, morally, than Jackson, and he knew it. Perhaps he believed them rare, but he knew that some existed, for the old General's conscience was not quite clear. His homicides, indeed, sat lightly upon him, for he considered them, without exception, virtuous acts; but he knew it was not right to swear the way he did, nor to stay away from church as often as he did, and, above all, he knew that his careless haste in the matter of his marriage had inflicted a grave wrong upon the one person who held his complete devotion. The evidences of moral uncertainty in Jackson's career are, indeed, rare and inconspicuous; but there is at least his confession at the end of his life that he had done wrong not to shoot Henry Clay and hang John C. Calhoun, so he evidently had some moments of dubiety.

If Jackson was not quite completely self-righteous, it is hardly necessary even to glance at any of the rest. Neither Webster nor Clay was in position to cast the first stone at any sinner, and while John Quincy Adams was austere enough in his private life, he was too introspective to have developed Calhoun's impervious shell. As for the others prominent in public life, their frailties were obvious. Calhoun was the man without reproach, and Calhoun it was who hardened into "the cast-iron man." If it is impossible to prove a causal relation between these facts, it is equally impossible to prove that none existed; and psychologically the inference that one existed is plausible.

By the time Van Buren took office a wide gulf had opened between Calhoun and the other members of the Triumvirate. It was not political—indeed, they had never been united, politically, except for brief periods to gain limited objectives. This separation was much more profound than any disagreement over politics. The difference was that by 1837 Calhoun was no longer a political Argonaut, perpetually seeking the Golden Fleece of American politicians, the Presidency. It would be rash to assert that by 1837 he had surrendered all hope of ever securing the prize; but he had realized that if he were to approach it at all, he must come by a long and devious path. It was apparent that the indispensable first move must be to purge the Democratic party of Jacksonism, which was patently a large job in itself; but only after he had remolded the party into an instrument suitable to his purpose would it be worth while to think seriously of the Presidency. As it turned out, by the time he had pretty well finished the first part of his program, it was too late to run for the Presidency; his name had been put before the country once or twice and he was "mentioned" in every campaign, but from the time of Van Buren it is doubtful that he cherished much hope of ever winning the great prize and he certainly made no wholehearted effort to grasp it.

This detachment from the great quest that has absorbed the time and energy of most American statesmen of the first rank for much, if not most, of their careers, enabled Calhoun to concentrate upon winning the Democratic party. His success in that endeavor is, considering that he was a sectional candidate representing an obviously failing cause, nothing short of amazing.

Whenever they came into collision, Andrew Jackson beat

Calhoun without much effort; in the end, the Tennesseean ejected Calhoun from the party—"purged" him, in the terminology current a century later—and apparently finished his political career forever. Nevertheless, within ten years of the day when Jackson left the White House, the Democratic party was Calhoun's party and he was "purging" such old Jacksonians as Benton, although he did not live to see the downfall of that stalwart. The party continued to represent the ideas of Calhoun, rather than those of Jackson, until the explosion of 1861 blew it out of power for twenty years.

Without a doubt Calhoun owed part of his success in this remarkable achievement to his ability to concentrate on the task in hand. In these years he was practicing statecraft exclusively, while both Webster and Clay were practicing statecraft only intermittently, spending a great deal of their time playing politics. Even when they did emerge on the higher levels of public life they were ineffective because their motives were under suspicion.

This was vividly illustrated as early as December, 1837, when Calhoun moved his famous resolutions intended to commit the Senate flatly to the pro-slavery cause. Apparently he commanded votes enough to drive them through, but after the debate had raged for several days, Clay intervened with a substitute series; his resolutions admitted that Congress had no power to interfere with slavery in the States where it existed, and that petitions for its abolition were therefore to be rejected as demanding something palpably beyond the power of Congress. But he saved the faces of the Northern Democrats and some of his own Whigs by other resolutions asserting that petitions respecting the District of Columbia must be received and referred to the appropriate committee, as Congress did have the power to act there. Other resolutions deprecated the excesses of the abolition agitation and asserted that the Union must be preserved at any cost.

Clay's resolutions were seized with joy by a grateful Senate and rushed through. Yet they lost something of their effect by reason of the suspicion that they were intended to further his political ambition. Clay was in quest of the Golden Fleece, and everyone knew it; so it was widely assumed that the resolutions represented, not his sincere convictions, but an effort to collect votes on both sides. There is little doubt that his intervention on this occasion did win votes for Clay on both sides; at the same time it was thoroughly consistent with the man's attitude ever since he had entered public life. Like most of the reasonable men of his own day, and like his pupil, Lincoln, Clay, while opposing the principle of slavery, did not consider it an evil great enough to justify the destruction of the Union incidentally to its eradication.

Preston, of South Carolina, said, a short time after the incident, that Clay had consulted him about the resolutions and Preston prophesied that they would offend the extremists on both sides and might cost him the next election; to which Clay made his famous reply, "I had rather be right than be President."

Yet fifty years after the event Clay's ablest biographer made the acid comment, "What he called 'right' on this occasion he would not have called right at other periods of his life. He said it with the Presidency in his mind."[2] There spoke a man who had helped put down slavery by violence, and who could not differentiate between Clay's service to the Union and his incidental and unwilling service to slavery. What Schurz could not comprehend was that Clay actually stood, in those resolutions, not for slavery, but for union and peace; that was what he called right, and he called it right at every other period of his life. So, for that matter, did Carl Schurz.

But although Clay stopped him from harnessing the Democratic party to his sectional wagon in 1837, Calhoun soon found himself tremendously assisted by the course of events. Long before the administration was over every politician in the country realized that the panic of 1837 had ruined Van Buren. When he found himself confronted with the most fearful crisis in his career the Red Fox, to the amazement of all beholders, quit trying to be foxy and stood up like a man. There was little that he could do, but he did that little; and he stood like a rock against tremendous pressure to adopt all sorts of crazy financial schemes that might have been temporarily popular but that would inevi-

[2] Schurz, vol. ii, p. 169.

tably have multiplied the damage in the end. Naturally, he made enemies right and left, and although the Democrats had to renominate him, or confess responsibility for the panic, it was quickly evident that he would have no chance whatever at the polls. Long before the convention met it was clear that the Whig nomination would be equivalent to election.

This was the moment toward which Henry Clay had been working all his life, the supreme moment of his political career. He was not only the leader, but to a large extent the creator of the party. In point of ability no other man in it stood close to him save Webster and Webster was admittedly a sectional candidate, whereas Clay was national in the eyes of all men. The nomination was his by every right; but he was neatly tricked out of it.

However, the men who knocked his feet from under him at the moment when he was about to step upon the summit of political ambition did not include John C. Calhoun. They were Daniel Webster and Thurlow Weed, Whig boss of New York. They were assisted in the enterprise by the fact that Clay had run the party with too high a hand, and the lower ranks were filled with sullen resentment of his arrogance, while some of the upper party workers had grown superstitious about Clay as a candidate always doomed to defeat. The battering he had received at the hands of Jackson here began to tell heavily. At that, defeating him in the convention took some desperate and highly dubious manipulation; the delegates were not allowed to vote in the open; it was all done through committees meeting in secret, and even so the first ballot gave Clay a lead of eleven votes over his nearest rival. But at the proper moment General Winfield Scott, whom Webster and Weed had employed as a stalking-horse, was withdrawn and the party emerged with the ancient and decrepit William Henry Harrison as its candidate for the second time. To make the ticket more absurd they gave him as his running mate a renegade Democrat, John Tyler, of Virginia.

Clay's reception of the news from the convention has become

legendary. Henry A. Wise,[3] who was with him at the time, tells
the story. Clay, keyed up with excitement, had had a few more
drinks than it is advisable for a politician to take aboard, so
when the news arrived he was in the mood to say what he
thought, and he did.

"My friends are not worth the powder and shot it would take
to kill them!" he howled, and striding up and down the room he
proceeded to expatiate on the theme. "I am the most unfortunate
man in the history of parties:" he declared, "always run by my
friends when sure to be defeated, and now betrayed for a nomination when I, or any one, would be sure of an election." Finally
he made the deliverance that most impressed the spellbound
Wise: "If there were two Henry Clays, one of them would make
the other President of the United States."

The glaring improbability cast upon that by the late transac-
tion quite escaped him. If there were not two Henry Clays, there
were a Clay and a Webster, and one of them had just prevented
the other from becoming President of the United States. Two
Clays would undoubtedly have operated in the same way. The
apex of the political pyramid is narrow, and if two big men seek
to occupy it at the same time, one is reasonably sure to jostle
the other off.

However, the Kentuckian was quite right about the result at
the polls. "Tippecanoe and Tyler, too," were swept into office
by a huge majority after one of the most cynical campaigns in
American history. There was not even an attempt to make an
issue. There was not even any mudslinging comparable to that
in the campaign of 1828. They jeered Van Buren—"Van, Van is
a used-up man"—"With Taylor and Tyler, we'll bust Van's
b'iler"—but they hardly troubled to slander him in a serious
way. They simply shouted for log cabins and hard cider and let
nature take its course.

All this did Calhoun no particular good, unless he enjoyed a
certain satisfaction in seeing his ancient rival tumbled into a
pitfall, but his time was to come, with little delay.

Poor old Harrison all unwittingly was racing with an infi-

[3] Quoted by Schurz, vol. ii, p. 181.

nitely more formidable competitor than the Red Fox of Kinderhook; he had against him also the Rider of the Pale Horse, and
just thirty days after the inauguration that opponent won.
Pneumonia struck Harrison down while Van Buren was still
making his leisurely way to Kinderhook.

The death of the President was a thunderclap to Clay and
Webster. The New Englander had been invited into the Cabinet
by Harrison; so had Clay, but he haughtily refused to accept favors from the man who occupied the office he regarded as right-
fully his. Moreover, as the Whig leader in Congress he would
have a chance to drive through the party program of legislation.
These were sufficient reasons for sticking to the Senate, over and
above the fact that Harrison had seen fit to assume a pompous
and stuffy attitude toward his party leader. None of them, however, applied to Webster, who promptly accepted the offer of
the Department of State and already had in train several projects
of his own when Harrison died.

But the disaster to Clay and Webster was Calhoun's opportunity. Tyler, succeeding to the Presidency, promptly fell from
grace and became a thoroughpaced Democrat again, albeit a
Democrat of the Calhoun, not the Jackson, school. Clay, blithely
proceeding on the theory that, backed by a majority in both
House and Senate, he held control of legislation, was rudely
awakened. He promptly put through both houses a bill re-estab-
lishing the Bank of the United States. The President as promptly
vetoed it and Clay's plans instantly crashed. He had a majority,
but not a two-thirds majority. He could put through legislation,
but he couldn't override a veto. With Tyler in the White House,
he was helpless to undo the work of the Jacksonians.

The wrath and consternation of the Whigs, when the veto
was announced, surpassed description. They had won an election
by a popular majority of more than 150,000 and by an electoral
vote of two hundred and thirty-four to sixty; and now they were
about to lose the fruits of victory. It was no consolation to remember that they were the victims of their own slick politics.
Tyler had been put on the ticket partly as a sop to Clay, since he
was regarded as a Clay man, but largely because, as Thurlow

Weed candidly admitted, "we could get nobody else to accept." Clay's real friends were too much outraged by the intrigue that had deprived him of the nomination to be willing to occupy the second place.

The conventional Whig view of Tyler was, of course, that he was a Judas, and this view was accepted by Whig historians and historians with Whig sympathies for many years. But it is a view too simple to be supported by the facts; as later writers on this period have pointed out[4] John Tyler had never pretended to be a Whig, or anything other than an anti-Jackson Democrat. His resignation from the Senate was itself based on his objection, not to any of the great legislative projects of the Jackson administration, but to voting, as the Virginia legislature commanded him to do, in favor of Benton's resolution to expunge Clay's censure of Jackson from the Journal of the Senate. It is a little difficult to establish clearly his betrayal of a party to which he had never formally adhered and to whose principles he had never given assent, in so many words.

On the other hand, he had accepted the nomination for Vice-President on the Whig ticket, and no man with a nice sense of the proprieties would have done that unless he had been prepared to assist in carrying out the Whig program. Yet there was no law against it. If the Whigs chose to play the fool by putting a Democrat on their ticket, there was no statute compelling John Tyler to restrain them. Nor was his accession to the Presidency due to any act or omission of his. He hadn't poisoned old Harrison. His obligation to the Whigs was entirely moral, not legal, and his repudiation of it was trickery, not treason. To compare him with Iscariot or Arnold is to make too much of him, for he was essentially a small man with a large ambition[5] most astoundingly gratified.

---

[4] For example, Herbert Agar in *The Pursuit of Happiness*, says, "Tyler was one of the most firm, and most honorable, characters who have played a part in our political life," and Hugh Russell Fraser, in *Democracy in the Making*, paints him as a hero.

[5] John Quincy Adams wrote in his *Diary* on April 4, 1841, "Tyler is a political sectarian, of the slave-driving, Virginian, Jeffersonian school, principled against all improvement, with all the interests and passions and vices of slavery rooted in

But he was equipped with a full share of the small man's characteristic stubbornness. Nor did he lack courage. He had dared defy both Andrew Jackson and the legislature of Virginia; he was not likely meekly to submit to Henry Clay. It is reported that Clay had said, "Tyler dares not resist. I will drive him before me,"[6] but if he did say it, he sadly misjudged the capacity of a little man to resist when he thinks his dignity has been violated. A man capable of throwing down the gauntlet to Jackson on a point, not of principle, but of personal spleen, was a bad man to drive.

Even after the first veto Clay did not understand. Knowing Tyler for a trifler, he reframed his bank bill, eliminating the word "bank" and substituting "Fiscal Corporation"; but Tyler vetoed that bill, too, and the Whigs were stuck.

Furiously Clay ordered the Cabinet to resign, and they did, with the exception of Webster. He had two reasons for remaining, one highly meritorious, the other not so much so. He was engaged, at the moment, in some rather delicate negotiations with Great Britain concerning the northeastern boundary and the case of one Alexander McLeod, a British subject whom the State of New York was trying to hang for the murder of an American citizen, perhaps in New York, but perhaps in Canada. It is distinctly to Webster's credit that he was unwilling to abandon these negotiations on account of a party squabble. The second reason, which he could not very well avow in public, was that he was thoroughly sick of taking orders from Henry Clay.

There must have been, however, a third reason. Webster was an excellent Secretary of State. Perhaps the assertion of one of his biographers, "It may be fairly said that no one, with the exception of John Quincy Adams, has ever shown higher quali-

---

his moral and political constitution—with talents not above mediocrity, and a spirit incapable of expansion to the dimensions of the station upon which he has been cast by the hand of Providence, unseen through the apparent agency of chance." It is an estimate that has stood the test of time better than most of Adams' estimates of contemporaries.

[6] Schurz, vol. ii, p. 204.

ties, or attained greater success in the administration of the State Department, than Mr. Webster did while in Mr. Tyler's cabinet,"[7] is a little absurd, in view of the fact that Thomas Jefferson, John Marshall, James Madison, Edward Livingston and John Forsyth had all made fine records in that office before Webster came to it; but it is a fact that it was work for which he was well equipped by temperament and by training. The negotiations leading up to the Ashburton Treaty settling the Canadian boundary line—the man McLeod, when he came to trial, was proved to be an empty boaster who was nowhere near the scene of the crime he said he had committed, so New York had to let him go—were conducted by Webster with a high degree of competence. A disturbance raised by an unruly ambassador, Cass, at Paris, was handled with equal deftness and dispatch, and the internal affairs of the department moved with swift and smooth efficiency. Proverbially, a man who is doing good work enjoys his work and there is little reason to doubt that Webster liked being Secretary of State. This undoubtedly had some influence in making him stick to his place until May, 1843.

But by that time politics had built a fire under him that he could no longer ignore. The Cabinet was a spot too hot for any Whig and Webster jumped. At that, he was somewhat singed. The underlings of the party scoffed at his alleged desire to finish the Ashburton Treaty and described him as the sort of man who would willingly serve under Judas Iscariot, or under Beelzebub, for that matter, as long as he could hold a grand and gaudy job. The canard hurt. It was a canard, for Webster's reasons were not cheap; but a good many people, even in Massachusetts, believed it, and Webster's influence suffered as a result.

In the meantime Clay had retired from Congress. It "was something like the soul's quitting the body," wrote Crittenden, his successor, but everyone understood that it was no permanent withdrawal from public life. It was strictly a strategic retreat. As Clay could no longer hope to accomplish anything in the Senate, he was abandoning that position as untenable, but only

[7] Henry Cabot Lodge, *Daniel Webster*, p. 261.

On the Golden Fleece

in order to maneuver his forces on to a terrain more favorable for a grand assault on the White House in 1844.

But with Clay giving all his time to campaigning for the Presidency, and with Webster practicing law in Massachusetts, the field at Washington was left open to Calhoun, and "the cast-iron man" moved inflexibly to his purpose. Tragic chance came to his assistance. The explosion of a big gun on the warship *Princeton* during an official inspection killed Abel P. Upshur, who was trying to fill Webster's shoes, and Tyler invited Calhoun to become Secretary of State.

As an anti-Jackson Democrat himself the South Carolinian was unperturbed by the unpopularity of the President with Whigs and Jacksonians, and the State Department offered a glorious opportunity to strengthen the South, which was now his main object in life. In the closing hours of the Tyler administration he jammed through Congress a joint resolution admitting the Republic of Texas as a State.

In this Calhoun, for once, was moving with the trend of the times, instead of against it. A great deal of highly moral nonsense has been talked about the admission of Texas and the Mexican War, which it rendered inevitable. It was, as a matter of fact, ruthless conquest, but it was rather less ruthless than the seizure of Massachusetts by the Pilgrims. The Pilgrims actually ejected the Indians from land which they had occupied for untold generations. We did not eject the Mexicans from Texas, because they had never been there. The country was empty of white men until settlers from our southwestern States moved in. At the time of the revolt against Mexico, the Mexican population of the eastern part of the territory was inconsiderable. Texas was already American and its eventual incorporation into the Union was certain. The wrath aroused by this logical development was due entirely to the fact that the acquisition of Texas strengthened the South.

In the meantime, Clay had made his last great gamble for the Presidency and had lost again. Facetious destiny once more broke two of its toys that emerged from their proper characters. Once

[249]

more Martin Van Buren undertook to act like a statesman, and Henry Clay like a politician, with disastrous results to both. Abolitionism and the slave interest by this time were both rabid, and the annexation of Texas was the test by which they tried candidates. Van Buren, seeking the Democratic nomination, was questioned and he answered, not in the manner of a politician, but with a courage and frankness worthy of his hero, Jackson. He said, in effect, that he hoped to see Texas in the Union eventually, but that he was flatly against immediate annexation. Instantly the slaveowners proscribed him, and the nomination went to the relatively unknown James Knox Polk. Clay received the Whig nomination by acclamation and against such an opponent as Polk his victory seemed assured, but when he was questioned on Texas, instead of coming out flatly and firmly he equivocated, wriggled, squirmed, wrote a letter from Alabama that read one way, and another letter from Raleigh, North Carolina, that read another, and left everyone so bewildered that the wilder abolitionists in New York left him in disgust, nominated a man of their own and drew sixteen thousand votes away from Clay, giving Polk the State by five thousand. With New York went the election.

The abolitionists thus defeated their own cause and made the Mexican War certain, but they also defeated Clay, and many of them were so angry with him that they considered the price not too high. So the politician who tried to be a statesman and the statesman who tried to be a politician both went to ruin, while Calhoun gracefully stepped out of the Cabinet with his point gained.

For Clay it was irretrievable political disaster. The day the final news came in Lucretia met him, weeping, and folded in her arms he wept with her. Nor was political defeat the sum of his losses; he had spent all he had, and at this juncture one of his sons failed in business and Clay assumed the boy's debts. It meant placing a mortgage of $27,000 on Ashland, and for a time it seemed likely that Clay would repeat the fate of Jefferson, dying a ruined man. But here, all unexpectedly, there came one gleam of light. Clay went into the bank to make a small payment on the mortgage and the cashier refused it with the astonishing statement that the note was paid. But who had done this? Many people, said the banker, in many parts of the country, had been sending remittances of various sizes to clear Ashland; and now it was cleared. But what were their names? Mr. Clay must know, if only to thank them. The banker though, was smilingly obstinate. "Evidently they are not your enemies, Mr. Clay," was all that he would say.

After 1844 Webster was back in the Senate, his accounts, as Secretary of State, being investigated by a special committee, which reported finding nothing worse than some extremely slipshod bookkeeping. After March 4, 1845, Calhoun also returned. Polk had politely offered him the ministry to England, knowing that Calhoun would politely decline it; but Polk had no idea of having "the cast-iron man" in the Cabinet. It would have been too uncomfortable for a plaster President. So a Senator from South Carolina promptly resigned his seat and the legislature sent Calhoun back there.

But if Clay was out, if Webster could do nothing, Calhoun had little to do. His job was finished when he got the resolution of annexation of Texas through Congress, for the course of events thereafter was inexorable.

The Mexican War was fought. Colonel John Clay was killed in action at Buena Vista and his aged parents in Kentucky almost sank under the blow. Presently Scott was in Mexico City and Taylor held all the northern part of the country. Organized government in Mexico collapsed and dissolved, and momentarily there was no one with whom the victorious Americans could make peace. Then up rose the wilder expansionists demanding that the United States seize the whole country and retain it forever. Henry Clay was seventy years old, now, and time and sorrow had sapped his physical strength, but the threat of this outrage brought him into the lists again. The moral quality of the enterprise revolted him; it would be plain robbery by violence, he asserted. The country rallied behind him on this point, and the annexationists were put down:[8] but the idea of giving up all the western country occupied by Fremont was a little too much; so California and New Mexico were "bought" from Mexico at the price of fifteen million dollars. However, robbery with salve is definitely better than plain robbery.

Even in retirement the habit of years is strong. In 1848 Clay made a last, half-hearted sortie in the ancient quest. So did Webster. Clay was now seventy-one and Webster sixty-six, and both were definitely of the past. The new generation was already knocking at the door. In the House of the new Congress was a Representative named Abraham Lincoln, and in the Senate a member named Jefferson Davis. In both houses new voices were commanding more and more hearers. The new men were definitely of the opinion that Clay and Webster were worn out, and even as loyal a Clay follower as Crittenden confessed that he had no taste for following his flag into another defeat. Both the old statesmen were brushed aside and a man, as old in years but new in politics, was chosen to lead the Whigs. This was Zachary Taylor, another "military chieftain."

So at last the quest for the Golden Fleece was definitely ended. For both Clay and Webster it had meant fifteen years of relative futility, and fifteen of their best years. But it was exciting and absorbing while it lasted. After all, if they chose to spend their lives that way, whence comes our right to denounce them?

[8] Perhaps Clay's moral scruples were especially touchy at this moment, because it was about this time that he was recieved into the Episcopal Church, the rite of baptism being administered at his house, a huge, cut glass vessel presented to the statesman some years earlier being employed as a font. Gamaliel Bradford chuckled at the thought that this was probably a punch bowl. "Baptized at seventy in a punchbowl! Could there be a more delightful epitome of Kentucky life a century ago?" *As God Made Them*, p. 57.

CHAPTER XVI

ON THE FATALITY OF ACHIEVING GREATNESS

Telling how Mr. Clay and Mr. Webster combined to save their country once more and, having sacrificed ambition on the altar of patriotism, were hissed off the stage

THE fifteen millions that the United States paid Mexico bought not only a wide area on the Pacific Coast but a first-rate crisis in Washington, as well.

Northern historians pretty consistently give the impression that the South forced the fighting in the struggle that culminated in 1850, but this is not true. David Wilmot introduced his famous "proviso" in 1846, and David Wilmot was from Pennsylvania. The occasion was the request by the President for an appropriation of $2,000,000 to assist in negotiating peace. Everyone understood that this request envisaged the purchase of something, although no one knew exactly what; Wilmot therefore attached to the bill a proviso that slavery should be barred from any territory acquired from Mexico as a result of the war.

This was taking the offensive with a vengeance. It was evident that a great deal of any territory so acquired must lie below the line of the Missouri Compromise; hence the Wilmot Proviso was, in effect, a repeal of the Compromise. It was the North that launched the fight with a frontal assault on the settlement that had held the country together for seventeen years, and Calhoun and his forces were really fighting a defensive action. This perhaps accounts for Clay's singular tardiness in perceiving the extent and significance of the crisis. At any rate, even in 1849 he was writing, with reference to his return to the Senate, "I shall not place myself in any leading position . . . but . . .

seek to be a calm and quiet looker-on, rarely speaking, and when I do, endeavoring to throw oil upon the troubled waters."

He was, however, very nearly the only man in the country who cherished any such delusion. Everywhere else it was the common belief that The Day was at hand. Hitherto protest and expostulation had been the part of the South and the North had been content to deny that it had any design or desire to interfere with the domestic institutions or the prosperity of the South. With the Wilmot Proviso, however, all that was ended. This was not merely a chance blow struck at slavery in the pursuance of some other objective, as the tariff, for example, had been. This was deliberately aimed, and men knew it, North and South. The "cast-iron man" knew it and decided that the time had come. Calhoun was old and ailing, but he drew himself together now for the last great effort of his life, for he knew if this opportunity were allowed to pass the South was doomed.

The Legislature of Kentucky knew it, too, and acted remarkably. Kentucky was no longer dominated by Clay. It had revolted against him in the campaign for the nomination, and the legislature contained many men who were opposed to practically everything Clay stood for. Nevertheless, it was the belief of Kentucky that when a great crisis impended the country was entitled to the services of Henry Clay; therefore, in 1849 he was elected to the Senate without a single dissenting vote. The fact that a great leader was sent to meet a great crisis by the votes, in part, of men who were frankly his opponents is a refutation of the theory that blind partisanship must always defeat intelligent action in a democracy.

So once more, and for the last time, the great Triumvirate gathered on the field where their fame had been won, and girded themselves for the greatest struggle of all. They came to it in a different spirit. They were old men, now, and Calhoun was actually a dying man. Clay was seventy-three and his physical strength was nearly gone. Webster was sixty-eight and had only two more years to live. For two of them, Clay and Calhoun, the quest of the Presidency was over. They grappled for the last time with no personal ambition to serve, with nothing to lose and nothing to gain for themselves. After many years they stood clear of suspicion; seeking nothing whatever save their country's good, the politician's character burned away by the fires of frustration and disappointment, ambition killed by age and frailty, they were statesmen at last.

The great debate was heard by a brilliant audience. In the Senate itself were such men as Hannibal Hamlin, William H. Seward, James M. Mason, Willie P. Mangum, John Bell, Salmon P. Chase, Pierre Soulé, Jefferson Davis, Stephen A. Douglas, William R. King, Thomas H. Benton, Lewis Cass and Sam Houston. On the House side there was one great man missing. In the session of 1848, on the day before Washington's Birthday, John Quincy Adams suddenly slipped from his seat and only the arm of the member next him saved him from falling to the floor. The old Puritan was dead on the field of honor, as he would have wished to die. Yet the roster of the House for the session of 1850 is starred with names, some of them almost unknown, then, but which have not been forgotten—Elbridge Gerry, Horace Mann, Thaddeus Stevens, Robert M. McLane, James McDowell, Howell Cobb, Alexander H. Stephens, Robert Toombs, Robert C. Schenck, Humphrey Marshall, Andrew Johnson and David Wilmot.

The debate was infinitely complex, tortuous and involved, but the essentials of the question before the Senate were simple enough. It was Calhoun's counter-attack, following the Wilmot Proviso. The status of slavery in the area recently acquired from Mexico was to be determined. Since the proponents of the Wilmot Proviso had publicly repudiated the Missouri Compromise, seeing that a great deal of the new territory lay below that line, Calhoun struck back with a demand that slaveowners be allowed to enter any part of the western country, taking their slaves with them. It was a challenge, and was intended to be one; nor had the gauntlet more than struck the ground when it was snatched up.

Some of the angry Northerners may have been befogged, but Calhoun knew exactly what he was doing, and was prepared to abide the consequences. The South was weakening. Time was against her. But at this moment she had some troops and an array of brilliant young officers hardened and tempered by service in the Mexican War. Robert Edward Lee, Thomas Jonathan Jackson, James Longstreet and Pierre Gustave Toutant Beauregard had all been below the Rio Grande and learned to command in something other than maneuvers. If the Union ever was to be disrupted, now was the time. But Calhoun appreciated the psychological advantage of making your opponent strike the first blow. "It is our duty to *force* the issue upon the North," he wrote; yet in the same letter he declared that dissolution of the Union was not even to be looked to except in the last extremity. His strategy was to compel the North to abandon, not merely the Wilmot Proviso, but all that it implied, or of its own motion to force the South out of the Union. He did not wish the dissolution of the Union; he hoped for a surrender, but if the Union must be dissolved he preferred to make the North strike the blow.

Never did he grasp the truth that the North not only would not surrender, but could not surrender, even had it been in the mood to do so. That is to say, no surrender on its part would have been effective simply because it did not control the forces that were grinding the South to powder. Calvinist Calhoun was still doing battle with a personal devil. Evil, to him, was the result of wicked contrivance, nothing else. Abolitionism was the foe; and in abolitionism he saw never a glimmer of idealism, but only the offspring of a monstrous union of envy and hate. He was as honest as the witch-hunters of Salem, and as blind.

However, no one else saw clearly the trend of the giant struggle. It is easy for us, nearly a hundred years after the event, to perceive that the deadly foes of slavery were not the abolitionists and not the people of the North, but many impersonal forces, two of the most effective being steam and electricity. But before we plume ourselves on our great sapience and vent our scorn on Calhoun, Clay and Webster for not comprehending what was before their eyes, let us answer with easy assurance some of the comparable questions that we face—trace, for instance, the course of the British Empire now that the airplane has abolished the insularity of England, or explain precisely what will be the effect of continued technological advancement upon our own national economy.

Webster, Clay and Calhoun understood quite well that the world was changing around them—understood it quite as well as we understand that it is changing around us. Indeed, they knew it better than we do, for they had witnessed changes incomparably more radical than those the modern generation has seen. They had seen the country expand, physically, from the Mississippi to the Pacific; and at the same time they had seen it constricted by the railroad until Boston was closer in time to Washington than Baltimore had been when Henry Clay first came to Congress. They had seen the application of steam power well on its way to the demolition of the household crafts. They had seen the rise of the penny press that was revolutionizing not merely journalism, but American political thinking as well. If the modern generation seems, at times, hopelessly confused by the relatively slight changes it has witnessed, should it speak scornfully of the men of 1850 because they were confused, too?

Yet, while a certain modesty in passing moral judgments is becoming, it does not follow that we should pay much attention to the explanations they advanced to account for their actions and the results that flowed from them. Still less should we be impressed by the explanations of the generation that succeeded them, a generation whose judgment was warped by the passions of war. The biographers who wrote between 1865 and 1900 were, with a few honorable exceptions, as fanatically convinced of the existence of a personal devil, from whose machinations all evil arose, as was Calhoun. They merely changed the devil's name from abolitionism to slavery. Not until the intense emotionalism aroused by the conflict had subsided was it possible for men to perceive that both abolition and slavery were phases of the stress occasioned by a national economy that was changing with great speed, but unevenly.

Perhaps Henry Clay's strongest claim to fame is the fact that he seems to have guessed part of this. He never understood it clearly, nor did anyone else at the time. Even Schurz noted the peculiarity of Clay's behavior: "That nervous, sleepless, instinctive watchfulness for the safety of the peculiar institution, which characterized the orthodox slave-holder, was entirely foreign to him."[1] But even in 1887 Schurz could not quite comprehend that the basis of Clay's relative indifference to slavery was an intuition—it was too vague to be formulated into a belief—that slavery was not really at the bottom of the dispute that was rending the country. This accounts for the conduct that pained and bewildered the honest Schurz—that readiness with which Clay at times denounced the institution with startling virulence,[2] and at other times as Secretary of State negotiated with the British for the return of escaped slaves and as a Senator voted for the fugitive slave law. Clay was, in fact, consistent; he thoroughly disliked slavery, but he believed passionately that the only way of arriving at a just and equitable settlement of the question was through preservation of the Union. Whether he was right, we can never know; all we know is that the Union was not preserved and that an unjust and inequitable settlement of the question was attained.

Neither did Calhoun believe that slavery was the paramount issue. To say this of the man who declared slavery "a good—a positive good" and who was ready to split the Union in its defense may seem at first mere silly striving after paradox, but it is a fact. Calhoun was willing to split the Union on the tariff in 1833. He would have split the Union on anything, and slavery merely happened to be the most convenient instrumentality at hand. He saw, with appalling clarity, that this was the South's last chance; if she failed this time either to dominate the Union or to dissolve it, she must inevitably go into economic bondage. In that, he was right. His error was in supposing that permanent domination by the South was possible, or that dissolution of the Union could preserve its economic independence. Nothing could

[1] Schurz, vol. i, pp. 301–302.
[2] "If I could be instrumental in eradicating this deepest stain upon the character of our country . . . if I could only be instrumental in ridding of this foul blot that revered state which gave me birth. . . . I would not exchange the proud satisfaction which I should enjoy for the honor of all the triumphs ever decreed to the most successful conqueror."—Clay's speech to the Colonization Society, January, 1827.

have saved the old South, for it was defying, not merely the
abolitionists, but time and tide, human resourcefulness and ingenuity, all the processes by which mankind was securing firmer
control of the forces of nature.

Slavery was the summation, the portrayal, of the agrarian
economy, but slavery was finally abolished without saving that
economy. The economy itself was hopelessly obsolete in that it
was wasteful of time and energy. Southern orators made much
of the factory slavery which the North was instituting even as it
inveighed against the chattel slavery of the South. It was a fine
talking point, because the wage system of the North was then,
and continued to be appalling; in fact, in some of its manifestations it is appalling to this day. But at its worst, the application
of steam power to manufacturing processes, and the resultant
abolition of the household crafts did release human energy and
that energy was applied to the improvement of the standard of
living in the North. Greed allied with cunning did cheat the
people of the North out of many of the benefits of the new order;
but the benefits were so immense that even the Gargantuan robbery of the latter half of the nineteenth century could not steal
them all.

The final, irrefutable argument was stated clearly by Calhoun
himself—"We are now stronger relatively than we shall be
hereafter, politically and morally." In brief the South was dying.
It was not dying of wounds inflicted by enemies, regardless of
Calhoun's opinion, nor was it dying of slavery any more than a
man with smallpox dies of the eruption on his skin. What Calhoun never understood was that in the year 1850 slavery was
possible only in a dying civilization; yet the facts were before
him. The North was swiftly increasing, not in wealth and man
power, only, but in general intelligence, through the tremendous increase in readers of books and newspapers. The South
was increasing in these things, too, but much more slowly; and
the reason was that the South was clinging to an archaic economy, of which Negro slavery was only one expression. That
expression had once existed in the North, but the healthier civilization north of the Potomac had thrown it off. The application

of scientific and technological discoveries to the reduction of the
forces of nature resulted in enormous economy of man power;
and such huge reservoirs of man power as the slave system
represented became useless and wasteful.

Eli Whitney doubtless perpetuated slavery for the better part
of a century when he invented the cotton gin, thereby rendering
the cultivation of cotton apparently profitable. The cultivation
of cotton required then, and still requires, man power in quanti-
ties hardly equaled by any other crop; and when the South began
to cultivate cotton on a large scale, the slave system seemed to
be profitable, for awhile. As a matter of fact, it was not. It did
make possible the accumulation of a few large fortunes; but that
does not establish it as profitable. If depletion of the soil be
taken into the account, and if the loss sustained by the South
through the necessity of purchasing abroad supplies that might
have been made at home had the region been less intent on the
one money crop be added, it is probable that never in its history
has the South raised a crop of cotton that sold for as much as it
cost to produce.

The real misfortune of the South was not the existence of
slavery, which might have been eliminated as smoothly and as
painlessly—except to the unfortunate Negroes—as it actually
had been eliminated from New England. New Englanders had
either sold their slaves to Southerners, or had manumitted them
and blithely permitted them to perish of starvation, or of tuber-
culosis and pneumonia. By 1850 the Negro element had been
almost eradicated from the population of New England, not by
design, but by the necessities of an economy which demanded
labor of the highest possible efficiency and ruthlessly eliminated
all other. New England, throughout this period, held a subordinate position in national affairs and was filled with the discon-
tent, and so with the activity, that a position of subordination
breeds in an energetic and ambitious race.

The South, on the contrary, had been dominant in nearly all
of the seventy-five years of the nation's history. Her leaders
were content, and therefore conservative. The avidity with which
the North seized on every innovation, they did not share at all;

from their standpoint any change was likely to be for the worse. They had no reason to suspect, there was nothing in human history to lead them to suspect that they were entering a period when all phases of existence were to be tremendously accelerated, so that what had been, in the previous generation, mild conservatism was to become not merely reactionism but downright criminal apathy. Calhoun, in his later years, began to suspect this, but somehow he acquired the delusion that it was characteristic of the United States or, rather, of the northern part of this country. He deduced that the South must either dominate the rest of the country, or separate itself from the rest; he preferred dominance and called that preference love of the Union; but he was prepared for separation. However, he knew beyond any reasonable doubt that the South must achieve one or the other in 1850 if it were ever to achieve either.

He came into the debate with a grim resolution that made him formidable indeed. At the very beginning he seized the offensive and he maintained it for months. He drove his forces furiously. He taunted the North, he reviled it, he constantly demanded the impossible of it, he made the unattainable the *sine qua non* of all negotiation. Moderates, such as Benton, were bewildered and appalled. They could not bring themselves to believe what was as plain as a pikestaff, to wit, that Calhoun was moving heaven and earth to provoke a break. He hoped that what would break would be the North's determination to assume that place in the country to which its size and strength entitled it; but he was determined that if the North did not break, then the Union should. From the standpoint of the old South, he was absolutely right. It was the last chance. Let that opportunity pass and no other would ever arise.

But slavery he was defending only incidentally. The cause for which he was making this desperate stand was the preservation of an agrarian civilization of the eighteenth century. Naturally, it was hopeless. Had Calhoun succeeded, the South might have, probably would have, broken away from the Union and established its independence, for awhile; but it could not have preserved its civilization. Even if there had been no internecine disturbances, even if no military adventurer had overthrown it, even if it had maintained unbroken peace with the United States, it must inevitably have followed one of two courses—either it would have followed the rest of the civilized world, reconstructing its own way of life after the prevailing pattern, or, as its soils were exhausted and eroded, its forests swept away, its rivers and harbors silted up, it would have sunk to the present level of Chinese Turkestan. In either case, the old civilization must have disappeared, simply because it was far too wasteful of human energy to compete with civilizations based on lavish use of natural forces.

To meet the assault of this desperate and resolute fanaticism, the country turned with one accord to old Henry Clay. Webster could fight Calhoun. Benton could fight him. The new men, Seward, Chase, Douglas, could fight him. But that was exactly what Calhoun wanted. A decision, and a decision on the spot, was what he sought. To force the issue meant either dominance of the Union or its dissolution and the South Carolinian would have been satisfied with either. Time was the desperate need of the Union, as it was the desperate danger of the South, and all men agreed that there was only one man in the world who could stave off the crisis. Not all agreed that it should be staved off. The taunts, the abuse, the studiedly impossible demands of Calhoun had driven many Northerners into blind rage so that they were as ready to rend the Union as was Calhoun himself. Yet even the men of wrath admitted, disgustedly, that if any man could defeat their efforts to stiffen the resistance of the North, Clay was the man.

Yet while all the world said, "If anyone, then Clay," it was a big "if." Calhoun was ranging far beyond rejection of the Wilmot Proviso. He was demanding a fugitive slave law with more teeth than an army of crocodiles, but that wasn't half of it. He was demanding the summary rejection of all petitions against slavery anywhere, and a formal repudiation by Congress of any right to legislate on the subject of slavery; but he went further than that. He demanded that the United States mails be closed to antislavery propaganda and that a rigid censorship be exercised over newspapers, books and all other printed matter. Unsatisfied with demanding all this of Congress, he went beyond Congress and demanded that the Northern States themselves employ their police power ruthlessly to crush agitation against slavery. In short, not content with demanding that the North cease acting against slavery, he demanded that it cease thinking against it.

As a serious legislative program, this was insane, but Calhoun, while his physical powers were almost gone, was never in better command of his intellectual faculties. He was not proposing a serious legislative program; he was forcing a fight. From that standpoint his demands, far from being insane, were shrewdly devised and terrifically effective.

When Clay arrived in Washington, in December, 1849, the chances that Calhoun would get the fight he was seeking seemed excellent. Indeed, the odds in his favor were so heavy that many men regarded his success as a foregone conclusion and not even the appearance of Henry Clay on the scene altered their opinion. The old man had been good in his time, to be sure, but he was seventy-three, now, and to ride such a storm as was raging seemed to require an alertness, agility and endurance such as no man of that age could be expected to possess. The Mill-Boy of the Slashes, Harry of the West, the Great Pacificator, seemed to have come to his supreme test too late in life to have a chance.

He was doubtful, extremely doubtful, himself. Nevertheless, summoning all the old craft, he went to work, and on January 29, 1850, he unfolded his scheme to the House. It comprised eight points, embodied in resolutions to be followed by appropriate bills. The first was that California should be admitted as a free State—a sop to the North. The second was that, regardless of the Wilmot Proviso, Congress should make no regulation prohibiting slavery in New Mexico[3] and Utah—a sop to the South. The third and fourth regulated the boundary between Texas and New Mexico, restricting the territorial claims of Texas, but giving her an indemnity in money—a sop to each

[3] New Mexico included at this time not only the present state of that name, but Arizona and Nevada also.

[263]

contestant. The fifth declared it inexpedient to abolish slavery in the District of Columbia without the consent of Maryland— a sop to the South. The sixth proposed abolition of the slave trade in the District—a sop to the North. The seventh, calling for a more effectual fugitive slave law, and the eighth, declaring against interference with the slave trade among the slaveholding States, both went to the South.

This was the great Compromise of 1850. As its author expected, it was received with a storm of objurgation from both sides. Nobody liked it—but, for that matter, neither did Clay. Nevertheless, all his eloquence, all his extraordinary power of persuasion, all his charm, all his political skill, all his vast experience he threw into the effort to put it through. He was old and ill and very tired, but he worked as he had rarely, if ever, worked before, not even in the days when he was young and ardent, with the great prize of politics glittering in the distance. Now there was no prize ahead, nothing in it for Henry Clay; now it was no longer the most fascinating and thrilling of games, but hard, dull drudgery; now there was not even much hope of success, but he strove magnificently, without a prize, without a thrill, almost without a hope, with no motive save the desire to serve his country in the hour of her bitter need. For many years Clay was considered the greatest orator of his time and from countless platforms he had swept multitudes into a delirium of enthusiasm; but perhaps the greatest speech he ever uttered was made to an audience of one, from no platform, but on the steps of the Capitol. The old man was dragging himself up that long flight to make his famous address of February 5, so weak and ill that, even with the assistance of a friend's arm, he had to stop several times to recover his breath. The man with him, alarmed by his condition, suggested that perhaps the speech had better be deferred; but Clay replied, "I consider our country is in danger, and if I can be the means in any measure of averting that danger, my health and life is of little consequence." It was not rhetorical, it was not even grammatical, but none of his set orations surpass it for splendor.

They denounced him on the floor, bitterly. He, a southern

man, he, a slaveowner, to be making concessions to the enemies of the South and the enemies of slavery—it was treason to his section! He was betraying his people, he was renouncing his allegiance.

But the old man flung back the taunt in their faces. "Sir," he thundered, "I have heard something said about allegiance to the South. I know no South, no North, no East, no West, to which I owe any allegiance."

The great oration which he began on February 5 lasted two days. Instead of being destroyed by the exertion he seemed to gather strength; and although by the end of the second day the strain was obviously telling, he wound up with a burst of eloquence that brought a cheering throng rushing upon the Senate floor, men to shake his hand, women to kiss him.[4]

But that was only the beginning. All the rest of the month the great debate raged, slavery men and abolitionists denouncing each other, but both turning upon Clay with unbridled fury. He made no more set speeches, but he was on his feet frequently, replying to individual arguments, and he was incessantly at work behind the scenes, pleading, cajoling, threatening, using every art he knew to line up the votes. For a man of his age it was an amazing performance; "everyone was astonished," says Rhodes, "at the fire and vigor of Clay."[5] But the country was waiting to hear from the other two members of the Triumvirate.

On March 4 came the speech of Calhoun, a dramatic utterance made under dramatic circumstances. A pulmonary infection had lately been complicated by heart disease and the "cast-iron man" was so weak and ill that he could hardly crawl into the Senate chamber, much less speak. "Swathed in flannels"[6] he sat without motion or change of expression while Mason, of Virginia, read his manuscript. Only the keen, dark eyes searched the faces of Senators to mark the effect of the argument upon them.

The tone of the speech astonished many of the hearers. It was conspicuously free of vituperation and bitterness, in places curi-

[4] Schurz, vol. ii, p. 335.
[5] *History of the United States*, vol. i, p. 173.
[6] Rhodes, vol. i, p. 127.

ously gentle, but as keen and incisive as any argument Calhoun had ever made. Here, again, was no politician, seeking some ulterior personal advantage. Calhoun was addressed to the realm of death, and earthly honors could no longer have any meaning for him. The Senate knew it. It was not even Calhoun's voice that was in their ears, and as Mason read on the solemnity of the occasion became such as might have attended the hearing of a message from one already dead. Such is politics that rarely does the Senate listen to a speech absolutely certain that every word in it is utterly sincere; but the Senators knew it on this day.

The argument was clear and strong. It was addressed to the Northern Senators' love of the Union. "You have had forced upon you the greatest and gravest question that can ever come under your consideration: How can the Union be preserved?"[7] he began, and proceeded with an argument that the Union had existed up to 1850 only by virtue of an equilibrium between the sections which had recently been destroyed, not by the operation of economic forces, but by Federal legislation, with the result that the cords that bound the Union together were giving way. "Already the agitation of the slavery question has snapped some of the most important, and has greatly weakened all the others." He named them. Already the Methodist Episcopal Church had been sundered into two organizations, one North, one South. Next to go was the Baptist denomination. As he spoke the unity of the Presbyterians was in process of destruction. Finally, not only were the ecclesiastical cords breaking, but the political, also; the parties were becoming northern and southern. "If the agitation goes on, the same force, acting with increasing intensity, will finally snap every cord, when nothing will be left to hold the States together except force." But it would be tragic irony to call "Union" a group "when the only means by which the weaker is held connected with the stronger portion is force." He concluded by referring, in general terms, to a Constitutional Amendment which he proposed to introduce to restore the equilibrium. But it was not upon the amendment

[7] Excerpts from Calhoun's speech are taken from Benton's account in the *Thirty Years' View*, vol. ii, p. 744 ff.

that he counted; he hoped to persuade the Northern Senators to remove the necessity for it.

He was calling for the impossible. All through the speech the villain of the piece was "agitation" and "agitators." Hence the only way to eliminate the evil was to suppress agitation and agitators—that is to say, to gag, not the mouths, but the very minds of Northerners. Like many a conservative, before him and after him, Calhoun identified the trouble with the outcry it produced; perhaps by this time he had persuaded himself that what made the agitators agitate was nothing more respectable than envy, although it is hard to believe that a mind so keen could have gone so far in self-delusion.

The speech had two immediate and apparently contradictory effects. In the first place, it convinced everyone who listened to it that Calhoun was really devoted to the Union; and it stiffened the abolitionists in their conviction that there was no possibility of dealing with the South. If a sincere lover of the Union could see nothing but its dissolution ahead, what could be expected of those others whose professions of loyalty to it were mere lip-service? Momentarily it seemed that Calhoun had won—not, indeed, what he preferred, the abject submission of the North, but at least what he regarded as second best, to wit, a decision then and there.

There was, however, a third effect of the speech, not instantly apparent, but more powerful in the end than the immediate effects. This was Calhoun's success in convincing the moderates that the South, or at any rate he, its representative, really wanted a fight. There had been a widespread disposition, up to this time, to believe that the southern threats were mere bluff. It was not confined to the North, by any means; a good many Southerners, especially among the Whigs, felt sure that the South Carolina crowd were deliberately exaggerating their own ferocity and some of these moderates were not altogether unwilling to support the bluff as long as it was not carried too far. But as Mason read the cold, measured, unemotional argument, with that figure of death sitting by his side, a chill descended upon these Southerners. Here was no bluff. Probably the very mildness of Calhoun's language strengthened, rather than weakened, the feeling that it was deadly. Even the courts will receive the statement of a dying man without the support of an oath, and not a Southerner in the Senate doubted that this South Carolinian meant every word he said. That threw a different light on the compromise proposals of Henry Clay, and Southern Whigs, along with some Democrats, began edging over in the Kentuckian's direction.

Then, on March 7, Webster spoke, and when he ended such a hellish clamor burst forth as had not assailed the nation's ears since the roaring days of Andrew Jackson. Hisses, boos, jeers, objurgations of every sort were climaxed by the shrill catcall of John Greenleaf Whittier, that singularly bloodthirsty Quaker, who, fearing with reason that Webster had cheated him of the sight of a holocaust, screamed,

> . . . from those great eyes
> The soul has fled:
> When faith is lost, when honor dies,
> The man is dead.

Yet all Webster had said was, in effect, that since it had plainly come to a choice between abolition and the Union, he chose the Union. The Seventh of March speech is absolutely consistent with his stand throughout his whole career, and if it is at any point out of line with the general conception of his character, that point is the courage it took to make it, which was more magnificent than anyone was justified in expecting of Webster.

He had counted the cost. He knew the virulence of the abolitionists and he knew it would be turned upon him in full force. It must be taken into consideration, too, that he was the one member of the Triumvirate who had not quite persuaded himself to abandon the quest of the Golden Fleece; even in 1852 he was still cherishing some hopes of the Presidency. He knew that to make that speech would be terribly dangerous, probably fatal, to those hopes; but he made it.

It was no political claptrap, then, but plain statement of fact when he began, "I wish to speak today, not as a Massachusetts man, nor as a Northern man, but as an American. . . . I speak today for the preservation of the Union. 'Hear me for my cause.'" He then proceeded with a long review of the history of slavery in the United States so dispassionate, accurate, and fair that Rhodes says it "rises to the level of a judgment by a philosophical historian."[8] He made no concession to the institution itself; he branded it "an evil, a blight, a scourge and a curse." But as for the point then at issue, considering that by reason of their climates and geography "both California and New Mexico are destined to be free . . . I would not take pains uselessly to reaffirm an ordinance of nature, nor to reenact the will of God. I would put in no Wilmot Proviso for the mere purpose of a taunt or reproach."

As for the nonrendition of fugitive slaves, he thought the complaints of the South were just. It was the law that slaves should be returned, and the North had not obeyed the law; he was prepared to support a more effective statute. Nor was he in favor of the abolition societies, much as he opposed slavery. He thought the bitterness of their attacks had done the cause of freedom more harm than good. However, the thing that stirred him, the thing that had brought him to his feet in support of the compromise, was the ruin that would attend any other course. "Sir, he who sees these States, now revolving in harmony around a common center, and expects them to quit their places and fly off without convulsion, may look the next hour to see the heavenly bodies rush from their spheres, and jostle against each other in the realms of space, without causing the wreck of the universe."

His peroration Rhodes deems almost as fine as that of the reply to Hayne: ". . . instead of speaking of the possibility or utility of secession, instead of dwelling in those caverns of darkness, instead of groping with those ideas so full of all that is horrid and horrible, let us come out into the light of day; let us enjoy the fresh air of liberty and union. Never did there devolve on any generation of men higher trusts than now devolve upon us for

[8] *History of the United States*, vol. i, p. 145.

the preservation of this Constitution, and the harmony and peace of all who are destined to dwell under it. Let us make our generation one of the strongest and brightest links in that golden chain which is destined, I fondly believe, to grapple the people of all the States to this Constitution for ages to come."

So it was done. After long years of dubious service, largely to himself and after himself to the powerful financial and industrial interests of the North, the man with one superb gesture had flung everything upon the altar of his country. After being showered with riches and honor and fame for many years, the Contented Debtor had suddenly become discontented, and magnificently had repaid the nation. His reward was obloquy. Daniel Webster, nearing the end of his days, for the first time became truly and indubitably great, and in the same moment was damned.

After that climax the story of the Triumvirate sags to a dull and dispiriting end. It was no false premonition that made the Senators feel a chill in the air like the breath of the tomb on the day that Mason read Calhoun's speech. The Reaper was among them. Just twenty-seven days later the South Carolinian breathed his last, murmuring, "The South! The poor South! God knows what will become of her!" It was the utterance of a seer. What has become of her? God knows! She went out to battle and she fell. She has lain in economic bondage longer than the republic had lasted when Calhoun was in his prime. She has felt the lash of the taskmaster, and has made bricks without straw. She has been perverse, and froward, and indomitable, foul and magnificent. She has produced Robert E. Lee and Huey Long, *Deep River* and *Tobacco Road*, John Wilkes Booth and Sergeant York, Woodrow Wilson and *The Memphis Blues*. In the matter of Negro enfranchisement she has defied the Constitution of the United States and she has flung her sons by thousands upon the bayonets of its enemies. She has given us lessons in lynching and courtesy. Distracted, violent and tender, she is filled with loveliness and horror and drives her sons to revile while they adore her.

With Calhoun gone, Clay and Webster battled doggedly on. Month after weary month the struggle continued, Jefferson Davis taking command of one bitter wing and Seward the other. President Taylor died in July, and Fillmore, succeeding to the office, invited Webster into the Department of State. So he walked off the stage of the Senate for the last time, to the accompaniment of a few hisses, and soon thereafter the sinister figure of Charles Sumner appeared in his place.

Webster entered the Cabinet July 23 and Clay lasted just ten days longer. He had managed to get his resolutions referred to a special committee of thirteen and this committee had reported them out in three bills. The first of these, derisively called, on account of its length and complexity, "the Omnibus Bill," was slowly cut to pieces by the raiding squadrons of Davis, on one side and Seward, on the other. At last, when everything of importance had been ripped out of it, the combatants sardonically joined forces in passing the useless remnant with a whoop.

Henry Clay was beaten. He had done his best, but his best was not good enough, and the Compromise of 1850 lay in ruins around him. However, there was no surrender in him, and after the vote he staggered to his feet and gave them the last shot in his locker: "The honorable Senator speaks of Virginia being my country. This Union is my country; the thirty States are my country; Kentucky is my country. . . . Even if it were my own State—if my own State lawlessly, contrary to her duty, should raise the standard of disunion against the residue of the Union— I would go against her; I would go against Kentucky in that contingency, much as I love her."

On August 2, exhausted, ill, and despairing, he relinquished his leadership and allowed himself to be carried off to the seaside. The last of the Triumvirate had quit the stage, derided by the triumphant merchants of hate.

Calhoun was dead, Webster was translated, Clay was whipped. In Congress smaller men rubbed their hands and decided, now that the Triumvirate was no more, to get down to business. Busily they set about showing the world how to do what Clay and Webster couldn't do. Some sort of legislation had to be passed regarding all this newly acquired territory in the West; Clay's was preposterous and they had slain it; now they would prove to an admiring country how much more sensible they were by producing a group of better laws. So they went to work. Clay had introduced his compromise on January 29, and Congress had fought over it all winter, all spring and most of the summer, killing the Omnibus Bill late in July. On August 2, Clay withdrew. By September 10, this same dawdling Congress has passed all the legislation necessary—a lesson indeed, for the old man, proof positive that the new men were brisk fellows who knew how to get results.

But when the country lumped together all the legislation and took a look at it, a curious fact came to light. Each and every item of importance that Davis and Seward had torn out of the old Omnibus Bill had been revived and enacted as a separate law. In six or eight measures Congress had embodied also the substance of the other two bills originally presented by the special committee. There had been a stirring in the graveyard, a yawning and an emergence; back into Congress had come the late corpse, blithe and hearty. Although only four Senators are recorded as having voted for every measure on the list, what the Senate had accomplished in the end was to enact the Compromise of 1850 almost exactly as Henry Clay had originally proposed it.

Hissed off the stage, beaten and repudiated, Henry Clay *in absentia* had whipped them all. The Compromise was established and the Civil War was postponed for eleven years—postponed until the North was barely strong enough to win it.

Clay and Webster both lived for about two years longer. Webster permitted his name to go before the Whig convention in Baltimore in 1852, but Clay rejected the suggestion that he be a candidate and supported Fillmore, who had faithfully tried to carry out the Compromise. Webster was badly beaten by General Scott who, in turn, was beaten in the general election by the Democrat, Pierce. But neither of the old men lived to see the outcome. Clay died June 29, 1852, Webster on October 24 of the same year.

On the Fatality of Achieving Greatness

That was nearly ninety years ago, but to this day whenever the people are gathered for patriotic ceremonies and the chanter intones, "Let us now praise famous men," soon he interrupts the catalogue of individuals and introduces this group, Webster, Clay and Calhoun. What were they, really? Does it matter? More to the point is to ask, What are they, really? As is true of all great men, they have been many different things as the decades passed; and what they are to us presumably they will not be to our children. To us, they were men who fought their way blindly, but gallantly through a period like our own, in that the very foundations of the social order seemed to be dissolving and flowing away; and two of them for thirty years blocked the way of the Four Horsemen and gave their country peace.

Upon Clay's monument they carved, "No South, no North, no East, no West." If today it is somewhat less an aspiration and closer to being a fact, none did more than he to make it so.

THE END

[273]

Set in Monotype Bell type.
Format by A. W. Rushmore
Manufactured by the Haddon Craftsmen
Published by HARPER & BROTHERS
New York and London

INDEX

Abolition, as Calhoun saw it, 256
Adams, Henry, 5, 65, 101
Adams, John, 3, 56, 57, 59, 106, 191
Adams, John Quincy, 11, 13, 25, 63,
72; at Ghent, 83 ff.; his precision,
88; Secretary of State, 115; sup-
ports Jackson, 128; countenanced
secession, 147; candidate of New
England, 174; President, 178; rela-
tions with Clay, 186; defeated, 189;
supports Jackson on nullification,
216; death, 255
Adams, William, 87
Agar, Herbert, 8 n., 111 n., 246 n.
Alien and Sedition laws, 36, 86
America, size of important, 138
American System, 15, 36, 145, 169,
170, 185, 206, 216, 218, 220
Americanism of Washington, 3
Ames, Fisher, 62, 101
Arbuthnot and Ambrister, 126, 216
Aristocracy as seen by Clay and Jef-
ferson, 100
Army, reduction of, 61
Ashland, 32, 34, 250

Bacciochi, Felice Pasquale, Prince of
Lucca, 155, 158
Baltimore, failure of attack on, 93
Baltimore and Ohio Railroad, 237
Bank of the United States, 14, 54, 102,
103, 112, 117, 200, 206, 208, 227
Barlow, Joel, 68
Bassett, John Spencer, 214 n.
Bayard, James A., 82, 84
Benton, Thomas Hart, 33, 119, 131,
192, 196, 212, 218, 219, 226, 241,
255, 261, 262
"Best" people, designed for under-
lings, 101
Biddle, Nicholas, 34, 99, 208

Biographies of Clay, 15
Bismarck, Prince Otto von, 125
Blaine, James G., 6 n.
Bolivar, General Simon, 155, 158
Bonaparte, Elisa, Princess of Lucca, 155
Bonaparte, Joseph, 160
Bonaparte, Napoleon, 6, 15, 54, 67,
91, 131, 155
Bradford, Gamaliel, on humanness of
Clay, 5, 155; on his education, 11
n., 15
Brag, game of, 34, 45, 89
Briand, Aristide, 195
Buchanan, James, 117
Buenos Ayres commission, 156
"Build-up," 19
Burke, Edmund, 62
Burr, Aaron, 34, 48, 193
Bryan, William Jennings, 101, 102,
111, 195, 222

Calhoun, Floride Colhoun, 44; marries
John C. Calhoun, 45; in Eaton affair, 202
Calhoun, John Caldwell, describes
Clay, 4; virtuous, respected, 7;
modern supporters, 8; ancestry and
birth, 38; resembled Jackson, 39;
Yale, 39; influenced by Dwight, 41;
at Litchfield, 42; admitted to bar,
42; elected to Congress, 43; marriage, 45; contrast with Clay, 45;
self-righteousness, 46; effect of supporting bank, 113; attains national
status, 114; Secretary of War, 115;
fitness for Presidency, 121; Rhea
letter, 125; against Jackson, 127;
irritated by slavery debate, 137;
urges planned economy, 149; difficulty in realizing him, 154; attitude
toward South America, 157; candi-

Index

date, 175; elected Vice-President, 177; turns sectional, 184; joins Jackson, 192; breaks with him, 202; in earnest on tariff, 211; returns to Senate, 211; his terrible sincerity, 212; his courage, 215; compromise, 219; contrasted with Van Buren, 226; censures Jackson, 229; his prophetic vision, 235; his principles a rule of inaction, 238; abandons quest of Presidency, 240; captures Democratic party, 241; Secretary of State, 249; annexes Texas and retires, 250; returns to Senate, 251; challenges North, 255; uses slavery as a pretext, 258; his last great fight, 261; last speech, 265; death, 270

Cass, Lewis, 119, 196, 248, 255
"Cast-iron man," 46
Castlereagh, Robert Stewart, Viscount, 64, 84, 86
Caucus, 115, 123, 175, 176, 231
Cavell, Edith, 189
Charleston, South Carolina, Calhoun's comment on fever there, 46, 239
Chase, Salmon P., 255, 262
Cheves, Langdon, 63
Civil War, 8, 79, 116, 120, 210
Clay, Henry, reaches Washington, 1; physical appearance, 2; representative of the West, 4; linked with peace, 6; moral qualities, 9; epigram on Peggy Eaton, 11 n.; on compromise, 12; Speaker, 16; no proletarian, 17; ancestry and birth, 18; in Richmond, 22; under Wythe, 24; goes to Kentucky, 27; success there, 28; favors Negro freedom, 36; in legislature, 37; United States Senate, 37; defends Burr, 49; described by Plumer, 51; returns to Kentucky, 51; duel with Marshall, 52; returns to Senate, 53; attacks bank, 54; enters House and becomes Speaker, 55; grows warlike, 60, 65; named peace commissioner, 81; misjudged colleagues, 83; calls British bluff, 90; cured of war fever, 97;

national figure, 98; his qualified democracy, 99; objections to bank, 103; effect of supporting it, 113; opposes caucus, 115; fitness for Presidency, 121; attacks Monroe through Jackson, 123; speech against Jackson, 131; attitude toward slavery, 137; opposes Taylor amendment, 141; Missouri Compromise, 142 ff.; tricks Randolph, 144; conceives American System, 145; opposes Buenos Ayres commission, 156; Monroe Doctrine, 163; his great dream, 168; candidate of the West, 175; eliminated, 177; swings to Adams, 178; "bargain and corruption," 184; duel with Randolph, 184; Secretary of State, 185; domestic tragedies, 187; bewildered by Adams' defeat, 191; returns to Senate, 205; bank fight, 208; loses to Jackson, 209; his game turned to earnest, 211; sacrifices American System to union, 218; effects compromise, 219; arrogance as party leader, 222; mistakes Van Buren for Master Mind, 224; defeats his nomination, 226; censures Jackson, 229; might have worked with Jackson, 231; "rather be right than President," 242; defeated by Weed and Webster, 243; balked by Tyler, 245; orders Tyler Cabinet to resign, 247; retires from Congress, 248; defeated by Polk, 250; debts paid by friends, 251; baptized, 252 n.; defeated by Taylor, 252; unanimously re-elected to Senate, 254; Compromise of 1850, 263; his greatest speech, 264; beaten, 271; wins after all, 272; death, 272

Clay, Colonel John, 251
Clay, Reverend John, 17
Clay, Lucretia Hart, born, 32; marries Henry Clay, 33; character, 33; comes to Washington, 187; consoles Clay, 250
Cleveland, Stephen Grover, 104
Clinton, George, 57, 193

Index

Index